THE ARCHEOLOGY OF
WORLD RELIGIONS

D1158624

To aid readers making comparative studies of
the archeological backgrounds of the ten religions
contained in the casebound edition of *The Archeology of World Religions,* the publishers have
retained the original page, chapter, and illustration numbers, and have included in each of the
three paperbound volumes the complete index
to all ten religions that appeared in the original
edition.

Volume II
Buddhism, Confucianism, Taoism

Volume III
Shinto, Islam, Sikhism

THE ARCHEOLOGY OF
WORLD RELIGIONS

Primitivism
Zoroastrianism
Hinduism
Jainism

BY JACK FINEGAN

PRINCETON, NEW JERSEY
PRINCETON UNIVERSITY PRESS

153645

Copyright, 1952, by Princeton University Press
London: Oxford University Press

❖

ALL RIGHTS RESERVED
L. C. Card 52-5839

❖

First PRINCETON PAPERBACK Edition, 1965
Printed in the United States of America

BL
80
FБ
1965
v. 1

Preface

THERE are many living religions in the world today. In addition to the more prominent systems of belief and practice cherished by groups which have long recorded histories or political or numerical importance, there are the numerous forms of faith found among preliterate peoples in various parts of the earth. If the latter may be dealt with collectively under the heading of "primitivism" the major religions of the present world are at least twelve. They are Buddhism, Christianity, Confucianism, Hinduism, Islam, Jainism, Judaism, Primitivism, Shinto, Sikhism, Taoism, and Zoroastrianism.

The archeological background of the Hebrew and Christian faiths was the subject of my *Light from the Ancient Past* (Princeton University Press, 1946), and it is the purpose of the present book to give a similar account relative to the ten others.

In a study primarily archeological it is clear that the chief concern will be with the early history of the religions, rather than with their recent and contemporary aspects. A beginning of the entire inquiry will be made with Primitivism. Pertaining as the adjective primitive does to that which is earliest in time, this subject directs our attention to the first discernible evidences of religion, back in the mists of man's prehistory; but synonymous as the same adjective is with aboriginal, it also points to the faiths of native peoples still on earth today. Many of these may have been in existence for a very long time and even have had a history as long as that of men of literate cultures, but the facts that this history has not been recorded in writing and that these people have lived in relative isolation from advancing civilization, suggest that among them religion may be at least relatively simple and archaic. It will not be assumed in advance that the contemporary beliefs of such folks correspond with those of prehistoric men, but if similarities are actually observed they will be pointed out. Thus two glimpses will be had of Primitivism, one in prehistoric times, the other in the life of present-day preliterate peoples.

We shall then deal with the other religions, in an order suggested by both geographical and chronological considerations. As far as geography is concerned, the study will take us eastward from Iran to India, China and Japan, then westward to Arabia and back once more to India. Each of these lands will be described briefly when we

[v]

first come to it. In regard to chronology, it is of course often difficult or impossible to assign exact dates to the lives of the founders of religions or to crucial events in the history of religions. Evidence will be presented on such questions, however, and the order in which the various religions are considered will reflect at least to some extent the relative times of their emergence in world history. In each major geographical area the rise of human culture will be traced from the earliest times; in each religion the history of the faith will be followed from its origin to the point where its most distinctive emphases have come into view. Considerations of space as well as the archeological interest preclude any attempt to carry the history farther than such point as this. Inevitably the limitation means that a great many developments cannot be touched at all. In the case of Buddhism, for example, a relatively full story is told of its rise in India but to its later spread through many other lands only very brief references are made.

The archeological interest also determines the fact that attention is focused throughout upon the ancient monuments and documents of the various religions. The actual objects and manuscripts which archeology brings to light provide materials of tangible and fascinating sort for understanding the nature of the religions which produced them. Through the ancient writings and the monuments which are often far older than any written records, the religion speaks with its own authentic voice.

In order to make these fundamental materials known in as direct a way as possible, extensive quotations are given from the texts, and many of the monuments are reproduced in photographs. The work is based upon my own travel around the world, gathering of material from museums, libraries and other sources in Asia, Europe and America, and consultation of the literature cited. Except for books appearing in the List of Abbreviations, each work is listed fully upon its first mention.

I wish to express deep appreciation to various members of the staff of Princeton University Press, and especially to Miss Margot Cutter, Fine Arts Editor, for many courtesies.

JACK FINEGAN

Pacific School of Religion
Berkeley, California

Acknowledgments

SOURCES of photographs and quotations are given in the List of Illustrations and in the footnotes. In addition to these acknowledgments, appreciation is also expressed to the following for permission to make reproductions of pictures: to the American Council of Learned Societies, Washington, for Fig. 133; to the Director General of Archaeology in India, New Delhi, for Figs. 54, 61 and 65; to Ludwig Bachhofer for Figs. 89, 91, 92, 93, 94, 95, 96, 97, 99, 100 and 101; to Ernest Benn Limited, London, for Fig. 59; to the Bobbs Merrill Company, Indianapolis, for Fig. 187; to the Trustees of the British Museum, London, for Fig. 33; to W. Norman Brown for Figs. 82, 83, 84, 85, 86 and 87; to Avery Brundage for Fig. 141; to the Syndics of the Cambridge University Press for Fig. 115; to the Carnegie Institution of Washington for Fig. 46; to the Chicago Natural History Museum for Fig. 149; to the Clarendon Press, Oxford, for Fig. 238; to the Columbia University Library, New York, for Fig. 220; to Mrs. A. K. Coomaraswamy for Figs. 55, 56, 57, 62, 63, 64, 67, 72 and 114; to the John Day Company, Inc., New York, for Fig. 143; to Faber and Faber Limited, London, for Fig. 16; to the Freer Gallery of Art, Washington, for Figs. 82 and 83; to Librairie Orientaliste Paul Geuthner, Paris, for Figs. 154, 158, 159, 162, 211 and 219; to George G. Harrap and Company Limited, London, for Fig. 183; to Harvard University Press, Cambridge, for Fig. 129; to the late Ernst E. Herzfeld for Figs. 23, 32, 41 and 42; to the High Commissioner for India, London, for Fig. 128; to the Institut de Paleontologie Humaine, Paris, for Figs. 11, 12 and 13; to the Macmillan Company, New York, for Fig. 136; to the Matson Photo Service, Jerusalem, for Fig. 227; to the Museum of Navajo Ceremonial Art, Santa Fe, for Fig. 19; to the National Geological Survey of China, Nanking, for Figs. 137 and 138; to the National Museum, Stockholm, for Figs. 180, 184, 185 and 186; to the New York Public Library for Fig. 208; to Martinus Nijhoff, The Hague, for Figs. 124, 125 and 126; to Oxford University Press, London, for Figs. 37, 39, 40, 44, 45, 243, 244 and 250; to Oxford University Press, New York, for Fig. 23; to Pantheon Books Inc., New York, for Figs. 148 and 176; to Arthur Upham Pope for Figs. 37, 39, 40, 44, 45, 243, 244 and 250; to Presses Universitaires de France, Paris, for Fig. 237; to Princeton University Press, Princeton, for Fig. 131; to Routledge and Kegan Paul Ltd., London, for Fig. 136; to the Society

[vii]

of Antiquaries of London for Figs. 209 and 210; to the Society for Promoting Christian Knowledge, London, for Fig. 164; and to Van Oest, Les Editions d'Art et d'Histoire, Paris, for Figs. 110, 118, 167, 202, 205 and 206.

Certain material reproduced in this book, namely, seven pictures, three figures, two plates, and the reproduction of the first page of a preface of a work (in Japanese), which material is specifically identified in the acknowledgments in the List of Illustrations, was taken from six German works and two Japanese works, originally published in Germany and Japan, respectively. The German and Japanese interests in the United States copyrights in these works were vested in the Attorney General of the United States in 1950, pursuant to law. The works involved and the particular material taken therefrom are listed below. The use of this material in the present book is by permission of the Attorney General of the United States under License No. JA-1482.

1. William Cohn, *Buddha in der Kunst des Ostens*. Leipzig: Klink-hardt & Biermann, 1925. "Copyright 1924 by Klinkhardt & Biermann, Leipzig."
    (1) Picture on page 5, with title on page 4 (for my Fig. 102)
    (2) Picture on page 101, with title on page 100 (for my Fig. 132)
2. Ernst Diez, *Die Kunst Indiens*. Wildpark-Potsdam: Akademische Verlagsgesellschaft Athenaion M.B.H., 1925.
    (1) Figure 136, on page 115 (for my Fig. 105)
3. P. Andreas Eckardt, *Geschichte der koreanischen Kunst*. Leipzig: Karl W. Hiersemann, 1929. "Copyright 1929 by Karl W. Hiersemann, Leipzig."
    (1) Figure 178 on Plate LXII (for my Fig. 130)
4. Otto Fischer, *Die Kunst Indiens, Chinas und Japans*. Propyläen-Kunstgeschichte, IV. 2d ed. Berlin: Propyläen-Verlag, 1928. "Copyright 1928 by Propyläen-Verlag, G.M.B.H., in Berlin."
    (1) Picture on page 168 (for my Fig. 104)
    (2) Picture on page 247 (for my Fig. 77)
5. Helmuth von Glasenapp, *Die Literaturen Indiens von ihren An-fängen bis zur Gegenwart*. In Oskar Walzel, ed., Handbuch der Literatur-Wissenschaft. Wildpark-Potsdam: Akademische Verlagsgesellschaft Athenaion M.B.H., 1929. "Copyright 1929 by

Akademische Verlagsgesellschaft Athenaion M.B.H., Wildpark-Potsdam."

(1) Figure 26 on page 51 (for my Fig. 50)

6. Heinrich Glück and Ernst Diez, *Die Kunst des Islam*. Propyläen-Kunstgeschichte, v. 3d ed. Berlin: Propyläen-Verlag, 1925. "Copyright 1925 by Der Propyläen-Verlag G.M.B.H., Berlin."

(1) Picture on page 186 (for my Fig. 241)
(2) Picture between pages 188 and 189 (for my Fig. 242)
(3) Picture on page 338 (for my Fig. 252)

7. Mizoguchi, Teijiro and Eikyu Matsuoka, eds., *Nihon Emakimono Shusei*. Tokyo: Yuzankaku, 1929.

(1) Vol. III, Plate 64 (for my Fig. 193)
(2) Vol. IV, Plate 10 (for my Fig. 192)

8. Uematsu, Yasushi and Tatso Otsuka, annotators, *Kojiki Zenshaku*. Tokyo: Fukyusha-shoten, 1935.

(1) Facsimile in Japanese language of first page of Preface (for my Fig. 188)

Contents

Page

III. *HINDUISM*

IV. *JAINISM*

List of Illustrations

[xix]

LIST OF MAPS

LIST OF ABBREVIATIONS

AJA   *American Journal of Archaeology.*

ARAB   Daniel D. Luckenbill, *Ancient Records of Assyria and Babylonia.* 2 vols. 1926-27.

ARE   James H. Breasted, *Ancient Records of Egypt.* 5 vols. 1906-07.

BASOR   *Bulletin* of the American Schools of Oriental Research.

BEIS   Ludwig Bachhofer, *Early Indian Sculpture.* 2 vols. 1929.

CAH   J. B. Bury, S. A. Cook, F. E. Adcock, M. P. Charlesworth and N. H. Baynes, eds., *The Cambridge Ancient History.* 12 vols. and 5 vols. of plates. 1923-39.

CBC   Herrlee G. Creel, *The Birth of China, A Study of the Formative Period of Chinese Civilization.* 1937.

CEMA   K. A. C. Creswell, *Early Muslim Architecture, Umayyads, Early 'Abbāsids and Ṭūlūnids.* Part I, *Umayyads,* A.D. 622-750 (1932); Part II, *Early 'Abbāsids, Umayyads of Cordova, Aghlabids, Ṭūlūnids, and Samānids,* A.D. 751-905 (1940).

CHI   E. J. Rapson, Wolseley Haig, Richard Burn and H. H. Dodwell, *The Cambridge History of India.* 6 vols. 1922-37.

CHIIA   Ananda K. Coomaraswamy, *History of Indian and Indonesian Art.* 1927.

CRW   Carl Clemen and others, *Religions of the World, Their Nature and Their History.* tr. A. K. Dallas. 1931.

CSECC   Herrlee G. Creel, *Studies in Early Chinese Culture,* First Series (American Council of Learned Societies Studies in Chinese and Related Civilizations, 3). 1937.

CSHI   H. H. Dodwell, ed., *The Cambridge Shorter History of India.* 1934.

EB   *The Encyclopaedia Britannica.* 14th ed. 24 vols. 1929.

EI   M. Th. Houtsma and others, eds., *The Encyclopaedia of Islām, A Dictionary of the Geography, Ethnography and Biography of the Muhammadan Peoples.* 5 vols. 1913-38.

FAH   Nabih Amin Faris, ed., *The Arab Heritage.* 1944.

FHCP   Fung Yu-lan, *A History of Chinese Philosophy,* I, *The Period of the Philosophers (From the Beginnings to circa 100 B.C.).* tr. Derk Bodde. 1937.

FLP   Jack Finegan, *Light from the Ancient Past, The Archeological Background of the Hebrew-Christian Religion.* 1946.

GCBD   Herbert A. Giles, *A Chinese Biographical Dictionary.* 1898.

GCE   René Grousset, *The Civilizations of the East.* tr.

Catherine A. Phillips. I, *The Near and Middle East*. 1931; II, *India*. 1931; III, *China*. 1934; IV, *Japan*. 1934.

GJ   Helmuth von Glasenapp, *Der Jainismus, Eine indische Erlösungsreligion* (Kultur und Weltanschauung, Eine Sammlung von Einzeldarstellungen). 1925.

HERE   James Hastings, ed., *Encyclopaedia of Religion and Ethics*. 12 vols. 1910-22.

HHA   Philip K. Hitti, *History of the Arabs*. 2d ed. 1940.

JAOS   *Journal of the American Oriental Society*.

JGRMW   Edward J. Jurji, ed., *The Great Religions of the Modern World, Confucianism, Taoism, Hinduism, Buddhism, Shintoism, Islam, Judaism, Eastern Orthodoxy, Roman Catholicism, Protestantism*. 1946.

JNES   *Journal of Near Eastern Studies*.

LCL   *The Loeb Classical Library*.

MASI   *Memoirs of the Archaeological Survey of India*.

MHR   George Foot Moore, *History of Religions* (International Theological Library). I, *China, Japan, Egypt, Babylonia, Assyria, India, Persia, Greece,* *Rome*. rev. ed. 1920; II, *Judaism, Christianity, Mohammedanism*. 1919.

MPEW   Charles A. Moore, ed., *Philosophy—East and West*. 1946.

OIC   *Oriental Institute Communications*.

PSPA   Arthur Upham Pope, ed., *A Survey of Persian Art from Prehistoric Times to the Present*. 6 vols. 1938-39.

REJH   *Early Japanese History* (c.40 B.C.-A.D. 1167). 2 vols. Part A by Robert K. Reischauer; Part B by Jean Reischauer and Robert K. Reischauer. (Princeton University: School of Public and International Affairs). 1937.

SAOC   *Studies in Ancient Oriental Civilization*. Oriental Institute.

SBE   F. Max Müller, ed., *The Sacred Books of the East Translated by Various Oriental Scholars*. 50 vols. 1885-1910.

SJSCH   G. B. Sansom, *Japan, A Short Cultural History*. rev. ed. 1943.

SLR   Alfred Bertholet and Edvard Lehmann, eds., *Lehrbuch der Religionsgeschichte, begründet von Chantepie de la Saussaye*. 2 vols. 4th ed. 1925.

THE ARCHEOLOGY OF

WORLD RELIGIONS

CHAPTER I

Primitivism

THE account of world religions opens in prehistoric times. Archeological evidences, shortly to be described, attest the existence of religion at the dawn of human history. Among the simplest folk yet to be found on earth, too, there is religion. The faith witnessed to by the remains of prehistoric periods and that encountered among peoples far from civilization today may not be the same. Indeed there are many different configurations of belief and practice among contemporary preliterate groups, and there may have been many likewise among the men of prehistoric ages. In the two areas of exploration, therefore, we are confronted by a multiplicity of forms of faith. Nevertheless, despite this recognized diversity, the realms of ancient prehistory and contemporary preliterate life have this much in common, that they are the two places accessible to our investigation which are the farthest removed from the advances of civilization. In the earliest human times before civilization had hardly begun, and in the remotest regions where it has scarcely yet penetrated, we may reasonably expect to find a relatively simple and untutored kind of religious expression which has been largely superseded in the circles of civilization. To this we may properly give the name of Primitivism, since that which is primitive is what is first (*primus*) or earliest, and, by a ready extension of meaning, what is aboriginal or native. The number of persons living on the level of "primitivism" in religion is commonly estimated at about 175,000,-000.[1]

In actual practice, as anthropologists have studied preliterate peoples they have found not only that there are unmistakable evidences of religion among every folk of whom full ethnographic records have been made, but that in the midst of all the manifold data there are at least a few very widespread agreements.[2] Furthermore, some of

[1] For the statistical estimate of this and the other religions, which in every case is only approximate, see John Clark Archer, *Faiths Men Live By*. 1934, p. 2. Revised figures in latest printing.

[2] Ruth Benedict in Franz Boas, ed., *General Anthropology*. 1938, p.628. For scientific methods of ethnographic research among native peoples see, for example, Bronislaw Malinowski, *Argonauts of the Western Pacific*. 1922, pp.4-25.

the basic attitudes and ideas thus attested provide helpful clues for the interpretation of some of the findings made by archeologists working in the field of prehistory. Several of these fundamental ways of feeling, thinking and acting will now be described.

1. CHARACTERISTICS OF PRIMITIVE RELIGION

It is everywhere observable among preliterate peoples that some of their attitudes and activities are of the sort which we would describe as belonging to the realms of common sense or science and some as belonging to the areas of magic or religion.

COMMON SENSE AND SCIENCE

By common sense is generally meant the way of thought and body of opinions held about ordinary things by ordinary men. The ideas characteristic of common sense are usually based upon what can readily be seen in one's surroundings, or they are derived by inference from such observations. Preliterate people certainly employ common sense. They guide their lives to a considerable extent by what they have learned in everyday experience, and they deal with much of their environment in accordance with the obvious behavior which it manifests.

Science constitutes a system of concepts and techniques which has developed out of the common-sense approach to the world. Like common sense, science is based upon experience, but its observations are more methodical, its reasoning more rigorously logical, and its techniques more highly developed. At least the rudiments of science are also to be found among many preliterate peoples. Such a procedure, for example, as the chipping of a flint to produce a cutting edge, or the tilling of the soil to make a garden, exhibits to a degree the empirical basis and elaborated technique characteristic of scientific method.[3]

MAGIC AND RELIGION

When we speak of magic we have reference to ideas and practices which relate to more mysterious aspects of the environment. Visible objects still play a large part in magical procedures, of course, but instead of being taken at their face value and employed for workaday purposes they are now regarded as the bearers of invisible potencies and manipulated as agencies for the accomplishment of ends which are not attainable by common sense techniques. That much of the life of preliterate peoples is permeated by beliefs and occupied by activities which must be classified as magical is well known. As a single example, a practice of the aborigines of Central Australia may

[3] Bronislaw Malinowski, *Coral Gardens and Their Magic, A Study of the Methods of Tilling the Soil and of Agricultural Rites in the Trobriand Islands.* 1935, I, p.77.

be cited. Believing that the pearl shell contains the concentrated "essence" of water, they will suck out this "essence" and spit it into the sky in order that the drops may cause rain clouds to form.[4] The distinction between this practice and, for example, the use of a shell as an ornament in everyday life is perfectly clear and there is no doubt but that the ceremony just described must be recognized as belonging to the realm of magic.

Religion, for its part, also has to do with something more than the obvious surface of things. Like magic, it is oriented toward unseen forces. The forces are not necessarily the same as those with which magic is concerned, nor is the attitude of the person engaged in an act of religion necessarily similar to that of the practitioner of magic. Nevertheless, in religion as in magic, although perhaps in quite a different way, there is an attempt to relate life to a dimension of existence other than that with which common sense and science are concerned. What this something more is may be defined differently in different cultures, and the attitudes and acts judged appropriate in relation to it may likewise vary widely. It remains true that throughout all the ramifications of feelings, conceptions and practices there is an orientation toward a plus factor in existence. Whether this plus factor is apprehended and dealt with as fearsome or mysterious or wonderful or awe-inspiring or as possessing yet other attributes does not matter at this point; what we are here concerned to establish is that religion, like magic, represents a relationship of man to an aspect of the universe, real or imaginary, which is different from that with which common sense and science are habitually concerned.

Since religion and magic agree in their orientation toward aspects of the universe which transcend those dealt with by common-sense and scientific methods, how are they themselves to be distinguished from one another? In the case of the relationship of common sense and science it was suggested that the latter might be regarded as developing out of the former. The theory has not lacked for supporters that in a somewhat similar way religion arose out of magic. Thus Sir James G. Frazer maintained that the age of magic preceded the age of religion.[5] This supposition is not verified, however, by actual observation. Magic and religion are coexistent and even almost inextricably interwoven in too many instances to make it possible to

[4] Charles P. Mountford in *The National Geographic Magazine*. 89 (1946), p.101.
[5] See e.g. James G. Frazer, *Totemica—A Supplement to Totemism and Exogamy*. 1937, p.257.

believe that the one was the predecessor and the root of the other.[6] The distinction between magic and religion does not consist in the temporal priority of the one over the other. Rather, if it is to be found at all, the distinction must be sought in the nature of the two systems of ideas and practices.

Here it must be said that the drawing of a sharp dividing line is not always possible. There are practices which it is difficult to classify with confidence on one side of such a line or the other. On the whole, however, there are some broad differences in methods and attitudes which often appear. The tendency is for magic to be more mechanical in procedure and coercive in intent, religion more personal and supplicatory.[7] A characteristic act in the practice of magic, for example, is to prepare an object or medicine so that it will be charged with special potency, and then to manipulate it so that the potency will work effectively toward the desired end. All must be done in accordance with very precise rules, and it is believed that if the practitioner knows these rules and follows them accurately the effect will not fail to be secured. At this point there is a similarity between magic and science, in that both depend upon a knowledge of the laws involved in a given procedure, and assume that if man's knowledge is sufficient and his procedure flawless he can constrain the forces with which he is working to accomplish what he wishes. Nevertheless, magic remains unmistakably different from science, in that it professes to manipulate forces of a more mysterious sort than those with which science deals. Religion, for its part, often addresses itself to more mysterious forces of the universe not so much with the intent to constrain them by mechanical manipulations as to gain a favorable relationship to them by the establishment of such attitudes as those of submission and dependence and the performance of such acts as those of propitiation and petition. Of course, even a prayer may be uttered with a belief in the automatic efficacy of the pronunciation of certain syllables or in the compulsive effect of a sufficient number of repetitions, and thus the line of demarcation often remains indistinct between magic and religion.

THE NATURAL AND THE SUPERNATURAL

In the attempt, then, to classify ways of feeling, thinking and act-

[6] Bronislaw Malinowski, *A Scientific Theory of Culture and Other Essays.* 1944, pp.196-201.

[7] Bronislaw Malinowski in Joseph Needham, ed., *Science, Religion and Reality.* 1925, pp.71f.,81.

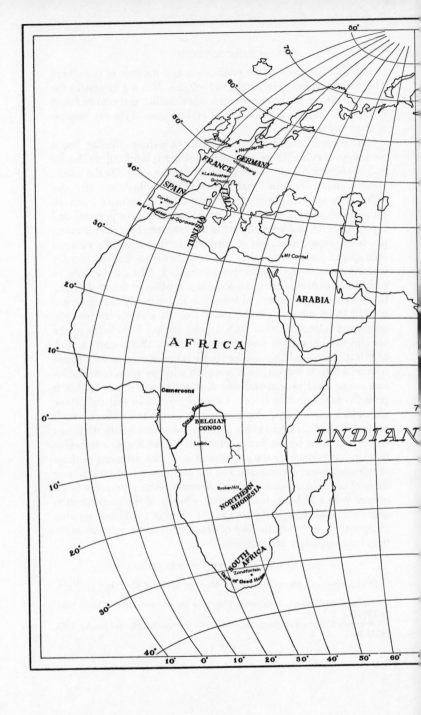

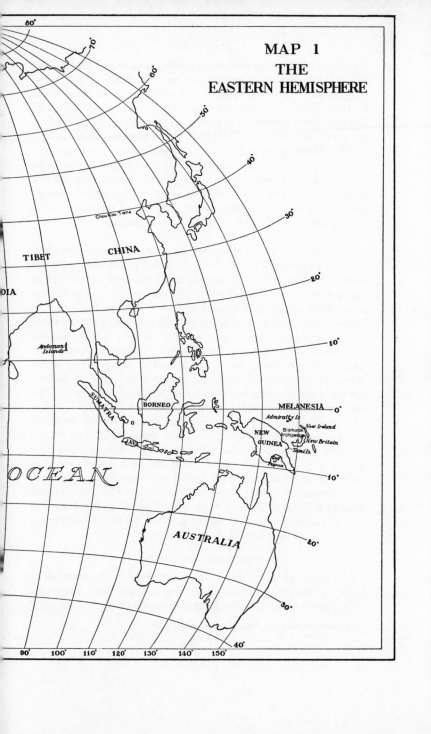

MAP 1
THE
EASTERN HEMISPHERE

ing encountered among preliterate people we have put together the things of common sense and science, and the things of magic and religion. Between common sense and science we have made a distinction, and likewise between magic and religion; nevertheless the first two have a discernible degree of affinity with each other and so, too, do the last two. Is it possible to give a name to the areas with which common sense and science, on the one side, and magic and religion, on the other, are concerned? In the English language the words most conveniently and frequently used to designate the two spheres are the natural and the supernatural. By the natural is meant the realm of everyday affairs, by the supernatural the realm that is more marvelous and mysterious, the "extra dimension"[8] of the universe.

While the employment of these terms is convenient and seems necessary, their use is not intended to suggest that preliterate man draws the line between the natural and the supernatural at the same place that a man of our own culture might, nor indeed that preliterate man himself always draws the dividing line consistently or clearly. Rather, the impingement of the supernatural in both time and space may be apprehended in varying ways in primitive thought. At one time a native's attention may be given quite exclusively to an undertaking in the workaday world, and at another every energy be devoted to a procedure related to the domain of the more mysterious; but again concern may be evident with both realms at one and the same time, as, for example, when the tilling of the tangible soil is accompanied by the performance of rites directed toward the forces believed to govern fertility. Likewise, a given object may on one occasion excite no particular interest whatever, but on another be treated as if it had been invested with the most remarkable attributes. Nevertheless, despite the fluidity or inchoateness of concepts, the difference is usually unmistakable between the attitudes and dealings which have to do with the natural and those which have to do with the supernatural. From this point on, we shall be concerned primarily with the realm of the supernatural.

DYNAMISM AND ANIMISM

It is clear that the realm of the supernatural is apprehended as having a bearing upon the life of man, and that both magic and religion are concerned with adjusting man's life effectively and satis-

[8] Benedict in Boas, ed., *General Anthropology*, p.631.

factorily to the forces that are operative in that realm. When we inquire as to what specific conceptions prevail about these supernatural
forces, we find, of course, a great variety of ideas. Broadly speaking,
however, they all fall within two general groups. A convincing explanation, moreover, has been advanced by Ruth Benedict to account for the rise of precisely these two types of thought. As she has
pointed out,[9] what preliterate man evidently has done has been to
extend to the area of the supernatural what he has learned in dealing
with the natural. Here in everyday life man has to do both with
impersonal things and with other persons. In both the impersonal
and the personal he encounters qualities and forces which affect him.
Even impersonal things exhibit attributes and manifest powers. A
stone is hard and heavy; a river flows and the wind blows. Other
persons make an impact upon him with their will and emotions.
Even so, in the realm of the supernatural it may be supposed either
that the operative forces are of an impersonal sort, or that they are
comparable to the intentions and drives of man himself. Thus, to
illustrate the one type of supposition, a particular stone may not
only possess the attributes of hardness and weight but also have the
quality of supernatural power pertaining to it, and thus be an amulet
of peculiar potency. And, to give an example of the other type of
supposition, a tree may fall upon an unfortunate individual because
it hates him and wishes to kill him.

To the first mode of thought, which conceives the supernatural as
operating in terms of impersonal forces, we may give the designation
dynamism. This word is derived from the Greek δύναμις, meaning
"power," and in the present sense has been introduced and employed
notably by Alfred Bertholet.[10] Dynamism means belief in and relationship to supernatural power, conceived of as impersonal, immanent and pervasive, a force which may be encountered anywhere
in the universe, a quality which may inhere in anything.

To the second way of thinking, which personalizes the forces of
the supernatural world, the name animism is applicable. This term
comes from the Latin anima, which basically means "breath" or
"breath of life," and therefore also has the connotation of "soul" or
"spirit." In the sense in which it is here used, the designation was
brought into currency by the writings of Edward B. Tylor.[11] It con-

---

[9] In Boas, ed., *General Anthropology*, pp.631f.

[10] Alfred Bertholet, *Das Dynamistische im Alten Testament*. 1926, p.6; Van der
Leeuw in RGG IV, cols.1366-1368.

[11] Edward B. Tylor, *Primitive Culture*. 1st ed. 1871; 6th ed. 1920, I, pp.425f.

notes belief in and relationship to supernatural powers insofar as they are thought of in terms of personal will and understood to exist in the form of spirits.

Of the two manners of thought just described, the impersonal might logically be supposed to have preceded the personal, and it has been said of what we have called dynamism that it "seems to be the first clearly formed religious idea."[12] In actual observation, however, dynamism and animism so often appear side by side, and indeed are so often inextricably interwoven, that it is perhaps safer not to attempt to attribute priority either to the one or to the other. Without hesitation, however, we may state that they are both extremely early and extremely widespread aspects of religion.

Concrete illustration of dynamism may be found in many places. One of its most characteristic and well-known formulations occurs in Melanesia. Here there is a widespread belief in a power which, while it may originate in a spirit or be manifest in a person, is essentially an impersonal potency and may equally well be effective in inanimate objects. The name of this power is *mana*. Robert H. Codrington has written about it and its significance in Melanesian religion as follows: "The religion of the Melanesians consists, as far as belief goes, in the persuasion that there is a supernatural power about belonging to the region of the unseen; and, as far as practice goes, in the use of means of getting this power turned to their own benefit. The notion of a Supreme Being is altogether foreign to them, or indeed of any being occupying a very elevated place in their world. . . . There is a belief in a force altogether distinct from physical power, which acts in all kinds of ways for good and evil, and which it is of the greatest advantage to possess or control. This is Mana. . . . It is a power or influence, not physical, and in a way supernatural; but it shows itself in physical force, or in any kind of power or excellence which a man possesses. This Mana is not fixed in anything, and can be conveyed in almost anything; but spirits, whether disembodied souls or supernatural beings, have it and can impart it; and it essentially belongs to personal beings to originate it, though it may act through the medium of water, or a stone, or a bone. All Melanesian religion consists, in fact, in getting this Mana for one's self, or getting it used for one's benefit—all religion, that is, as far as religious practices go, prayers and sacrifices."[13]

[12] A. Campbell Garnett, *God In Us*. 1945, p.100.
[13] R. H. Codrington, *The Melanesians, Studies in Their Anthropology and Folk-*

Looking elsewhere, we find that in Africa the Bantu people have a very strong belief in a sort of universal energy or potency. This is an intangible, all-pervasive something which is immanent in and flows through all things, but which comes to a focus in special objects. It can be used for either good or evil, and at all times it must be approached and employed with circumspection. The religion of the Bantu, according to Edwin W. Smith, "consists very largely in getting this power to work for his benefit and in avoiding that which would bring him into violent and harmful contact with it."[14]

In America a similar concept is met with among many families of Indians. The Algonquins believe in a great power which permeates all things and orders all happenings. This is known as *manitou*.[15] The Iroquois explain all the activities of life and nature as due to an immanent, impersonal energy which they call *orenda*.[16] The Sioux think that a mysterious, superhuman power pervades the world and manifests itself in both fortunate and unfortunate happenings. Its name is *wakanda*.[17]

In Australia the aboriginal Arunta believe in a supernatural power which seems always to work in a harmful way, and which may be employed for the accomplishment of evil. They give the name *arung-quilta* both to this evil influence itself and to an object in which it is supposed to reside.[18]

While in the last instance the supernatural power appears to be altogether evil and dangerous, in the other cases it is clearly capable of doing good as well as working harm. Likewise, while it might be supposed that the impersonal nature of the dynamistic power would render it specially amenable to the relatively mechanical procedures of magic rather than to those of religion, the foregoing illustrations have made it plain that this type of belief functions perfectly well as

---

Lore. 1891, p.118 n.1. Cf. Codrington in HERE VIII, p.530; R. R. Marett, *The Threshold of Religion.* 2d ed. 1914, pp.99-121; and in HERE VIII, pp.375-380; Nathan Söderblom, *Das Werden des Gottesglaubens, Untersuchungen über die Anfänge der Religion.* 2d ed. 1926, p.27.

[14] E. W. Smith, *The Religion of Lower Races as Illustrated by the African Bantu.* 1923, p.10.

[15] Clark Wissler, *Indians of the United States* (The American Museum of Natural History Science Series, I). 1940, pp.103f.

[16] J. N. B. Hewitt in *Report of the Bureau of American Ethnology.* 43 (1925-26), p.608 n.3.

[17] Alice C. Fletcher and Francis La Flesche in *Report of the Bureau of American Ethnology.* 27 (1905-06), pp.597f. (for the Omaha tribe of the Siouan family); Edwin T. Denig, *ibid.,* 46 (1928-29), pp.486f. (for the Assiniboin).

[18] Baldwin Spencer and F. J. Gillen, *The Arunta, A Study of a Stone Age People.* 1927, II, p.414 n.1.

a basis not only for magic but also for religion. The purposes and feelings with which men approach the unseen power are varied. The attitudes exhibited run the gamut all the way from fear to trust. If it is possible to name one attitude as most characteristic of all, it is perhaps that of awe, in which fear and trust are commingled, and in which there is a strange compulsion not to flee from the unseen power but to draw near to it.[19]

To give illustrations of animism is almost unnecessary, it is so widespread and well known.[20] Animism peoples the world with spirits, and their number is legion. Any object whatsoever may have its individual soul, and free spirits may be anywhere and everywhere. The Bantu of Africa think that spirits dwell in springs, rivers and lakes, in rocks and piles of stone, in trees, caves and hills.[21] The Arunta of Australia have a firm belief in the existence of spirits, which are thought to live in trees and rocks, to prowl about especially at night, to travel long distances rapidly and easily, and to be capable of both cruel and beneficent deeds.[22]

In man's response to the spirits there is the same ambivalence which appeared in his relation to the dynamistic power. He is both repelled and attracted, both made fearful and moved to trust. Fear of the spirits may seem to predominate, as in this description of the Guiana native given by a traveler in that land: "His whole world swarms with beings. He is surrounded by a host of them, possibly harmful. It is therefore not wonderful that the Indian fears to be without his fellow, fears even to move beyond the light of his campfire, and when obliged to do so, carries a fire-brand with him, that he may have a chance of seeing the beings among whom he moves."[23] Yet the possible availability of superhuman assistance from the spirits may lead to a sense not so much of fear as of dependence and confidence. Similarly, it goes without saying that both the practices of magic and the procedures of religion are employed with relation to the spirits.

Such, then, are the two great ways of thought about the super-

[19] Karl Beth, *Religion und Magie bei den Naturvölkern.* 1914, p.125; John Murphy, *Lamps of Anthropology* (Publications of the University of Manchester, CCLXXXI). 1943, pp.38-49.

[20] George W. Gilmore, *Animism.* 1919.

[21] W. C. Willoughby, *Nature-Worship and Taboo, Further Studies in "The Soul of the Bantu."* 1932, pp.1-118.

[22] Spencer and Gillen, *The Arunta,* II, pp.421-428.

[23] E. F. Im Thurn, *Among the Indians of Guiana.* 1883. Quoted by Gilmore, *Animism,* p.99.

natural which we distinguish as dynamism and animism. Yet, as we have already said, the two are not always in fact sharply separated. In Melanesia, as we have seen, the ultimate source of *mana* is usually supposed to be a ghost or spirit, and there, too, it is correct to say both that a man has *mana* and that a spirit is *mana*.[24] Among a number of the Bantu tribes the word *mulungu* is applied to the vague, impersonal power in which they believe, but the same word is also used to designate all the spirits of the dead.[25]

THE SOUL AND ITS SURVIVAL

Thus far, then, we have described belief in, and a sense of relationship to, supernatural power or powers as a major characteristic of primitive religion. A widely encountered aspect of primitivism must now be mentioned. This is belief in the human soul and in its survival after death, together with the feelings and attitudes and practices that accompany such belief. While this may be a matter in which very diverse conceptions appear and which is correspondingly difficult to deal with, it is at the same time a matter which is unmistakably prominent in the thought and life of a great many nonliterate peoples.

A single example will illustrate one sort of practice which is widely encountered. The Bantu inter the deceased. It is their custom to wrap the corpse in skins and blankets and place it in an excavated grave. Then the members of the family kneel around the opening in the earth and place upon the body such things as a calabash of milk, a pipe and tobacco, and seeds. Finally they bid the deceased one farewell with some such words as these: "Good-bye! Do not forget us! See, we have given you tobacco to smoke and food to eat! A good journey to you! Tell old friends who died before you that you left us living well."[26]

Elsewhere in the world many forms other than that just cited are found for the disposal of the body of the deceased. The corpse is sometimes deposited in the jungle, exposed on a platform in a tree, placed in a hut, committed to the waters of a river or the sea, or cremated. Where a grave is employed it may be located beneath the hut in which the deceased lived, or in the enclosure for the cattle, or out in the forest away from the village. It may be sunk deep in the earth, or left shallow and covered with a pile of boughs, a mound

---

[24] Marett in HERE VIII, p.376.   [25] E. Sidney Hartland in HERE II, p.365.
[26] Smith, *The Religion of Lower Races as Illustrated by the African Bantu*, p.29.

of earth, or a heap of stones. The body is often placed in a crouching position, or flexed and laid on one side in the grave. In some cases the position may have been determined by the binding of the corpse; again these may have been considered natural attitudes of rest.[27]

Throughout the world it is customary to place food and property in or upon the grave. Sometimes the objects left at the grave are broken or burned, the principle involved evidently being that the things themselves must be "killed" in order to go with and be of service to the dead. Animals are also slaughtered that they may continue to be available to their deceased owner, and until recent times the custom has existed in some parts of the earth of slaying wives, slaves or other dependents, that they may accompany their dead master into the other world. The severity of some of these customs has often been mitigated and the economy of property and life promoted by the substitution in the grave of models for the actual objects, of figures for the slaughtered animals, and of statuettes for the slain persons.[28]

The wide variety of beliefs entertained concerning the state of the dead seems to have included the idea that the deceased person lived on in the grave in bodily form. At any rate the apprehension sometimes appears that the dead may come forth in the body from the grave, and the opinion is frequently found that the ghost or soul lingers for a time at the place of burial. Most generally, the principle of life which animates the body is considered to be the soul, and the soul is regarded as separable from the body and capable of living on after it.

Fundamentally, the soul is the life of the body, and as such it may be identified with the blood, the heart, the breath, the shadow, the name, or with light or fire. The separability of the soul from the body may have been suggested even in life by experiences in dreams, unconsciousness and illness. In death the separation of the soul from the body is sometimes thought of as attended by great difficulty and as requiring considerable time for its complete fulfillment.[29]

After death the soul is often expected to survive indefinitely or forever, but again it may be thought that it will live on for only a limited time until it reaches a final end in a second or third death. The place of life after death is variously supposed to be in caves,

[27] E. Sidney Hartland in HERE IV, pp.420-426.
[28] *ibid.*, pp.428-431.
[29] H. B. Alexander in HERE XI, pp.725-731.

hills or rocks, in a distant forest, valley or mountain, in a subterranean region, in a land near where the sun rises or sets, in the sky, or among the stars. In other cases the lot of the soul is imagined to be that of rebirth in human form or transmigration into animal form. Often the state of the dead is expected to be similar to earthly life, but again it is anticipated that it will be much happier, or it is believed that it will vary in accordance with the status or character of the person, or the circumstances of his death, or the conditions of his burial.[30]

For illustrations of these beliefs we may adduce examples from among the Melanesians and the American Indians. On one of the Melanesian islands a lake fills the crater of an ancient volcano. To this lake the dead man's soul is believed to make its way after it has quitted its former habitation. Sometimes men notice recent footprints on the mountain path which leads thither, and they go down to the villages to ask who has died and just gone up that way. Near the lake is a volcanic vent by which the soul is supposed to descend to the abode of the dead. In the nether world there are trees and houses, it is thought, and the deceased live a happy life, free from pain and sickness.[31]

Among the American Indians, those of the Thompson River think that the land of departed souls is in the underground, toward the sunset. It is reached by a long track, at the end of which is a large lodge with doors at the east and west, and a double row of fires extending throughout its length. When the spirit reaches this place, he finds his deceased relatives assembled there, talking, laughing and singing. They welcome him warmly, and he finds a land of abundant grass and flowers and perfumed air, and enters among a people who are joyful and happy.[32]

Since primitive man seems usually to think of the dead as living unseen by mortal eye and with a certain independence of everyday limitations, he can also easily assume that the deceased possess some power which the living man does not have. This power may be expected to bring help to the living in such pursuits as hunting, fishing or agriculture, or it may be thought to bring harm in the form of famine, sickness or death. Therefore the attitude toward the dead may be that of trust, or of fear, or a mingling of both. Hence there

[30] J. A. MacCulloch in HERE XI, pp.817-828.
[31] Codrington, *The Melanesians, Studies in Their Anthropology and Folk-Lore,* pp.285f.
[32] MacCulloch in HERE XI, p.822.

may arise various practices of sacrifice, propitiation and ancestor worship, in which the purpose is to obtain the assistance of the departed spirits, or to ward off their malevolent influence.[33]

However ramified and variegated the customs and conceptions concerning the dead, basic to them all is the belief in the continuance of the personality beyond death. So widely encountered is this fundamental idea that Émile Durkheim has not hesitated to say that "the idea of the soul seems to have been contemporaneous with humanity itself";[34] and Sir James G. Frazer has spoken of belief in the immortality of the soul, in the sense of the indefinite persistence of personality after death, as "remarkably widespread and persistent among mankind from the earliest times down to the present."[35]

We have now noted two major aspects of primitive religion: on the one hand, the belief in supernatural power or powers, together with the attitudes and practices connected therewith; on the other, the belief in the soul and its survival of death, together with the feelings and procedures related to that conception. In fact, these two ideas seem to approach the status of universal beliefs as nearly as anything that can be found in the entire realm of primitive religion. Analyzing primitive beliefs and customs from the standpoint of anthropology, Bronislaw Malinowski points to the basic nature and universal extension of these beliefs in the following words: "Two affirmations preside over every ritual act, every rule of conduct, and every belief. There is the affirmation of the existence of powers sympathetic to man. . . . This is the belief in Providence. . . . The second belief is that beyond the brief span of natural life there is compensation in another existence. . . . In their deepest foundations, as well as in their final consequences, the two beliefs in Providence and Immortality are not independent of one another. . . . The unity of religion in substance, form and function is to be found everywhere. Religious development consists probably in the growing predominance of the ethical principle and in the increasing fusion of the two factors of all belief, the sense of Providence and the faith in Immortality."[36]

[33] James G. Frazer, *The Fear of the Dead in Primitive Religion.* 1933; Paul Radin, *Primitive Religion, Its Nature and Origin.* 1937, pp.221-227.

[34] Émile Durkheim, *The Elementary Forms of the Religious Life.* tr. Joseph W. Swain. 1915, p. 240.

[35] Frazer, *The Fear of the Dead in Primitive Religion,* p.6.

[36] Bronislaw Malinowski, *An Anthropological Analysis of Primitive Beliefs and Conduct with Special Reference to the Fundamental Problems of Religion and Ethics* (Rid-

[18]

OTHER IDEAS

Around the two basic ideas just presented cluster many subsidiary concepts. Of the most widely encountered of these, a very few may now be mentioned. The conception of taboo is a frequent concomitant of dynamistic and animistic belief.[37] The term is derived from the Polynesian *tabu* or *tapu*, and means something which is marked off, or not to be lightly approached. Anything which partakes of superhuman force, or anything connected with a spirit, may be taboo. Objects, plants, animals, persons, places and activities all may upon occasion fall within this category of the sacred or prohibited. A state of taboo may be inherent in something or in somebody, as in a mother or baby, a warrior on a campaign, a stranger, king or priest, a sick or dead person, a sacred place or object, a time, number or name. Taboo may also be imposed by a superior authority, as when a chief or priest declares some act or place to be forbidden; and it may likewise be acquired by contact with an object or person already tabooed. The entire system is easily capable, therefore, of building up into a very complex body of compulsions and restraints. It is understandable that in such a set of taboos fear may be a prominent motive. Nevertheless, something of the same ambivalence already noted in the entire relationship of man to supernatural power or powers may also appear here. That which is marked off because of its connection with the supernatural is certainly dangerous but it may also be potentially helpful. Therefore the attitude of shrinking away from what may cause evil may be balanced at least in part by the mood of interest in and approach to what may bring good. And, as R. R. Marett says, "fear tempered with wonder and submissiveness, and thus transmuted into reverence, is the forerunner of love."[38]

Closely related to taboo, and like it an expression of dynamistic and animistic belief, is fetishism. A fetish is a visible medium of the supernatural power or powers. It is generally a material object in which *mana* or a spirit dwells either temporarily or permanently. It may be a natural thing, such as an unusual stone, or a manufactured instrument or a strange concoction. In West Africa, for example, one fetish was simply a mixture of clay and various roots in an earthen

dell Memorial Lectures · 1934-1935, University of Durham). 1936, pp.60f. Quoted by permission of the publishers, Oxford University Press, London.

[37] James G. Frazer, *The Golden Bough, A Study in Magic and Religion*. 3d ed. 1911. Part II, *Taboo and the Perils of the Soul*; Hutton Webster, *Taboo, A Sociological Study*. 1942.

[38] In HERE XII, p.183.

pot. Another was a household broom which had been brought by the medicine man into contact with every sort of tabooed object, and before which he had uttered every forbidden name which might not ordinarily be spoken aloud. Thus the broom itself was invested with concentrated taboo, and became a fetish. By its nature a fetish lends itself to the manipulations of magic, yet it may also be a symbol and an object useful in the practices of religion.[39]

Another conception which appears in nonliterate society is that of totemism. Here a group of kindred people is regarded as related to a species of natural objects, usually animals or plants.[40] The term comes from the Indians of America, and the totemic organization of society appears in many other places too, notably including Australia. The Arunta of Australia believe that every individual has a special relationship to some animal or plant. His ancestors are often supposed to have been transformed into human beings out of this animal or plant, and by birth he himself was introduced into the totem group which bears its name and uses its symbol.[41] A possible explanation of totemism relates it to a dynamistic background. The men of the clan, the emblems of the totem, and the individuals of the totemic species, it may be supposed, all share in and are animated by a common principle or force comparable to *mana*. "This is what the totem really consists in," writes Émile Durkheim, "it is only the material form under which the imagination represents this immaterial substance, this energy diffused through all sorts of heterogeneous things, which alone is the real object of the cult."[42]

Reference must also be made to the idea of "high gods." Whether this conception arose through the personifying of *mana*, as might be supposed in the light of our previous discussion, whether it is always an importation due to missionary or other influence which is no longer traceable, as some observers believe, or whether it is evidence of the existence of an original monotheism, as has been argued notably by Wilhelm Schmidt,[43] is not yet clear. At any event, the idea,

[39] W. G. Aston in HERE v, p.896; Wilson D. Wallis, *Religion in Primitive Society.* 1939, p.33; William Howells, *The Heathens, Primitive Man and His Religions.* 1948, pp.59f.

[40] James G. Frazer, *Totemism and Exogamy.* 1910, IV, pp.3f.

[41] Spencer and Gillen, *The Arunta,* I, p.67; Frazer, *Totemica,* p.252.

[42] Émile Durkheim, *The Elementary Forms of the Religious Life.* tr. Joseph W. Swain. 1915, p.189.

[43] Wilhelm Schmidt, *Der Ursprung der Gottesidee, Eine historische-kritische und positive Studie.* 4 vols. 1912-33; *The Origin and Growth of Religion, Facts and Theories.* tr. H. J. Rose. 1931; *High Gods in North America.* 1933; *Primitive Revelation.* tr. Joseph J. Baierl. 1939.

although conspicuously lacking in some places, is indubitably present in others. Thus among the Melanesians there is reported to be no thought whatsoever of a Supreme Being,[44] but among the Bantu there is stated to exist a belief in a personal Being, who is the Creator of all things.[45] This deity is associated with the sky, and thought of as the determiner of all human destiny. For the practical purposes of everyday religion, however, attention remains centered on the spirits and on *mana*, while this deity for the most part occupies a place only on the fringe of consciousness. Similar ideas of one Supreme Being, who is Creator, Lord or Father, occur also among a number of other preliterate peoples in Africa, Australia, America and the Arctic regions.

PRIMITIVE ART

Many of the ideas and practices which are a part of primitivism are such as to encourage the employment and fabrication of sacred objects. These may be of the crudest, such as the pot of roots and clay which was a West African fetish; or they may exemplify the application of no little technical skill and artistic ability. Those which we will adduce in illustration are ones in the making of which at least some artistic effort is evident.

Among the widely varied sorts of objects found in primitive religious art, three are specially prominent, namely fetishes, masks and ancestral images. Fetishes or charms, being the dwelling places of supernatural power or powers, are often manufactured with elaborate ceremonial procedure and no little artistic labor. Two examples of such charms will be presented. The first (Fig. 1) is a war charm, twenty-four inches high and decorated with frigate bird feathers. It came from the Admiralty Islands, and is now in the collections of the American Museum of Natural History in New York City. The second (Fig. 2) is also a fighting charm. It is not quite twelve inches high, is made of cocoanut fiber and adorned with feathers, shells and seeds. It was made on the Gulf of Papua, New Guinea, and belongs to the collections of the Buffalo Museum of Science in Buffalo, New York.

The mask is another kind of artistic object which may represent a spirit or serve as a concentration point for spiritual power.[46] As

44 Codrington, *The Melanesians*, p.118 n.1.
45 Smith, *The Religion of Lower Races as Illustrated by the African Bantu*, pp.54-61.
46 Eckart von Sydow, *Die Kunst der Naturvölker und der Vorzeit* (Propyläen-Kunstgeschichte, 1). 2d ed. 1927, pp.32-36.

practiced for example on the Gulf of Papua, New Guinea, the making of such masks is strictly governed by taboos and surrounded by ritualistic procedures. Years may be required for the completion of the work, and when the masks are at last ready they are brought forth before all the people in ceremonial dances. Each mask is named after some spirit who figures in Papuan mythology, and the use of the objects is one of the chief means of perpetuating the mythical and totemistic ideas which prevail. The masks are generally made of bark-cloth stretched over cane and palm-wood frames, and painted with various designs.[47] In Fig. 3 we show an elaborate example of a bird mask, seventy-two inches high, from the Papuan Gulf, and in Fig. 4 a group of other smaller masks also from New Guinea. All are now in the Newark Museum, Newark, New Jersey.

The making of such masks is done in many other places too. We will turn for further illustration only to Borneo and West Africa. The mask pictured in Fig. 5 is from Borneo. It is of wood, painted. That in Fig. 6 is from the Cameroons, West Africa. It is of brass, with ornamented headdress, heavy eyebrows, filed incisors, and chin beard. Both of these masks are now in the American Museum of Natural History, New York City.

The importance in primitive religion of the worship of ancestors and of the dead explains the prominence of ancestral images among the works of primitive art.[48] The making of an image of this sort is usually done ceremonially, and in case it is so constructed that this is possible magical substances may be placed within it in order to assure that it will be the bearer of supernatural powers. As a potent fetish it may be employed for such purposes as to drive off enemies or to cure sickness. The making of such ancestral figures must have played a large role in the development of cult images and idols in general, and it is by no means always certain when a statuette should be specifically described as an ancestral image or just called a cult figure. The images shown in Figs. 7 and 8 are probably to be identified as ancestral figures. Both are from New Zealand, and are now in the M. H. de Young Memorial Museum, San Francisco. Mention may also be made here of the colossal stone idols of Easter Island (Rapa Nui), which in origin may have been conceived as ancestral images. They were cut out of the tufa of the crater of the volcano

[47] Ralph Linton, Paul S. Wingert, and René D'Harnoncourt, *Arts of the South Seas.* 1946, pp.96-98.
[48] Von Sydow, *Die Kunst der Naturvölker und der Vorzeit*, pp.37-42.

Rano-raraku, on the slopes of which they still stand looking out to sea. Shown in Fig. 9, they are probably the most powerful of all known expressions of primitive art.[49]

Certain outstanding characteristics found in primitive religion have now been described in general terms. Necessary as such a generalized treatment is in order to provide initial familiarity with basic concepts, it constitutes only an introduction to the further task of studying specific cultural groups with the purpose of comprehending the configurations of belief distinctive of each.[50] The remainder of this chapter will be devoted to an account of the religions of prehistoric man and of several groups of preliterate people today. While the relative scantiness of archeological remains from the very ancient past makes it impossible to reconstruct full pictures of the practice of religion at that time, there is at least enough to provide definite glimpses of the kind of faith which then existed. Among various folk living on a preliterate level today, there is abundant opportunity for observing different and developed configurations of religious belief and practice.

[49] *ibid.*, p.41; Linton, Wingert and D'Harnoncourt, *Arts of the South Seas*, pp.44-46; cf. Thor Heyerdahl, *Kon-Tiki, Across the Pacific by Raft.* 1950, pp.176-185.
[50] Ruth Benedict, *Patterns of Culture.* 1934, pp.xiii,49f.

2. THE RELIGION OF PREHISTORIC MAN

As we look back into the remoteness of prehistoric antiquity, it is not possible to discern any absolute beginning of religion. Rather, religion may be said to be as old as man himself. As R. R. Marett puts it: "The principle that everything must have a beginning does not seem to apply to any of the major institutions of mankind—to family, tribe and state, to government and law, to morality and fine art, and finally, and above all, to religion. In every case alike, if we work backwards from the present, traces of them persist until they fade out together precisely at the point at which Man himself fades out also."[51]

THE DIMENSIONS OF PREHISTORY

Man and his religion are at least dimly within the focus of our vision as far back as in the Old Stone Age. Speaking of the stratified rock formations which comprise the outer covering, perhaps fifty miles thick, of our planet, geologists distinguish four principal rock systems or periods, namely the Primary, Secondary, Tertiary and Quaternary. From the standpoint of the plant and animal fossils imbedded in these rocks, four successive eras are recognized, to which are given the names Eozoic (dawn life), Paleozoic (ancient life), Mesozoic (middle life), and Cenozoic (recent life). The Cenozoic era has numerous subdivisions, of which the last two are the Pleistocene and the Holocene. The Pleistocene epoch was that in which "most of the new" or present-day animals were in existence, and the Holocene is that in which "all of the new" or present-day fauna are known. The Quaternary rock period includes both the Pleistocene and the Holocene epochs of life.

In relation to climate, the Pleistocene was the epoch of the Ice Age. Within this period there were four major times when the great glaciers crept down out of the north, and three intervening occasions when they withdrew again. Since the advancing ice sheets also brought more abundant rainfall, the glacial and interglacial periods were correlated with pluvial and interpluvial phases of climate. When the last great ice sheets retreated, the transition was made to the Holocene or recent epoch in which the climate became much as it is at present.

[51] R. R. Marett, *Head, Heart and Hands in Human Evolution*. 1935, p.81. Quoted by permission of the publishers, Hutchinson and Company, Ltd., London.

As far as human life and culture are concerned, the Pleistocene corresponds approximately to the Paleolithic or Old Stone Age, a period which in Europe is customarily subdivided into Pre-Chellean, Chellean, Acheulian, Mousterian, Aurignacian, Solutrean and Magdalenian epochs. The Holocene is the period of modern man, and includes the Mesolithic, Neolithic, Chalcolithic, Bronze and Iron Ages. We have to do here with the Pleistocene epoch and the Paleolithic Age.

Estimates of geological time are based chiefly upon the counting of varves, which are the annual deposits of sediment left by the melting of the retreating ice sheets; upon observation of the extent to which uranium in the rocks has been transformed into lead in the very slow course of its radioactive disintegration; and upon comparison with astronomical results in the study of solar radiation. By such methods of investigation it is now calculated that the duration of the Pleistocene epoch was something like 600,000 years.[52] It lasted, of course, until the Holocene epoch, which began some ten thousand years ago. Thus the Pleistocene epoch and the Paleolithic Age have occupied over ninety-eight per cent of the total time span of human culture, leaving less than the last two per cent of the time to be filled by the Mesolithic, Neolithic, Bronze and Iron Ages combined.[53]

HOMO NEANDERTALENSIS

The appearance of man upon earth probably fell within the Pleistocene epoch. Fossil remains of anthropoid creatures are found first. These include the skeletal remains of *Pithecanthropus erectus*, the "erect ape man," discovered near Trinil, Java, in 1891 by Eugène Dubois, and *Sinanthropus pekinensis*, the "Chinese man of Peking," unearthed in 1927 and afterward by Gunnar Andersson near Chou K'ou Tien, forty miles from Peiping, China. Both belong probably to the Middle Pleistocene epoch (around 400,000 years ago), and both are considered "hominids," that is extremely early members of the great family now represented on earth by the genus *Homo*, or mankind.[54]

[52] Frederick E. Zeuner, *Dating the Past, An Introduction to Geochronology.* 1946, pp.144f.; Carey Croneis and William C. Krumbein, *Down to Earth, An Introduction to Geology.* 1936, pp.294-297,444.

[53] William Howells, *Mankind So Far* (The American Museum of Natural History Series, v). 1944, pp.120f.

[54] Franz Weidenreich, *Giant Early Man from Java and South China* (Anthropological Papers of the American Museum of Natural History, xl, 1). 1945; *The Skull of Sinanthropus Pekinensis* (Palaeontologia Sinica, n. s. d., 10. Whole Series, 127). 1943;

Elsewhere in the world, probably including Europe, at least equally primitive forms must have existed. In the east it is possible to trace the line of development from *Pithecanthropus erectus* through *Homo soloensis* (found at Ngandong on the Solo River six miles from Trinil, Java), to fossil forms and modern primitive types in Australia; and from *Sinanthropus pekinensis* to modern Mongoloid groups which have comparable physical characteristics. In the west a like development may be presumed to have taken place antecedent to the appearance of the relatively advanced types of which we will now speak.

For our purposes it will suffice to tell of *Homo heidelbergensis* and *Homo neandertalensis.* "Heidelberg man" is known only insofar as inferences are possible from an unquestionably human jaw discovered at Mauer, near Heidelberg, Germany, in 1907.[55] His date was perhaps in the Second Interglacial Period.[56] "Neandertal man" is more fully revealed by modern discovery. The first fossil human skeleton so designated was found in the Neander valley, not far from Düsseldorf, Germany, in 1857, and since that time skeletal remains of a similar type have been found elsewhere in Europe all the way from Russia and Yugoslavia to Belgium, France, Italy and Gibraltar. Other remains also related, but less closely, have been unearthed at points as far distant as Mount Carmel, Palestine (*Paleoanthropus palestinensis*) and Broken Hill, Northern Rhodesia (*Homo rhodesiensis*).

The date of Neandertal man in Europe was probably during the Third Interglacial and Fourth Glacial Periods, or perhaps from 100,-000 to 50,000 years ago. In its cultural aspects this epoch is known in Europe as the Mousterian. The name is derived from the village of Le Moustier, France, near which numerous flint implements of characteristic kind were found.[57]

Primitive as he was, *Homo neandertalensis* was indeed a human being, and probably in the direct line of evolution leading to *Homo sapiens.* In physique, Neandertal man was heavily built and of great strength, while his low, broad skull contained a brain as large or a

---

and *Apes, Giants and Man.* 1946; Hellmut de Terra in *The Scientific Monthly.* 51 (July-Dec. 1940), pp.112-124; Robert J. Braidwood in JNES 6 (1947), pp.30-42.

[55] For geographical details, particularly European sites not shown on our Map I, see the maps in Henry F. Osborn, *Men of the Old Stone Age, Their Environment, Life and Art.* 2d ed. 1915; and *The National Geographic Magazine.* 94 (1948), p.774.

[56] James H. McGregor in Boas, ed., *General Anthropology,* p.60.

[57] George G. MacCurdy, *The Coming of Man.* 1932, pp.35,51f.; Howells, *Mankind So Far,* p.165.

little larger than that of modern man. His flint tools were skillfully edged, and included scrapers, cleavers, drills and knives. He had fire, as even *Sinanthropus pekinensis* before him had had, and he lived on the cold-weather animals of the time.[58]

For the story we have to tell, however, the immensely significant fact is that Neandertal man had at least some conception and practice which may properly be termed religious. The evidence appears in the burials of the Mousterian Age. Previous to this time there is no indication of the practice of burial. The extant skeletal remains were generally found lying in the bed of a stream or lake, and if they were in a cave there was no sign of interment with care. Nor was interment unanimously practiced by Neandertal man, there being no trace of any burial, for example, in connection with the important Mousterian remains discovered at La Quina, France.

But at a number of other notable Mousterian sites, Neandertal man was found to have buried the dead with care. At Le Moustier the skeleton of a Neandertal youth of about sixteen years of age was unearthed. The body had been placed in a rock shelter in the side of a cliff. The right arm was bent so that the right side of the skull rested on it. The left arm was extended, and lying near the bones of the left hand were a beautiful stone cleaver and a scraper. Many other flint artifacts were immediately about. In similar fashion at La Ferrassie several adults and children were buried in a rock shelter, and stone tools were placed at their hands. Also at La Chapelle-aux-Saints a skeleton of the Mousterian epoch was found interred, together with beautifully made implements, in a rectangular burial pit which had been sunk in the floor of a cave.[59]

This burial of the dead with care which is so marked a feature of the Mousterian epoch is, to be sure, capable of various interpretations. It may be supposed that we have here evidence of natural affection. The bodies were placed with a certain tenderness, we may think, in the position of one asleep, and familiar implements were put near by. But it has also been argued that it was fear which accounted for such treatment of the dead. Perhaps the manner of burial and the placing of gifts in the grave show an intent to restrain and appease the deceased. It is not impossible, indeed, that both motives were at work. However that may be, one fact is unmistakable. Man believed in life after death. He thought that the departed would

[58] Howells, *Mankind So Far*, pp.148,164-170.
[59] George G. MacCurdy, *Human Origins*. 1924, I, pp.359-362.

continue to lead a life at least to some extent comparable to that lived here. In that life there would be need to have objects and implements like those which had been of service here. If fear of the dead entered the picture, then living man evidently believed in the possibility of a continued relationship in which the deceased might do him harm if not propitiated. All of this is sometimes called the "cult of the dead"; certainly it reveals attitudes, ideas and practices which must properly be designated religious.[60]

HOMO SAPIENS

The successor of *Homo neandertalensis* was *Homo sapiens*. This is "man the wise," the species which today inhabits the earth and not infrequently belies its anthropological designation by its actual behavior. The date of appearance of *Homo sapiens* is about the beginning of the Upper Paleolithic or most recent period of the Old Stone Age, say fifty thousand years ago.[61]

Carmel man (*Paleoanthropus palestinensis*) may have been an intermediate or transitional type,[62] Rhodesian man (*Homo rhodesiensis*) displays features which suggest the *sapiens* species,[63] and Solo man (*Homo soloensis*) has been called "the oldest at present known representative of *Homo sapiens fossilis*."[64] Fossil *Homo sapiens* is also represented by Wadjak man (*Homo wadjakensis*) in Java, and by the Upper Chou K'ou Tien cave types in China.[65] But it is Cro-Magnon man in Europe of whom we have the fullest knowledge and through whom we can best picture the life of prehistoric "man the wise."

Cro-Magnon is French patois for "great hole," and is the name of a rock shelter at the village of Les Eyzies, France. Parts of five skeletons were uncovered here in 1868, and became the type specimens of the race to which the name Cro-Magnon is given. Similar remains have been found at numerous other locations in western Europe.

As revealed by his skeletal remains, Cro-Magnon man was tall of stature and had a prominent chin and high forehead. Both physically and mentally he was much like the succeeding races of Mesolithic

[60] G.-H. Luquet, *The Art and Religion of Fossil Man.* tr. by J. Townsend Russell. 1930, pp.151-179.

[61] Lewis G. Westgate in *The Scientific Monthly.* 51 (July-Dec. 1940), p.157.

[62] J. Philip Hyatt in *The Journal of Bible and Religion.* 12 (1944), pp.235f.

[63] McGregor in Boas, ed., *General Anthropology*, pp.87f.

[64] W. F. F. Oppenoorth in George G. MacCurdy, ed., *Early Man.* 1937, p.359.

[65] De Terra in *The Scientific Monthly.* 51 (July-Dec. 1940), p.124.

and Neolithic times, which in turn were closely similar to modern races of men.[66]

The culture of Cro-Magnon man passed through three stages, known as Aurignacian, Solutrean and Magdalenian, and taken as a whole was much in advance of that of Neandertal man. Many kinds of stone instruments were manufactured, and the technique of chipping flint was developed to the highest degree in the entire Paleolithic Period. Other materials such as ivory, bone and reindeer horn were also employed extensively in the making of such things as needles, javelin points and harpoons.

Like Neandertal man, Cro-Magnon man lived in rock shelters and caves, and there buried his dead. Typical burials of the Aurignacian epoch have been found at Paviland in Wales, where the skeleton was deeply stained with red ocher and accompanied by implements and ornaments; at Grimaldi on the Italian frontier, where among others a man, young woman and youth were interred with a covering of red ocher, and an old woman and a young man were buried beneath a flagstone supported by two upright stones to protect their skulls; and at Combe-Capelle in France, where the skeleton of a tall man was surrounded by flints and shells. A burial of the Solutrean epoch was discovered at Klause in Bavaria, where the body was surrounded by a mass of powdered ocher. Magdalenian interments were found in France at the Laugerie-Basse rock shelter near Les Eyzies, where perforated shells remained at the forehead, elbows, knees and feet of the skeleton; and at Les Hoteaux, where again the body had been enveloped in powdered ocher and accompanied by various implements.[67]

A photograph of the Aurignacian burial at Combe-Capelle, mentioned in the preceding paragraph, is reproduced in Fig. 10.[68] There it may be seen that small shells, some perforated, had been placed about the head, and flint implements near the head, right arm, right leg and left foot.

Generally speaking, then, Cro-Magnon burials were comparable to those of Neandertal man, but showed certain advances. The richer culture of the period provided finer tools and weapons for the dead than were previously available, as well as numerous personal ornaments, including necklaces and other adornments made of such ma-

[66] MacCurdy, *The Coming of Man*, p.41.
[67] MacCurdy, *Human Origins*, I, pp.380-405.
[68] H. Klaatsch and O. Hauser in *Praehistorische Zeitschrift*. 1 (1909-10), p.276, Fig. 2.

terials as perforated shells and animal teeth. A prominent feature was the strewing of many of the graves with red ocher, but the significance of the practice is not known. One hypothesis is that the red color was intended to represent the blood, and that the application of the ocher was therefore meant to convey life-giving qualities to the corpse.[69] Whatever the correct solution of this particular problem, the total evidence leaves no doubt that Cro-Magnon man, like the Neandertal before him, believed in some kind of continuing and real existence beyond death.

PREHISTORIC ART

The love of ornament revealed in objects like necklaces found in Cro-Magnon graves was only one aspect of an extensive interest in art, which notably characterizes this period. As far as is now known, the first appearance of the fine arts in prehistory was during the Aurignacian epoch. Sculpture, drawing and painting were all included.

In part it was tools and weapons which were decorated with engravings; again fragments of stone, bone, ivory and horn were carved into various shapes; and also figurines and statuettes were produced. Prominent among the figurines and statuettes is a whole series of sculptured figures of women, dating from the Aurignacian epoch, and giving exaggerated and even grotesque emphasis to the female characteristics. A probable explanation of these is that they were employed within the framework of dynamistic and magical belief, where like was thought to have the power to produce like, and where such representations consequently could be expected to be powerful aids to fertility.[70]

The first discovery of Paleolithic paintings was a dramatic event. This was in 1879, when Don Marcelino de Sautuola was investigating the cave of Altamira not far from Santander in northern Spain. While he searched for relics of ancient man in the floor deposits of the vestibule, his small daughter, María, aged five, went under the low roof of the cave. Looking upward, she cried out, "Toros!" (bulls). When her father came he saw that the painting of a bison was on the ceiling. Upon closer examination, extensive frescoes were discovered and it was found that a large group of animals was depicted, includ-

[69] CRW p. 5; Phyllis Ackerman in Vergilius Ferm, ed., *Forgotten Religions*. 1950, pp.3f.

[70] William F. Albright, *From the Stone Age to Christianity*. 1940, p.92.

[30]

ing not only the bison but also the hind, the horse, the wild boar and others.[71]

One of the paintings at Altamira is shown in Fig. 11, as reproduced by the Abbé Breuil.[72] The animal is a bison, of an extinct species, with long slender horns. The ancient artist has evidently portrayed his subject with the greatest faithfulness.

This discovery was greeted with skepticism and was soon almost forgotten by the world. Then in 1895 a farmer, digging in a field south of Les Eyzies in the Dordogne region of France, found a hitherto unknown passage leading into the rock. A boy crawled into the hole with a candle and upon emerging declared that the walls of the tunnel were covered with pictures of wild animals. Thus was discovered the grotto of La Mouthe, where the scholar Émile Rivière soon confirmed the existence of prehistoric engravings. These were crude and only in part painted, but many different animals were recognizable, including the bison, horse, reindeer, mammoth and ibex. Edouard Piette, a magistrate who pursued the subject of prehistoric art as an avocation, connected the newly found pictures with those of Altamira and thus gave a new impetus to the study of the whole subject. While Piette was at the time almost seventy years of age, his work was continued by a pupil who attained the highest distinction in the field. This was l'Abbé Henri Breuil, who became Professor at the Institute of Human Palaeontology in Paris.[73]

In 1901, Breuil, Capitan and Peyrony studied more engravings and paintings in the caves of Les Combarelles and Font de Gaume, both also in the vicinity of Les Eyzies. The cavern of Combarelles is a low narrow winding tunnel extending underground for seven hundred and twenty feet. Its drawings begin about three hundred and fifty feet from the entrance and extend to the end of the passage, some of the finest being in a small chamber just before an extremely constricted place. Some three hundred pictures have been counted, and among them appear representations of the bison, horse, reindeer, mammoth, ibex, stag, rhinoceros, lion and wolf, as well as of men both masked and unmasked.[74]

[71] Émile Cartailhac and Henri Breuil, *La Caverne d'Altamira à Santillane près Santander (Espagne)*. Peintures et gravures murales des cavernes paléolithiques. 1906.
[72] *ibid.*, Pl. xxiii.
[73] M. C. Burkitt, *Prehistory, A Study of Early Cultures in Europe and the Mediterranean Basin*. 2d ed. 1925, pp.13,249; Osborn, *Men of the Old Stone Age*, pp.392f.
[74] L. Capitan, H. Breuil and D. Peyrony, *Les Combarelles aux Eyzies (Dordogne)*. Peintures et gravures murales des cavernes paléolithiques. 1924.

Fig. 12 is a photograph of one of these engravings in the cave of Les Combarelles.[75] The animal is a rhinoceros, and the head and horns are portrayed with special effectiveness. A later drawing, turned at right angles and cut across the withers of the pachyderm, is of the head of a hind.

The cave of Font-de-Gaume opens high on the side of a valley and extends back into the hill for nearly five hundred feet. Far back within the cave, almost half of the distance from the entrance to the end, there is a very narrow passage now called the Rubicon. Beyond this is the Grande Galerie des Fresques, where relatively smooth, concave surfaces provided unusually favorable opportunities for murals. Here there are both simple drawings and fine polychrome paintings. Great processions of bison, reindeer and mammoths appear, while pictures of the horse, rhinoceros and wild boar are also found. Even in a narrow fissure at the extreme end of the cavern, known as the Diverticule Final, there are engravings of the lion and horse and paintings of the rhinoceros. Also on the walls are certain schematic drawings now designated as tectiforms. These are more or less in tent form and are believed to represent shelters or dwellings of some kind.[76]

One of the polychrome paintings at Font-de-Gaume is selected for illustration here (Fig. 13). The reproduction is by the Abbé Breuil.[77] Two reindeer face each other, their horns rising in splendid curves.

In 1906 the great cavern of Niaux became known with its impressive array of prehistoric pictures. The cave is in the Ariège region of southern France, on the slopes of the Pyrenees not far from Tarascon. With its entrance high on the sloping side of a river valley, this grotto extends almost horizontally into the mountain for a distance of forty-two hundred feet. In the year mentioned, a French officer, Commandant Molard, retired from the Engineers, was surveying this cave with his two sons, Paul and Jules. Far back in the cave, Paul, who had been reporting surveying measurements, suddenly exclaimed, "Drawings!" The pictures thus first noticed by any modern observer were found to include a splendid series of black paintings of bison and horses, as well as engravings of the ibex, the chamois, the ox and two trout. There are also various signs including

[75] *ibid.*, Pl. xxv.

[76] L. Capitan and H. Breuil, *La Caverne de Font-de-Gaume aux Eyzies (Dordogne).* Peintures et gravures murales des cavernes paléolithiques. 1910.

[77] *ibid.*, Pl. xxviii.

dots and tectiforms and outlines which look like clubs and arrows. In some cases the bison are shown with arrows in their sides, and in the case of the figure of a bison drawn upon the ground, engraved arrows are directed toward small cavities in the floor evidently intended to be taken for wounds.[78]

Fig. 14 is a representation from the so-called Black Salon in the Niaux cave.[79] Depicted are two bison, with black and red arrows in their sides; and also a small horse. The white marker was inserted to provide a reference scale, and is itself about sixteen inches long.

In 1912 another notable cavern on the northern slope of the Pyrenees in the Ariège district of France was explored. This was the Tuc d'Audoubert, which was first entered in modern times by the Comte de Bégouen and his three sons, Max, Jacques and Louis. Since a subterranean river flowed out of the cave, it was necessary to use a small boat in order to gain access to the inner recesses of the grotto. Then, leaving the boat, a veritable labyrinth of corridors and chambers was negotiated on foot and by climbing and crawling. Many engravings, some with splashes of color, were found. They represented the hind, horse, reindeer and bison. In an upper cave, which it was very difficult to enter, were clay statues of two bison, a male following a female. The figures were placed against a rock, and where the sides of the animals leaned against this rock they were not modeled. Otherwise, however, they were excellently sculptured. Each figure was about two feet in length. Despite some cracks, the state of preservation was remarkable, due to the perpetual dampness of the cave, free however from running water.[80]

The foremost of the two clay bison is shown in Fig. 15.[81] The work of the prehistoric artist has been executed with realism and a keen sense of observation. Although the figure is made to lean up against the rock, it is executed in such high relief that the ears and curved horns stand out as if on a fully detached statue. The treatment of the eye, with a small hole marking the pupil, the nostrils, mane and beard, is also noteworthy.

Only two years later, near the Tuc d'Audoubert, the Bégouen boys went down a vertical shaft and found themselves in yet another cave. Named by their father in their honor, Trois Frères, this cave, too,

[78] E. Cartailhac and H. Breuil in *L'anthropologie*. 19 (1908), pp.15-46.
[79] *ibid.*, p.27, Fig. 10.
[80] Bégouen in *Académie des Inscriptions et Belles-Lettres, Comptes rendus*. 1912, pp.532-538.
[81] *ibid.*, Pl. II following p.532.

was adorned with numerous pictures. On the walls were the figures not only of the bison, reindeer, horse, mammoth, rhinoceros, lion and bear, but also of birds something like owls, and of a man wearing stag's antlers on his head, and a tail, presumably a prehistoric sorcerer.[82]

In 1922 the previously unknown cave of Montespan, in the district of Haute Garonne, west and somewhat north of the region in which the caverns of Tuc d'Audoubert and Trois Frères were found, was discovered and explored by Norbert Casteret. While once probably dry, a subterranean stream was now flowing here through an underground tunnel two miles in length. When the grotto was first entered by Casteret, a water-filled siphon blocked the way completely at one point, but was passed through by swimming. Within, rich discoveries awaited the explorer, including some fifty engravings of animals and thirty specimens of modeling in clay. Many of the engravings were in a sloping tortuous passage. They pictured the horse, bison, stag, reindeer, hind, hyena, ibex, chamois and wild ass. In many cases the animals were represented as wounded. The clay sculptures included statues of a bear and two large lions or tigers, as well as relief models of horses. The clay bear was of particular interest. It was a headless statue, three and one half feet in length and two feet in height. Fallen between the front paws of the statue was an actual bear's skull, suggesting that at one time a real bear's head had surmounted the model. The sides of the figure were scarred with the marks of more than thirty blows from spears or arrows.[83]

The most remarkable cave of all, as it is generally recognized to be, was discovered in 1940.[84] This is the cave of Lascaux, above the village of Montignac, in the Dordogne. The discovery was made by a seventeen-year-old youth of Montignac, Marcel Ravidat, and three companions. Indeed it was their dog that was truly responsible for the find, for this animal accidentally fell into a hole hidden by bushes. Seeking to retrieve the pet, Ravidat descended into what seemed a natural well but actually gave access to a large cavern. Here, in the subterranean recesses of a grotto which had long been sealed up by a cave-in, were the finest and best preserved prehistoric paintings yet found. A veritable cavalcade of animal figures, four hundred in

[82] Burkitt, *Prehistory*, pp.257f.; José Pijoán, *El arte prehistórico europeo* (Cossío-Pijoán, Historia general del arte, vi). 1934. pp.113f.

[83] Norbert Casteret in *The National Geographic Magazine*. 46 (1924), pp.123-152.

[84] *Life*. Feb. 24, 1947, pp.62-69; Norbert Casteret in *The National Geographic Magazine*. 94 (1948), pp.771-794; Fernand Windels, *The Lascaux Cave Paintings*. 1949.

number, painted in red and black colors that are still fresh and vivid, appears upon the walls and ceilings. Bison, rhinoceroses, bears, stags, antelopes, cattle, deer and horses, and occasionally men as well, are seen. Many of the animals are depicted in more than life-size, as for example a gigantic black bull eighteen feet long. Some of the animals, including a red horse and a black bison, are pierced in vital places with arrows. In one picture a barred rectangle may represent a trap; in another, there is a stampede of horses, one of which is falling backward over a cliff or into a trap. At the bottom of a very narrow rock well are paintings of a rhinoceros, and of a bison the flanks of which have been torn by the spear of a hunter. The enormous beast has turned to charge the hunter, and the latter, pictured with a long body and birdlike head, is falling over backward with his arms flung out on either side (Fig. 16).

In addition to such finds as these already described on the mainland of Europe, other discoveries of prehistoric engravings and paintings have been made all the way from Scandinavia to South Africa.[85]

As far as chronological sequence is concerned in the mural art of Cro-Magnon man in Europe, four chief phases of development are distinguished.[86] The first corresponds with the Lower Aurignacian Period, and characteristically includes rude, deeply incised animal figures, ordinarily shown in absolute profile with only a single fore-leg and a single hind leg. Examples are to be found at Altamira, La Mouthe, Les Combarelles and Font-de-Gaume. The second is Upper Aurignacian in date, and is marked by the combination of engraving with painting. The figures are now far more lifelike. Altamira, La Mouthe, Les Combarelles and Font-de-Gaume again all provide illustrations. The third phase is that of Lower Magdalenian times. Here the animal outlines are generally incised deeply but are followed by light contour lines. In the painting, shading is practiced and color is sometimes used almost to excess. Early Magdalenian engravings and paintings are found at Altamira, Les Combarelles, Font-de-Gaume, Niaux, Tuc d'Audoubert and Montespan. Animal sculpture also appears, as notably illustrated by the bison of Tuc d'Audoubert. The fourth and climactic phase in the development of Paleolithic art was reached in the Upper Magdalenian Period. In

[85] Leo Frobenius and Douglas C. Fox, *Prehistoric Rock Pictures in Europe and Africa.* 1937; Frederick R. Wulsin, *The Prehistoric Archaeology of Northwest Africa* (Papers of the Peabody Museum of American Archaeology and Ethnology, Harvard University, XIX, 1). 1941, pp.114-137.

[86] cf. Osborn, *Men of the Old Stone Age*, p.395.

the drawings we now witness a perfection of animal outlines and an attention to detail which extends even to the employment of fine lines to indicate the hair. In the paintings, brilliant polychromes are produced which are truly magnificent. Splendid examples are to be seen on the famous ceiling at Altamira and on the walls of Font-de-Gaume and Lascaux. Here, too, there are human representations, of which one of the most remarkable is that of the disguised man with the stag's antlers and tail in the cave of Trois Frères.

By what methods were these remarkable pictures made in the recesses of these subterranean caverns? Some kind of illumination was obviously necessary, and it is surmised that this was furnished by small stone lamps. A lamp of this sort was found, for example, in the Magdalenian layer of the cave of La Mouthe. Bits of carbonized matter remaining on it suggested that an animal fat had fed its wick. The wick itself might have been of moss. The incised drawings, often involving extremely fine lines, must have been executed with various types of flint graving tools. The painting was presumably done most often with some sort of brush, although for some of the work it appears as if the fingers were used directly, while again there are examples which suggest that the paint was applied in a powdered form through a blowtube such as a hollow bone. The paint itself was probably made of ocher, oxide of manganese and other mineral materials, which were ground up and mixed with animal oils or fats.[87]

More important for our inquiry is the question as to the purpose which was served by the execution of these paintings and other works of art in the caves of the Paleolithic Period. It should be made plain that the interiors of the caves were not the places of habitation of Cro-Magnon man. We know little about where and how these people lived, although the tectiforms already mentioned have been believed to represent their huts or hide-covered shelters. In the mouths of the caves, also, deposits have been uncovered containing implements and traces of fire, suggesting human residence. But back in the caves there are no evidences of permanent habitation, nor would the deep interiors have provided satisfactory or safe places for living. Not only were the subterranean recesses generally uncomfortable for human dwelling, they also offered the dangerous possibility that the men within would be trapped by enemies, men or beasts, occupying the entrance. Nevertheless, it was into these inner reaches of the caves, and even into chambers and fissures which

[87] Osborn, *Men of the Old Stone Age*, pp.401,415; Burkitt, *Prehistory*, pp.205f.

were most extremely difficult of access, that the prehistoric artists went to accomplish their works.

It seems impossible, therefore, to give a satisfactory explanation of the art of the caves in terms of esthetic impulse alone. Without question many of the paintings and other works of art have a high value as measured by artistic criteria. The prehistoric artist certainly observed the animal life about him with extreme care and reproduced it with a vivid realism. In the creation of such fine images as he produced he may well have taken pleasure of an esthetic sort. Some of the pictures may have been intended to serve a purely decorative purpose. But if this were the only motive involved, why were many of the works put in such almost inaccessible places?

Furthermore, we note that the animals most frequently represented were precisely those upon which prehistoric man was chiefly dependent for his food and livelihood. They are most often shown as near at hand, which is the way they would have appeared to the Paleolithic hunter who had to contend with them at relatively close quarters. In some cases there seems to be an emphasis upon the fertility of the animals; often, as we have seen, they are shown with wounds, with darts or arrows hanging from their sides, or with clubs placed about them or traps near them.

Even a cautious evaluation of these facts leads to the conclusion that the raison d'être of this art included elements beyond the esthetic. In part at least, particularly where the figures are in relatively inaccessible places and where wounded animals are shown, the work must have been done because it was thought it would exercise some potent influence. The purpose was undoubtedly that of wielding power over the animals whose capture was desired. To portray the animal was to give the hunter some control over it, and to show the weapons with which it was attacked was to heighten the efficacy of those arms in the actual chase. The power of the representation extended to the thing represented. And some relation to this dynamistic and magical play of force was as necessary as life itself to prehistoric man.[88]

[88] Beth, *Religion und Magie bei den Naturvölkern*, pp.111-115; Ernest A. Parkyn, *An Introduction to the Study of Prehistoric Art.* 1915, pp.118f.; G. Renard, *Life and Work in Prehistoric Times.* tr. R. T. Clark. 1929, p.171; Miles C. Burkitt in EB II, pp.240f.; Luquet, *The Art and Religion of Fossil Man*, pp.96-113: Albright, *From the Stone Age to Christianity*, p.93; Max Raphael, *Prehistoric Cave Paintings* (The Bollingen Series, IV). 1945.

3. THE RELIGION OF PRELITERATE MAN

WE TURN now from religion as we have glimpsed it in prehistoric times to religion as it may be seen among preliterate peoples of the present. Brief descriptions will be given of several contemporary preliterate groups, in which at least certain highlights will appear of the configurations of religious and magical belief and practice prevailing among them. The groups selected for mention will be the Congo Pygmies, Bushmen, Andaman Islanders, Azande, Navaho, Chiricahua and Mescalero Apache, and Zuñi Pueblo Indians. At least the first three of these groups are among the rudest peoples on the globe.[89] All of them have been the object of scientifically dependable studies and publications, upon which we shall draw for the very short narratives which can be given here.

CONGO PYGMIES

The Pygmies are a dwarf folk living in equatorial Africa. Under five feet in height, they have skins which are dark, yet lighter than those of true Negroes, and are usually classified among the Negrito peoples, otherwise represented elsewhere in Africa and also in Oceania.

Among the Pygmies a practice has been seen by a modern observer which is strikingly parallel in significance to the dynamistic meaning which we have inferred for the cave art of the Old Stone Age. In the two hundredth century B.C., prehistoric man was painting pictures of the animals he wished to catch, and showing them with darts piercing their sides. In the twentieth century A.D., Professor Leo Frobenius of the *Forschungsinstitut für Kulturmorphologie* (Research Institute for the Morphology of Civilization) at Frankfort-on-the-Main was traveling in the Congo. In the jungle district near Luebo his expedition was guided for a time by three men and a woman who belonged to a hunting tribe of Pygmies. "One afternoon," relates Professor Frobenius, "finding our larder rather depleted, I asked one of them to shoot me an antelope, surely an easy job for such an expert hunter. He and his fellows looked at me in astonishment and then burst out with the answer that, yes, they'd do it gladly, but that it was naturally out of the question for that day since no preparations had been made. After a long palaver they declared themselves ready

[89] Robert H. Lowie, *Primitive Religion.* 1925, p.124.

to make these at sunrise. Then they went off as though searching for a good site and finally settled on a high place on a near-by hill."

"As I was eager to learn what their preparations consisted of," continues Frobenius, "I left camp before dawn and crept through the bush to the open place which they had sought out the night before. The pygmies appeared in the twilight, the woman with them. The men crouched on the ground, plucked a small square free of weeds and smoothed it over with their hands. One of them then drew something in the cleared space with his forefinger, while his companions murmured some kind of formula or incantation. Then a waiting silence. The sun rose on the horizon. One of the men, an arrow on his bowstring, took his place beside the square. A few minutes later the rays of the sun fell on the drawing at his feet. In that same second the woman stretched out her arms to the sun, shouting words I did not understand, the man shot his arrow and the woman cried out again. Then the three men bounded off through the bush while the woman stood for a few minutes and then went slowly towards our camp. As she disappeared I came forward and, looking down at the smoothed square of sand, saw the drawing of an antelope four hands long. From the antelope's neck protruded the pygmy's arrow. . . . That afternoon the hunters appeared with a fine 'buschbock,' an arrow in its throat."[90]

For the purpose of our study, it suffices to point out the remarkable correspondence in conception between this practice in the heart of contemporary Africa and the cave paintings of prehistoric man in Europe. Whether the agreement is evidence only of comparable ways of thought, or proves an actual cultural continuity, is not here of great importance. The latter possibility, however, certainly exists. In earlier times the Straits of Gibraltar probably had not been formed, and Europe was more intimately connected with Africa than now. As was thus geographically possible, and as is suggested by the existence in various parts of Africa of prehistoric rock pictures comparable to those of Spain and France, one culture doubtless then overspread the regions both to the north and the south of the Mediterranean lake. When the last ice sheet retreated and northern Africa turned into a desert, the African branch of this culture naturally moved southward into the moist interior. Thus it is understandable

[90] Frobenius and Fox, *Prehistoric Rock Pictures in Europe and Africa*, pp.22f. Quoted by permission of the publishers, The Museum of Modern Art, New York.

that, as Frobenius states, "that which existed once in Europe lives on among its epigones in Africa today."

BUSHMEN

The Bushmen of South Africa are also a Negrito people, small in stature, living normally as nomadic hunters. Rude as their existence is, they have a decided artistic sense and possess a wealth of folklore.

Their chief artistic expression has been in the form of rock paintings which are found scattered all over South Africa. More permanent than the sand drawing of the Pygmies just described, these pictures are like that one and like the cave pictures of prehistoric man[91] in that their subjects are most often the animals which are objects of the chase. The animals represented include antelopes, elephants, boars, leopards and lions, and the portrayals are usually very realistic. Since the hunting of these animals is often depicted, it may be believed that the pictures have more than a purely artistic significance, and, like those we have discussed already, were intended to bring success in the actual hunt.

One example of the Bushmen paintings is reproduced in Fig. 17 from a copy made by M. Helen Tongue. This picture is in a cave at Zandfontein, Cape of Good Hope. The animal is a fearsome hippopotamus, and is charging into a trap while under attack by natives. This method of hunting large game is, of course, well known among the Bushmen.[92]

The extensive folklore of the Bushman was made available for scientific study only through the learning by western scholars of the guttural, clicking language of these people and the recording from the lips of various narrators of the stories which had hitherto been told only orally. The collection of Bushman folklore which was made in this manner and published by Dr. Wilhelm H. I. Bleek and Miss Lucy C. Lloyd contains descriptions of wild animals and their habits, accounts of Bushman customs and practices, myths, legends, fables and poetry.[93]

The sample selected for presentation here is a myth called The

[91] For comparison of prehistoric man and the Bushman see Burkitt, *Prehistory*, pp.306f.

[92] *Bushman Paintings Copied by M. Helen Tongue*. 1909, p.13, Pl. IV. For these paintings see also *Rock-Paintings in South Africa from Parts of the Eastern Province and Orange Free State, Copied by George William Stow, with an Introduction and Descriptive Notes by Dorothea F. Bleek*. 1930; Herbert Kühn, *Die Kunst der Primitiven*. 1923, pp.31-39.

[93] W. H. I. Bleek and L. C. Lloyd, *Specimens of Bushman Folklore*. 1911.

Origin of Death.[94] This takes the form of a story about the Moon and the Hare. The hare, it appears, was at one time a human being but came to have his present animal form as a result of the happenings recited in the present story.

It occurred, the narrative begins, that the hare's mother died. He thereupon lamented grievously and declared emphatically "that he would not be silent, for his mother would not again living return; for his mother was altogether dead. Therefore, he would cry greatly for his mother."

To this the Moon replied that he should cease to cry, for his mother was not altogether dead; she would indeed again living return. Despite this, the hare maintained his stubborn belief that his mother was irrevocably lost, and contradicted all the assurances given by the Moon. At that the Moon became angry and struck the hare with his fist, cleaving the hare's mouth. Then he pronounced this curse: "This person . . . his mouth shall altogether be like this, even when he is a hare; he shall always bear a scar on his mouth; he shall spring away, he shall doubling come back. The dogs shall chase him; they shall, when they have caught him, they shall grasping tear him to pieces, he shall altogether die."

Not only was the hare thus made to assume permanently his animal form and become subject to death; the curse of death was also placed upon all men. The Moon continued: "And they who are men, they shall altogether dying go away, when they die."

One vestige of its former human status remains with the hare, according to Bushman belief. This is a certain small part of the flesh of the animal which is still human flesh, and consequently is scrupulously avoided when the rest of the hare is eaten.

As for man himself, he remembers his lost estate sadly and blames his subjection to death upon the deed of the hare. "The hare's doings," says the Bushman, "are those on account of which the Moon cursed us; that we should altogether die." The original intention of the Moon had been that man should be like itself, seeming to die indeed but then coming back again alive. "For I," said the Moon, "when I am dead, I again living return. I had intended that ye who are men, ye should also resemble me and do the things that I do; that I do not altogether dying go away." If only the hare had assented to the Moon's suggestion and said, "Yes, my mother lies sleeping; she will presently arise," then "we who are people, we

[94] *ibid.*, pp.57-65.

[41]

should have resembled the Moon; for the Moon had formerly said
that we should not altogether die."

When the new moon first becomes visible, the Bushman addresses
to it this prayer: "Take my face yonder! . . . Thou shalt give me thy
face—with which thou, when thou hast died, thou dost again living
return; when we did not perceive thee, thou dost against lying down
come—that I may also resemble thee. For, the joy yonder, thou dost
always possess it yonder, that is that thou art wont again to return
alive, when we did not perceive thee. . . . Thou didst formerly say
that we should also again return alive when we died."

Thus it is that the passing of the moon through its successive
phases suggests to the Bushman not only the transition from life to
death but also from death to life again. To pass from life to death
he knows is now his lot. To go from death to renewed life he believes
once was possible and wistfully hopes and prays may yet again become his privilege.

ANDAMAN ISLANDERS

The Andaman Islands lie in the Bay of Bengal between India and
the Malay Peninsula. The inhabitants are also a Negrito people,
short and black-skinned, with frizzly hair. Anthropological researches
were carried out among this folk by A. R. Brown in 1906-1908 and
were published more recently.[95] From the detailed information here
provided about their social organization, customs and beliefs, myths
and legends, we select for condensed report certain materials concerning their belief in spiritual beings.[96]

The Andaman Islanders believe in a large number of supernatural
beings. These may be divided into two classes. The first is that of
the spirits which inhabit the jungle and the sea and are thought to
be the ghosts of human beings. Whenever a man or woman of the
Andamans dies, he or she becomes one of these spirits. In the mythology of the Islands there is reference to the remote ancestors of the
Andamanese people, and these are believed to be spirits now, too.
They are thought of as occupying positions of prominence among
the other ghosts, and are called "big" spirits.

All of these spirits are under ordinary circumstances invisible.
From time to time the report is heard, however, that a human being
has seen them. When described, they are often spoken of as being

[95] A. R. Brown, *The Andaman Islanders, A Study in Social Anthropology.* 1922.
[96] *ibid.*, pp.136-166.

light skinned and having long hair and beards, in all of which features they contrast with the Andamanese themselves. Their bodies are thought to be small, their arms and legs extraordinarily long. On the whole, the impression they make is that of grotesqueness and ugliness. They are believed to carry lights, and sometimes men see these without glimpsing the spirits themselves.

The spirits have their own villages or camps in the forest and in the sea. Their customary sustenance is the flesh of dead men and women. The spirits of the jungle devour the bodies of those who are buried in the earth; the spirits of the sea consume those who are drowned or lost there.

It is evident that the spirits are fearful beings. Men wandering in the jungle by themselves run the danger of being taken captive by the spirits. It is said that when this happens, if the individual shows fear he is slain but if he manifests bravery is released after a period of detention. In the latter case, the man himself is henceforth endowed with magical powers. Aside from such individuals as have had experiences of this kind through which they have become friends of the spirits, men do well to avoid every contact with these beings. It is they who cause sickness and death resulting therefrom. Danger from the spirits is greater at night than in the day, greater when one is alone than when in company, greater when one is in a strange region than when in the precincts of home.

The second class of supernatural beings is that of the spirits associated with the heavenly bodies, with thunder and lightning, and with the monsoons. The sun and moon, it is usually held, are wife and husband respectively, and the stars are their children. One tribe believes that upon occasion the moon turns himself into a pig and comes down to earth in that form. All the tribes hold that when the moon rises in the early evening, he will be extremely angry if he sees any fire or bright light. Therefore fires and lights are extinguished or dimmed for a time at moonrising.

Thunder and lightning are also personal beings. Lightning lives in the sky and produces the familiar phenomenon associated with himself by shaking his foot. Thunder lives there too, and makes his great rumbling noise by rolling a stone about over the sky.

Of the monsoons, the chief ones to affect the Andamans are the northeast and the southwest. These, too, are personified, the northeast wind being known as Biliku, the southwest as Tarai. The entire year is divided between these two beings, the Tarai season being

[43]

the period of usually four or five months while the southwest monsoon is blowing; the Biliku season being the remainder of the year including not only the stormy season of October and November but also the cold season of December to February and the hot season of March and April.

Biliku and Tarai are often considered wife and husband; again they are said to have been friends who experienced an estrangement. The tale told by one tribe is this: "Once upon a time Puluga (Biliku) and Daria (Tarai) were great friends, but they quarreled. Puluga said that he was the bigger (more important). Daria said that he was. So now they are always quarreling. Puluga sends the wind for one period. Then Daria sends his wind."

When bad weather comes it is because Biliku or Tarai has been angered. Three actions by men are specially offensive to these beings: (1) burning or melting beeswax; (2) killing a cicada or making a noise, particularly chopping or banging wood, during the time in the morning or evening when the cicada is singing; (3) using certain foods including specified kinds of yams and edible roots. Actually the special seasons of the year for honey, for cicadas and for the yams and roots, are when stormy weather is beginning; hence the conclusion in the native mind that deeds in connection with these things are responsible for causing anger to the beings who control the weather. Thus it is clear that Biliku and Tarai are personifications of natural forces, and the myths and customs associated with them are expressions of the social value of natural phenomena.[97]

AZANDE

The Azande are a Negroid people who live in the southern Sudan, on the divide between the Nile and the Congo Rivers. Extensive ethnological researches were conducted in Zandeland in 1926 and following by Dr. E. E. Evans-Pritchard, and his detailed account of Zande witchcraft will provide the basis for the following short sketch.[98]

Witchcraft occupies a place of dominant importance in the configuration of belief and practice characteristic of the Azande. It is ubiquitous. It plays a part in agriculture, hunting and fishing, in domestic and communal life, in law, morals and religion. In any

[97] *ibid.*, pp.351-376.
[98] E. E. Evans-Pritchard, *Witchcraft, Oracles and Magic among the Azande.* 1937.

realm, an unfortunate event will probably be attributed to witch-craft.

The Azande have a perfectly good understanding of the normal sequences of events which we describe as cause and effect. But the particular conditions in any chain of causation which bring an individual into relation to natural happenings in such a manner that he sustains injury, are due, it is most often believed, to witchcraft. Thus when a Zande boy struck his foot against a small stump of wood in the center of a path in the bush, and the wound became infected and caused him much pain and inconvenience, he declared that it was the result of witchcraft. With the argument that it was not witchcraft which had placed the stump of wood in his path, since it had grown there naturally, he was entirely willing to agree. But to him the proof that witchcraft was involved lay in the fact that, whereas he had been as careful as ever to watch for obstructions, he had actually struck the stump; and whereas such a wound ordinarily heals quickly, this one had festered and become very painful. These unfortunate circumstances in a chain of happenings otherwise not out of the ordinary were the proof, to his mind, that witchcraft had been involved.

What, then, is witchcraft? It is evident that it is a normal thing in everyday life, just as normal as the misfortunes which constantly plague the steps of any native. Perfectly familiar as it is, witchcraft still has about it something peculiar. Men know that it exists and that it accomplishes evil, but the way in which it works eludes their understanding. They have a feeling about it rather than any clear-cut comprehension of it. In their feeling concerning it there is a sense of a mysterious hidden side, an inherent power, a soul of the thing. When witchcraft causes death, as it constantly does according to Zande thought, it is the soul of witchcraft which goes forth by night and devours the soul of its victim.

Suprasensible as it is, the power of witchcraft emanates from a tangible substance. This substance exists in the bodies of persons who are witches. Witchcraft-substance is inherited by a child from its parent, and grows more and more powerful as the person grows older. The individual may be unaware of his endowment, or even if aware of it may not make use of it. If others, however, suspect him of being a witch, upon his death an autopsy may be performed to discover whether witchcraft-substance is present. Those who are skilled in such matters are able at once to recognize the mysterious substance if they see it in the body of the deceased.

It is much more important, however, to be able to recognize a witch while he is still alive, for then it may be possible to avert his evil machinations or take vengeance on him for them. The ways in which witches may be identified are chiefly through oracles. Of these, the poison oracle is the most important. So important is it, indeed, that it is probably the most cherished of all Zande institutions of any kind.

In typical employment, the poison oracle works as follows. A death takes place. This, to the Azande, is never a purely natural happening. Natural causes may be and doubtless are involved, but the peculiar concatenation of them is obviously, to the Zande mind, due to the operation of witchcraft. It is therefore incumbent upon the kinsfolk of the deceased to ascertain the witch who is responsible for this murder, and to avenge upon him the death of the relative. In earlier days the vengeance might take the form of the slaughter of the witch, particularly if he were known to have committed several such murders. Today the duty of vengeance may be considered fulfilled if compensation is obtained from the witch, or if magical processes are instituted which lead to his death through the working of such mystical forces as he himself has unleashed.

But how can it be found out who the guilty witch is? This can be accomplished best of all by the poison oracle. Known as *benge*, the oracular poison is a red powder made, under strictest ceremonial conditions, from a forest creeper and mixed with water to form a paste. So reverentially is it treated, there is little doubt that *benge* possesses a supernatural dynamism. The employment of the poison as an oracle consists essentially in the administering of it to fowls and the observation of the results.

The usual place for consulting the oracle is in some secluded spot in the bush, and the normal time is from about eight to nine o'clock in the morning. Any male may conduct the séance, but it is usually done by a married householder who enjoys sufficient prosperity to have available the necessary fowls. Women are quite debarred, and normally neither operate the oracle nor consult it.

Ordinarily two chickens are used, and two consecutive tests are carried out. For the first test the poison oracle may be addressed somewhat as follows:

Poison oracle, poison oracle, if it is Bazugba who killed Bafuka, let this chicken die, if it is not he, let the chicken live.

After this the operator administers a dose of poison to the fowl, and all who are participating in the séance watch closely to see if it will die or survive. After the answer has been obtained, the second test is conducted. This must corroborate the first, otherwise the verdict is invalid. Also it is customary for the question in the second test to be framed in such a way as to require opposite behavior on the part of the second chicken in order to give agreement with the first. That is, if a fowl dies in the first test, then another fowl must live through the second test, and if a fowl survives the first ordeal then another must perish in the second, for the judgment to be accepted as valid. Thus, in the hypothetical case we are using for illustration, where we may suppose the first chicken died, the address introducing the second test might run like this:

The poison oracle has declared Bazugba guilty by slaying the fowl. If its declaration is true let it spare this second fowl.

If, then, the second fowl lives after being given the poison, the verdict is valid, and Bazugba is indubitably guilty.

While we have illustrated the use of the poison oracle in relation to the ascertainment of a witch's guilt for the death of a person, which is perhaps the most important single legal problem in Zandeland, the same oracle is also employed to obtain answers to questions about a great variety of other matters of significance to individuals and society. Typical situations occasioning consultation of the poison oracle are: before the marriage of a daughter; in the sickness of any member of the family; to discover the agent responsible for any misfortune; in cases of sorcery, adultery, or disloyalty to a prince; before long journeys; before hunting.

Other oracles are also employed, however, although none has as great an authority as that just described. Next in esteem is the termites oracle, and since it does not involve the possible sacrifice of chickens, it is more readily available to the poor man. The procedure is to find a termite mound and insert into it two branches of different trees. The next day the interrogator gets his answer by observing which branch the termites have eaten. Yet somewhat lower in authority, but used most widely of all because of ease and expeditiousness of operation, is the rubbing-board oracle. The rubbing-board is something like a miniature table with a tail, and with a separate lid having a vertical handle. The operator sits on the ground and steadies the

[47]

board by holding his right foot on its tail. Holding the handle of the lid between his thumb and first finger, he jerks the lid backward and forward. Prior to use, the table has been made ready by placing on its surface plant juices or grated wood, and during the operation the lid is dipped from time to time into a gourd of water. The oracle answers the questions which are put to it by sliding back and forth smoothly or by sticking in place firmly, the two responses corresponding to "No" and "Yes" respectively.

Oracles, therefore, constitute the first and most distinctive means by which the Azande cope with witchcraft. By oracles it is determined who has injured or is about to injure another by witchcraft, and whether or not witchcraft threatens a projected undertaking. The second thing of importance in dealing with omnipresent witchcraft is magic. By magic men can guard themselves against witchcraft and destroy it. The main purpose of magic is to combat the mystical forces of witchcraft. When a man dies, the cause is, as we have seen, witchcraft, and vengeance-magic provides a way of dealing with the ascertained culprit. When a man falls sick, witchcraft is attacked by the making of magic. Likewise the other misfortunes of life may be dealt with by the practices of magic.

The third channel through which the Azande are able to contend against the dangers of witchcraft is provided by the witch doctor. He serves both as diviner and as magician. As a diviner he exposes witches in their nefarious deeds; as a magician he performs the rituals which thwart them in their evil undertakings. Such is the threefold structure of defense which is erected in Zandeland against the perils of witchcraft by which man is so constantly surrounded.

NAVAHOS

The Navaho and Apache Indians belong to the southern branch of that extensive linguistic family of North American Indians known as Athapascan, the Pacific branch of which is found in California and Oregon, the northern in Canada and Alaska. Encountered first by the Spaniards near a Tewa pueblo called *Navahú*, or "great fields," the Navahos, as they thus came to be known, live now on a reservation occupying parts of Colorado, Utah, Arizona and New Mexico. A file of Navaho singers is shown in Fig. 18.

The Navaho people believe in the supernatural as a realm of power and of danger.[99] In order to influence the forces of the supernatural

[99] Clyde Kluckhohn and Dorothea Leighton, *The Navaho*. 1946, p.121.

and thereby affect the course of human events, various techniques have been elaborated. Of these some are socially approved and some socially disapproved. The two classes of procedures will be illustrated by reference to ceremonies and witchcraft respectively.

Navaho religious ceremonies follow for the most part a single general pattern. Ordinarily they center around a patient, perhaps a person who is actually sick, perhaps one who has been frightened by a dream. They are conducted at and in the hogan or dwelling of the patient, and are in the charge of a medicine man who is assisted by various helpers. Before a medicine man can give a healing ceremony he must have had the same conducted on his own behalf, and needless to say must have mastered all the intricate details of procedure and accompanying songs as well as the myth material basic to the ceremony.

Originally each ceremony was of nine days' duration, although now many are conducted more briefly. The first days of the ceremony have to do with cleansing from evil. At the outset the hogan is blessed and then various procedures are employed for cleansing the patient, such as sweat baths for the body and passing through a series of hoops to mark the shedding of the old personality. Herbs are infused, the patient's body painted, and prayers uttered as dictated by the medicine man. On the sixth day of a nine-day ceremony, after the patient has again been ceremonially bathed in the morning, the sand paintings begin.

The art of sand painting, also called dry painting and not unknown elsewhere in the world, has been carried to a very high degree of perfection by the Navahos. The actual work of the sand painting is done by relatives or friends of the patient and by other assistants, but under the immediate direction of the medicine man. Pieces of white, red, and yellow sandstone are ground to make the colors; charcoal is used for black, and blue is made by mixing charcoal and white sand. Instead of mineral colors, cornmeal, pollens and powdered flowers or plants may also be used for the various colors; but the background is still usually of sand and the method of work the same, hence the term sand painting still applies.

The sand or other material is taken up by the painter in his hand, a small amount at a time, and poured out on the background area, beginning at the center and working out toward the edges. The rate of flow and consequent thickness of line is controlled by letting the material escape from beneath the thumb and through the nearly closed joint of the index finger. A high degree of precision is attained by skilled workers.

The stylized figures and symbols which are wrought out in the sand painting have to do with the myth which underlies the ceremony. The course of man's life and the supernatural powers which play about it are vividly portrayed. A series of such sand paintings, depicting successive phases of the myth, may be executed on successive days, each painting being destroyed in turn to make way for the next. Indeed the life of the painting, painstakingly executed though it is, is in any event not long. In climactic parts of the ceremony the patient is caused to sit on the sand painting, and the medicine man takes his place on it, too.

One ceremony is the Hozhonji, or Blessing Chant. This blessing is conceived in terms of an appeasement and control of the supernatural powers, and of an achievement of right relationship between the individual and the universe. When this is accomplished, the person enjoys blessing or happiness.

The mythical materials employed in the Blessing Chant are from the Navaho Creation Myth, or Story of the Emergence. This myth was narrated to Mary C. Wheelwright, who recorded it in permanent form,[100] by Hasteen Klah, an aged and honored Navaho medicine man living at Nava, halfway between Gallup and Shiprock. The story begins in the dark First World, where were Begochiddy, the blue-eyed and yellow haired great god; Hashjeshjin, the fire god, son of the Fire and a Comet; Etsay-hashkeh, the Coyote Man; Asheen-assun, the Salt Woman; and Etsay-hasteen and Estsa-assun, First Man and First Woman, the prototypes of the human beings on this earth. All of these went upward to the Second World which is the blue world. There Begochiddy created twin men and twin women, only to have them destroyed by Hashjeshjin. From their bodies, however, Begochiddy created new twins, the Ethkay-nah-ashi, and breathed his spirit into them. In the yellow Third World, to which the powers later ascended, Begochiddy made many things, mountains, water, animals, birds, fishes, and the first four men and four women. Taking a bamboo and breathing through the Ethkay-nah-ashi, he gave life to all that he had created. There was no sun or moon in this world but the mountains gave plenty of light. Here the first marriage took place, and the first misunderstanding and sin. When big storms and

[100] *Navajo Creation Myth, The Story of the Emergence,* by Hasteen Klah, recorded by Mary C. Wheelwright. Navajo Religion Series, I. 1942.

hot waters poured upon this world, all the creatures went up a rapidly growing bamboo to reach the white Fourth World, which is this
present world.

The waters from the lower world kept threatening to overwhelm
the Fourth World. The reason lay in the fact that Coyote had stolen
a baby from the lower world, and when this was discovered and the
baby returned there, the waters ceased to rise toward this world and
ever after remained at a constant level. Gathering his people together
in a sweat house, Begochiddy led a conference on the creation of
the new world. He and the other powers there planned the mountains, the sun, moon and stars, and the months. In each case, as the
work of creation proceeded, the spirit of the thing about to be created
was made first. When all was ready, these spirits went into the places
where they belonged. The universe did not begin to move, however,
until the first person, called Etsay-dassalini, died. Then, the first time
the sun crossed the sky it was too near the earth and was too hot;
not until its fourth crossing was it in exactly the right spot where it
has stayed ever since.

Finally the powers began to make a new kind of human being.
Distinct from Hahjeenah-dinneh, The-People-Who-Came-Up, the
new people were called Anlthtahn-nah-olyah, meaning Created-from-
Everything. The feet and ankles of the new man were made of soil
of the earth, his legs of lightning, his knees of white shell and his
body of white and yellow corn. His heart was of obsidian and his
breath was the white wind. They made animals, too. When the new-
ly-made people arose they ate some white corn, for although they
were made of corn it was good for them to eat it, and the Navahos
live on corn even until now.

Thus was ended the creating of human beings and creatures, and
Begochiddy was glad and laughing, it is said, when he had finished
the creation.

One of the sand paintings of the Blessing Chant is shown in Fig.
19.[101] This is from the ceremony as conducted by Hasteen Klah, and
the sand painting was recorded by Franc J. Newcomb. The background was of sand, the colored designs of corn meal, pollen and
powdered flowers or plants. At the bottom of the illustration is a
rainbow path, leading from the east, with white footsteps on it. This
is man's path from the unknown. The white oblong is enclosed with
four lines, black, blue, yellow and white, signifying the four worlds

[101] *ibid.*, Set I, First Sand Painting.

through which man made his ascent, as told in the Creation Myth. Near the center, the circular figure represents the place of emergence, through which mankind came out into the present fourth, white world. In the making of this figure the ground is first colored all black, the blue is placed over that, then the yellow and finally the white. Thus the painter symbolically passes through the four worlds. On either side are the insect figures of the mythical Messenger Fly, Dontso, while at the top is the blue bird of happiness. Approaching the center, the path of man and his footsteps are made of yellow pollen, signifying prayer, blessing and fertility.

Turning from the socially approved religious ceremonies of the Navahos to the socially disapproved techniques of relationship to supernatural powers, we encounter witchcraft. Although a subject only reluctantly discussed by most Navahos, through long acquaintance Clyde Kluckhohn has gathered extensive data relating to witchcraft among these people.[102]

Four distinct types of malevolent activity in relation to the supernatural are recognizable and may be referred to as Witchery, Sorcery, Wizardry and Frenzy Witchcraft. It is Witchery which is most often mentioned. According to the stories on this subject, both men and women may become witches, the profession most often being learned from a parent or other relative, the initiation requiring the killing of a near relative. The witches are said to constitute a group and to hold meetings in a cave by night, presided over by a chief witch. Naked save for masks, beads and jewelry, they sit in a circle surrounded by baskets of human flesh. The evil counterpart of a religious ceremonial is conducted, with songs and sand paintings. Going forth upon their nefarious missions, the witches roam at great speed, clothed in skins of the wolf, coyote or other animals. Having made a powdered poison from the flesh of corpses, they drop it through the smokehole of their victim's hogan or blow it into his face from a furrowed stick. The poison at once causes fainting, lockjaw or a swollen tongue, and from the ensuing illness there is no recovery since in such a case the usual curing rituals are ineffective.

Ceremonial knowledge does give an advance protection against the attacks of witches, however, and certain small sand or pollen paintings are made by family members for the same purpose. The most potent protection of all is gall medicine, made from the gall of the

[102] Clyde Kluckhohn, *Navaho Witchcraft* (Papers of the Peabody Museum of American Archaeology and Ethnology, Harvard University, xxii, 2). 1944.

eagle, bear, mountain lion and skunk. This acts, it is believed, as an immediate antidote to the fainting caused by corpse poison, and is kept in most Navaho homes and carried by many Navahos when traveling or going into crowds.

After a person has fallen ill from Witchery the most effective cure consists in finding the witch and extracting, by questioning or by force, a confession. Capital punishment is said to have been visited not infrequently upon witches. Specific prayer ceremonials and chants also are designated for the cure of victims of witchcraft.

Sorcery is practiced by obtaining a part of the victim's clothing or hair or nails and uttering spells over it; or by making an image of the one to be attacked and "killing" or "torturing" this effigy. Wizardry is believed to depend upon the injection of some foreign particle such as a stone or bit of bone or ashes into the body of the victim. The shooting of such projectiles is accomplished by an incantation. Frenzy Witchcraft is essentially a love magic, involving the use of medicines made out of certain plants, especially including Datura or Jimson weed.

As Kluckhohn has shown, the Navaho belief in witchcraft has created a veritable pageant of everything that is most evil in society and has provided in the supposed witches an object upon which anxieties may be focused and against which animosities may be released.

CHIRICAHUA AND MESCALERO APACHES

The Chiricahua and Mescalero tribes of Apache Indians live together on the Mescalero Reservation in southern New Mexico. It is their common belief that a mighty force pervades the universe and works through natural phenomena to reach man.[103] This supernatural power may be conducted through anything and it may come to anybody. The sun, the lightning, the bear, the snake, the owl, the coyote, all these and other things may be the channels through which power communicates with human beings. There is no restriction on those to whom the communication may come. Any man or woman may upon occasion have "something speak to him." The message, whether it comes as a vision in a dream or as a word reaching an individual in the midst of a crowd, is always highly individual, meant for the person to whom it is addressed alone. Thus Bear may appear in a vision to a man, offering him power to cure bear sickness. The latter

[103] Morris E. Opler in *American Anthropologist.* New Series 37 (1935), pp. 65-70.

illness is incurred when a person has an unfortunate contact with a bear, as for example upon being frightened by one. The man to whom the curing power is offered is free to accept it or reject it. Indeed a considerable palaver may take place on the subject, Bear stating that he has studied this individual carefully and singled him out as the proper recipient of the gift, the man suggesting that others might be better qualified for it than he. If the man does accept, then he is given directions for the conduct of a ceremony through which power will be effective to the end specified.

The same general pattern is discernible in all the ceremonies. There is at first a ceremonial smoking, then a casting of pollen in the four directions, then prayer, and then the singing of a set of songs. The proper actions, prayers and songs of the particular ceremony having been made known to the individual recipient, he is henceforth their custodian. If any man should attempt to perform a ceremony to which he has not been granted the supernatural right, it would be fatal. If it is in accord with the wishes of his power, the owner of a ceremony may, however, transmit it to another. Usually this is from an older person to a younger, with the intent that the ceremony not be lost upon the death of the former. If the ceremony is handed down to another member of the same family, there is no fee; if it is transmitted outside the family, the payment of a fee is necessary. It is possible for the custodian of a ceremony to employ it privately on behalf of his own family, or also to use it for others. In the latter case, certain gifts are asked in return for the service, for which an extensive demand may develop.

There is a certain ambivalence about the supernatural power. It may bring benefit or work harm. It may be manipulated malevolently by a sorcerer or employed benevolently by a shaman, in either case to the accomplishment of extraordinary ends. Wonderful as it is, the power always remains dangerous. Especially if it is employed with notable success over a long period of time, it is apt to demand in payment the life of the one who has used it, or of a near relative of his. If consent is given to the latter sacrifice, for example, the relative will soon fall in battle or be destroyed by an accident.

In some ceremonies, masked dancers play an important part. Like the other ceremonies, these too originate in personal experiences with the supernatural. One Chiricahua shaman received such a ceremony in the following way. A spirit told him to go into a certain mountain. Led by a clown, he passed through four stone doors, some guarded by snakes and mountain lions. Within, an old man who controlled the whole mountain asked him what kind of power he wanted. To show the various ceremonies which were available, many Indians, dressed in buckskin, and Mountain People came in, dancing, followed by all kinds of birds, snakes and animals. Recognizing the Mountain Spirits to be the leading personages, the man chose them. For four days he stayed on in the mountain, learning the ceremony they had to impart. At last the old man of the mountain told him, "You may go home and use the ceremony according to what the Mountain People want you to do." From that time on, whenever the shaman held his ceremony, the Mountain People sent messages to him. When he wanted to know how to cure a man, they would come and tell him.[104]

In the case of such a ceremony, the masked dancers impersonate the Mountain People. The costuming and painting of the dancers is done under the immediate direction of the shaman, and to the accompaniment of full ritual details. During the painting the shaman beats upon his drum and sings songs about the Mountain People, their holy home, and the protection which may be expected from them against sickness and danger. The costume of the dancer includes high moccasins and a buckskin shirt, colored yellow. The arms and upper part of the body are painted with designs in black, white, yellow and blue colors. On the head a buckskin mask is worn, surmounted by a superstructure of painted wooden slats, while in each hand a sharp painted stick is carried. The dancing, angular and spectacular, is carried out around a blazing fire. No one confuses the masked men with the Mountain People themselves; it is clearly understood that they are only their impersonators. Nevertheless, through the ceremony the mighty power of these spirits is brought to bear upon the affairs of men.[105]

A photograph of two Mescalero Apache masked dancers together with a shaman is reproduced in Fig. 20.

Turning to the mythology of the Apaches, it will be readily understood that in it the Mountain People, whom we have just met, play an important part. They are described in various legends as protectors of the tribal territory. An even more important role, perhaps, is assumed by White Painted Woman and her son, Child of the Water. The latter is the Apache culture hero, and his exploits in the conquest

[104] Morris E. Opler, *An Apache Life-Way, The Economic, Social, and Religious Institutions of the Chiricahua Indians.* 1941, pp.269-272.
[105] *ibid.,* pp.100-115.

of numerous monsters provide the mythological background for much ritual. Still more popular, no doubt, is the character named Coyote, whose escapades are the subject of an entire cycle of accounts. Always a prankster, Coyote appears at the beginning of his travels and adventures with the characteristics of a human being, but at the end loses the ability of speech and assumes the appearance and manifests the traits of the animal whose name he bears. Actually, Coyote is not so much either an individual beast or human being, as a type; he has been called a self-portrait of the Apache character and a satire upon its weaknesses. While to their audience the stories about Coyote are entertaining in and of themselves, they also provide, through their narrative of the misdeeds of the chief character and his subsequent embarrassments, a certain amount of moral teaching. Also the Coyote cycle has been utilized as a vehicle for an account of the creation, a matter with which Child of the Water and White Painted Woman also are concerned.

As told by the Mescalero Apache, the story of Coyote and the Creation has been recorded by Harry Hoijer, during researches conducted from 1930 to 1934. His principal informant for this and other mythological materials of the Mescalero was a member of the tribe named Charles Smith. Ethnological notes have been provided by Morris Edward Opler.[106]

Coyote, the episode begins, informed his family that he was going away. When they expressed displeasure at being left alone so often, Coyote explained that he was learning as he traveled about, and that he would doubtless bring back something good from the new journey. He would go, he declared, to the Frog people, who were of high repute. The journey involved the crossing of broad rivers, deep canyons and high mountains, but was facilitated by directions kindly vouchsafed him both by birds and by a bear en route. Like Coyote, these animals manifested human qualities and spoke one universal language. Meanwhile, however, Coyote was taken possession of by Child of the Water, the culture hero of the Mescalero, who henceforth talked and worked through him. Through Coyote, Child of the Water made known that the things of earth were to be changed. When Coyote comes and speaks to the animals they will lose their

---

[106] Harry Hoijer, *Chiricahua and Mescalero Apache Texts*, with ethnological notes by Morris Edward Opler. The University of Chicago Publications in Anthropology, Linguistic Series. 1938, pp.170-181,217-219.

human attributes and common language; they will become as they
have remained ever since:

Earth! Now, for some reason, that which lies upon your surface, those
who live upon your surface, [and] those animate beings who exist upon
your surface, none of them disappearing, will all be transformed in a
place similar to this one which he will make somewhere. The people to
whom I am going, on the very day that I come to them, will become like
those in that place. Then, when they have spoken to me and I have spoken
to them, from that moment on, they, their words and their bodies by means
of which they customarily move about on the surface of the earth, will
change. I will not have heard them.

Coyote arrived finally at a region where were four small mountains,
with four cliffs. Under the cliffs, in turn, were four lakes, and on the
east side of the uppermost lake were four rivers which flowed into
it. On the farthest river bank on the uppermost clump of tule was
a black rock. There sat the Frog chief.

As Coyote stopped before him, the change took place which had
already been predicted. "The Frog chief was transformed exactly as
[Coyote] had said he would be transformed. Right at that moment
he became an ordinary frog. [Coyote] was unable to talk to him at
all. And therefore he did not talk to him. [The frog] jumped away
from him into the water."

"So that one was the first of all living creatures to be transformed,"
the account continues. "From this time on, everyone that [Coyote]
looks at, whoever it is, will be changed in this way. He walked about
sadly. He looked at the water. He also tried in vain to speak."

Then the work of creation proceeded. The voice of Child of the
Water spoke to Coyote, putting into his mind the names of many
plants. As he thought of these things, they were created. " 'Tule,
spike rush, sedge, slender tule, carrizo, water cress, white violet,
asphodel, side oats grama, blue-eyed grass, [and] everything, though
it does not [now] exist, of whatever sort that grows in the water will
be created,' [the voice] said to Coyote. [The voice] made him think
only of these things. From here [Coyote] went on. 'And right now
all the varieties of grass on the earth's surface: grama grass, false flax,
big blue-stem grass, buffalo grass, corn grass, wild violet, salt grass,
black grama grass, red columbine, wild barley, side oats grama, big
blue-stem grass, and blue grass. Whether or not I've been heard to
name all the varieties, let all of the other kinds come with [those I
have named] also.' All of them were created."

These and many other plants and trees were named and created, and then the voice of Child of the Water addressed them: "All kinds of people, all people, will repeatedly make use of you in some good way."

After that, hills and mountains were made. "Then Coyote looked about everywhere. Whatever he thought of became so. 'Let green hills extend upward everywhere,' he, thinking, thought so. Beautiful hills with all sorts of green plants growing on them came into existence. Big mountains also arose everywhere."

Then Coyote thought about all kinds of snakes, lizards and rodents, all varieties of antelope, deer, bear and mountain lions, and all varieties of birds both small and large, and as he thought about them they were created.

At last, Coyote himself was caused to change in condition and appearance, just as he had been the instrument through whom the other plants and animals had been transformed. "Now I have become very tired. He has made me in the form of a man. Therefore, I shall make my body small. [So will change] my ears, my nose, my eyes, my body hair, [and] my teeth. My legs will be four, my tail will be bushy, I shall howl and bark, my feet will be bunched, and I shall close up my arms and my hands. Coyote is no more. Now I will return as coyote the animal [to] my wife [and] my children. Wherever I go, wherever I live, I will sleep well everywhere. Only all varieties of meat will be my food and I will drink only water. I will howl."

Once again the mysterious voice spoke, and this time Coyote challenged: "Who is this person who is speaking to me again? Now, come before me!"

At that juncture a roar of thunder was heard from inside a cloud. "A rainbow had come down on both sides from inside the cloud. He who was its power came down. The whole earth began to shake. . . . The being who had just come, he of whom one could certainly not say that he was an evil man, had come down. He stood facing [Coyote]. 'Now, since you do not want to be human, you may go away. Humankind will do to you whatever they will. They will give you troubles that do not exist for human beings.' At this point, Coyote trotted away. There stood Child of the Water."

Child of the Water was now heard to opine that much was still lacking in creation. Forthwith, therefore, he proceeded to further acts of creation. "The voices of all sorts of birds that do not [now] exist will be heard singing and making a noise," he declared. "People made in my image will follow me. . . . There will be lightning . . .

water will rain down. Let it come!" said Child of the Water. "Everything happened just so."

Still there was something wrong. Mankind was subject to disease. "Since disease will be among them," said Child of the Water, "make something that will cure it that they can prepare. I ask my mother for this." Thereupon White Painted Woman, the mother of Child of the Water, came to him and spoke as follows: "You will make for them all sorts of herbs, all of which will cure [diseases]. Some they will boil, some they will chew, some they will paint on, some they will customarily burn for their smoke, some they will drink, [and] they will breathe the vapors of some. There will be names for these things. They will be called medicines. They will make them for whatever purpose they want. These medicinal herbs will be called 'medicines which are holy.'"

At this point in the story there follows a detailed inventory of medicinal herbs and sacred rocks and mineral substances, together with enumeration of ceremonial gestures and practices which accompany the employment of these substances for the purpose of curing disease.

Child of the Water then spoke again and uttered a final, solemn word of adjuration, promise and warning to his creation. "Now then, there is nothing more of value to me that I can set down on the surface of the earth for you. You are my people, my children. I am right here. Think about me. I have done everything for you. Now I shall put you all together. Even if you speak in many different ways, I shall do so for you. Thereby, I have given you a chance [to live together peaceably (?)]. You will do whatever you like with your minds. In spite of that, there will be difficulties everywhere. I have made witches and disease to live among you."

And the episode of creation comes to a conclusion with a description of the dispersion of human beings over the earth and their division into peoples and tribes.

ZUÑIS

Even before the Navaho and Apache tribes came in from the north, the Pueblo Indians were living in the great American southwest. Themselves the successors of the yet earlier Basket Makers, the early Pueblo people lived in the cliff dwellings and semicircular valley cities the ruins of which are still so impressive in the valley of the San Juan. Prior to the advent of the Spaniards in the sixteenth century, the cliff dwellings and semicircular citadels had been abandoned and their inhabitants had settled in the pueblos which are still occupied in the Rio Grande valley and the deserts of New Mexico and Arizona.

The configuration of religious belief and practice distinctive of the Pueblo Indians may be described as a ceremonious collectivism. Whereas the Apaches emphasize the vision or dream experience of the individual shaman and the Navahos are not free from a tendency toward the violent and the frenzied, the people of the pueblos characteristically make their approach to the supernatural through group rituals marked by the greatest formality and sobriety. For concrete illustration, we turn to the Zuñi Pueblo and the kachina cult.

Zuñi Pueblo was first viewed from afar by Friar Marcos de Niza in 1539. Back in Mexico, his glowing account of the great city which he had seen led to the expedition of Coronado. A procession of present-day women of Zuñi led by the governor of the Pueblo is shown in Fig. 21. For modern research in the religion of Zuñi we will turn to the works of Ruth L. Bunzel and Ruth Benedict.[107]

To the Zuñi people the entire world appears animate. All matter is alive and has a spiritual essence. Sun and earth, clouds and rain, trees and plants of corn, all are living beings. Thus the Zuñi prays:

> When our earth mother is replete with living waters,
> When spring comes,
> The source of our flesh,
> All the different kinds of corn,
> We shall lay to rest in the ground.
> With their earth mother's living waters,
> They will be made into new beings.
> Coming out standing into the daylight
> Of their sun father,
> Calling for rain,
> To all sides they will stretch out their hands.
> Then from wherever the rain makers stay quietly
> They will send forth their misty breath;
> Their massed clouds filled with water will come out to sit
>   down with us;
> Far from their homes,

[107] Ruth L. Bunzel in *Forty-Seventh Annual Report of the Bureau of American Ethnology to the Secretary of the Smithsonian Institution 1929-1930.* 1932, pp.467-1086; Benedict, *Patterns of Culture*, pp.57-129. For Zuñi mythology also see Ruth Benedict in *Columbia University Contributions to Anthropology*, XXI. 2 vols. 1935. cf. also Frank Waters, *Masked Gods, Navaho and Pueblo Ceremonialism.* 1950, pp.277-280.

With outstretched hands of water they will embrace the corn,
Stepping down to caress them with their fresh waters,
With their fine rain caressing the earth,
With their heavy rain caressing the earth,
And yonder, wherever the roads of the rain makers come forth,
Torrents will rush forth,
Silt will rush forth,
Mountains will be washed out,
Logs will be washed down,
Yonder all the mossy mountains
Will drip with water.
The clay-lined hollows of our earth mother
Will overflow with water,
From all the lakes
Will rise the cries of the children of the rain makers,
In all the lakes
There will be joyous dancing—
Desiring that it should be thus,
I send forth my prayers.[108]

Of this animated universe man is an integral and harmonious part. In it he is not the master but only one being among many, an equal with the rabbit, the deer and the corn plant. In order that his hunting or his agriculture may go well, the Zuñi must therefore request the aid of the supernatural and perform with punctilious accuracy the ceremonies by which his own life is kept in proper relationship with the spiritual forces about him. Granted exactitude and precision in the conduct of the ritual, the desired results must automatically follow.

There are no less than six esoteric cults in existence, each devoted to the worship of a special supernatural being or group of supernatural beings, each possessing a secret body of ritual knowledge, and each bound to the preservation and performance of certain distinctive ceremonies. To the work of these cults a large part of the collective effort of the people of Zuñi is devoted. The cults are those of the sun, of the water spirits, of the kachinas, of the kachina priests (related to but distinct from the foregoing), of the war gods, and of the beast gods respectively.

The kachina cult is widespread among almost all the Pueblos, but has developed most richly among the Hopi and the Zuñi. Its fundamental elements include belief in the existence of a large group of supernatural beings, the kachinas, who live in a lake and are identi-

[108] Bunzel in *Forty-Seventh Annual Report of the Bureau of American Ethnology*, p.484.

fied with clouds and rain as well as with the dead; the practice of the impersonation of these supernaturals by masked dancers; the initiation of all the men of the community into the cult and the custom of ceremonial whipping as a part of the initiation; the extreme sanctity of the masks, which can cause death to the careless wearer; and the complete identification of the one wearing the mask with the supernatural being who is thereby represented.

According to their myth of origin, the Zuñi people were long ago searching for the middle land where they might dwell in peace. Having to cross a stream, the first group of women were horrified to see their children turn into water snakes, turtles and frogs. The mothers cried out and dropped them into the water. Later the twin heroes of the Zuñis went back to see what had become of the children. They found them dwelling happily at the bottom of a lake. They had been transformed into kachinas, that is, supernaturals. They were adorned with beads and feathers, and they spent their days happily in dancing and singing.

To their parents the kachinas sent word that only one day's journey remained to reach the middle land, and that they themselves would stay at the lake forever in order to be near them and be able to help them in time of need. Thus the kachinas addressed the twin heroes: "You will tell our parents, Do not worry. We have not perished. In order to remain thus forever we stay here. To Itiwana but one day's travel remains. Therefore we stay near by. When our world grows old and the waters are exhausted and the seeds are exhausted, none of you will go back to the place of your first beginning. Whenever the waters are exhausted and the seeds are exhausted you will send us prayer sticks. Yonder at the place of our first beginning with them we shall bend over to speak to them. Thus there will not fail to be waters. Therefore we shall stay quietly near by."[109]

Pitying the loneliness of their people, the kachinas used to come often to Zuñi and dance for them. But every time they went away they took someone with them, that is, someone died. Therefore they decided not to come any more in person. They told the people to make headdresses and costumes like their own, and to imitate their dances. When the people did that, the kachinas were with them in spirit and everybody was happy.[110]

In the kachina ceremony, the dancers wear leather masks adorned with eagle feathers and spruce boughs. Their faces and bodies are

[109] *ibid.*, p.597. [110] *ibid.*, p.607.

painted, and they usually wear a kilt and moccasins. From the back of their belt a fox skin is suspended, and numerous necklaces of white shell, turquoise and coral are worn. A small package of seeds is placed in the belt, gourd rattles are carried in the right hand, and spruce in the left.

Thus accoutered and wearing the mask of the kachina, the impersonator becomes the very supernatural being he represents. The mask is the corporeal substance of the kachina, and in putting it on the man assumes the personality of the god. As the entire company of dancers executes its precisely ordered and synchronized steps, to the rhythmic and melodic accompaniment of drum and song, it is the kachinas themselves who are joyously dancing in the midst of their people. They will not fail to visit them thereafter in life-giving rain.

Here is a portion of one of the prayers in the kachina cult. It is prayed by the impersonator of Pautiwa, the latter being the kachina chief at the lake village of the kachinas. In address to this supernatural, he is referred to by the double name, Kawulia Pautiwa. The one praying refers at the outset of our quotation to his assumption of the personality of the god in the putting on of his mask. The plume wands which he mentions are the staves of office made by the priests and covered with sacred paint.

Representing my father,
Kawulia Pautiwa,
I assumed his person.
Carrying his waters,
His seeds,
And carrying my fathers' perfect plume wands,
I made my road come hither.
I offered my fathers plume wands. . . .
I prayed that throughout the country of the Corn priests
Our earth mother might be wrapped
In four layers of green blanket,
That the land might be full of moss,
Full of flowers
Full of corn pollen. . . .
Then far off to his own country
My father
Made his road go forth
Carrying my fathers' plume wands,
Carrying his prayer meal,
I made his road go forth.
Far off at the place of the first beginning

Touching them with my plume wands,
With all the others he will hold discourse.
Our fathers will take hold of our plume wands.
Then in that way
Their long life,
Their old age,
They will grant to us.
That our roads may reach to where the life-giving road of our
    sun father comes out,
That we may finish our roads—
This they will grant us.
This day in accordance with whatever you wished,
Whatever you wished when you appointed me,
I have fulfilled your thoughts.
With thoughts in harmony
May we live together.
For even while I call myself poor,
Somewhere far off
Is one who is my father.
Beseeching the breath of the divine one,
Kawulia Pautiwa,
His life-giving breath,
His breath of old age,
His breath of waters,
His breath of seeds,
His breath of riches,
His breath of fecundity,
His breath of power,
His breath of strong spirit,
His breath of all good fortune whatsoever,
Asking for his breath
And into my warm body drawing his breath,
I add to your breath
That happily you may always live.
To this end, my fathers,
My children:
May you be blessed with light.[111]

[111] *ibid.*, pp.699-701.

CHAPTER II

Zoroastrianism

THE homeland of Zoroastrianism was on the great Iranian plateau which stretches from the valley of the Indus on the east to that of the Tigris on the west. The eastern portion of this plateau is occupied by Baluchistan and Afghanistan, and the western by Iran. Iran, with which we are chiefly concerned, lies between the Caspian Sea on the north and the Persian Gulf on the south, and extends from the edge of the Tigris valley on the west to boundaries along the Tejen River or the Hari Rud (as it is known in its upper course), the Helmand swamps and the Talab River on the east.

There are also mighty mountain ramparts on most sides of the land. Curving south of the Caspian Sea is the Elburz range, whose Mount Demavend (Fig. 22) attains a height of about 18,600 feet and is the loftiest Asian mountain west of the Himalayas. In the extreme northwest beyond Lake Urmia is the massif of Ararat, with the highest peak known as Great Ararat rising to some 16,916 feet. On the west are the Zagros Mountains, while yet other ranges alternate with deserts in the south and east.

In this mountain-buttressed upland of Iran the chief cities are situated at considerable elevations, Isfahan and Kerman being over five thousand feet high, Tabriz over four thousand, and Meshed and Teheran over three thousand. In the center of the country there is a great desert, generally known as the Lut, the elevation of which is about two thousand feet.

1. EARLY IRAN

THE CASPIANS

THE life of man on the Iranian plateau began in early prehistoric times. The discovery of three human skeletons of the Old Stone Age in Hotu Cave near the southern Caspian shore has recently been announced by the Iranian Expedition of the University Museum of the University of Pennsylvania. The remains are reported to have been found in gravel of the last Glacial Period, but to resemble Cro-Magnon rather than Neandertal man and definitely to represent *Homo sapiens*. With the skeletons were large numbers of flint tools.[1]

Dwelling like their Paleolithic predecessors in the general region of the Caspian Sea and hence commonly designated as Caspians, the inhabitants of Iran in the Neolithic Age presumably lived long in a hunting stage of existence and then eventually developed the practice of farming. At any rate in the fifth millennium B.C., at the end of the Neolithic Period, a sedentary population was settled in large villages the maintenance of which would hardly have been possible without agriculture.

One of these villages was excavated by Professor Ernst E. Herzfeld in 1928 and 1931 at a small mound about two miles from Persepolis. The buildings were of stamped earth, and constituted a continuous agglomeration of rooms and courts suggesting that the community lived in clans. Numerous stone, flint and clay implements and instruments were found, but weapons of warfare were almost nonexistent. There were many human figurines of clay which were probably idols. The female ones may have represented a mother goddess. The making and decorating of pottery provided the chief avenue of artistic expression, and both unpainted and painted pottery was found in abundance. The painted pottery exhibits a great variety of designs, including symbols, geometrical patterns, animal representations, and, rarely, human figures. On a spherical vase a great ibex, an animal which still abounds in the rocks around the plain of Persepolis, is painted in profile. Its horns, as its most characteristic feature, are exaggerated in size and pictured as sweeping back in splendid curves. On the bowl shown in Fig. 24 a thrice-repeated triangle provides the background for a figure in human form. The body is shown in a front view, the feet are turned outward, and the heavy forearms and five-fingered hands are raised. The head is small, and it is difficult to tell whether it is human or animal. Perhaps it is an animal head, and the entire figure may well represent a demon.[2]

Similar fine pottery, displaying a yet more sophisticated art, was also found in the lowest levels at the famous site of Susa on the plains of Elam just west of the Iranian plateau proper. Susa was probably founded about 4000 B.C., and its inhabitants had implements not only of obsidian but also of copper, and thus had already entered the

---

[1] *Life.* May 21, 1951, pp.113-116; *Science News Letter.* Nov. 24, 1951, p.325.
[2] Ernst E. Herzfeld, *Iran in the Ancient East.* 1941, pp.9-62, Pl. v,lower.

Chalcolithic Age. It is thought probable that the first discovery in the Middle East of the use of metal was made by the Caspians. At any rate their lofty plateau contains an abundance of mineral de posits, and at its numerous Bronze Age sites, dating from arounc. 3000 to 1000 B.C., a wealth of metal objects has been recovered. Of these the famous bronze bits, rings, weapons and ornaments found in Luristan in western Persia, dating probably from the second millennium to the Assyrian Period, may be specially mentioned.[3]

Other important prehistoric sites in Iran include Tepe Giyan, Tepe Hissar and Turang Tepe. Tepe Giyan is in central Iran near Nehavend, and has been excavated by G. Contenau and R. Ghirshman.[4] Its pottery appears to be approximately contemporary with the early levels at Susa, and features among other motifs an ibex painted in a style clearly descended from the representation found on the pottery at the mound near Persepolis.

Tepe Hissar is in the north near Damghan, and has been excavated by Dr. Erich F. Schmidt.[5] This site seems to have been occupied from about 3500 to 1200 B.C., and then not again until the time of the Sasanians. Painted pottery, copper pins, needles and daggers, beads, stamp seals, and animal figurines probably used for purposes of sympathetic magic, were characteristic finds at Tepe Hissar. The painted pottery was decorated with geometric and animal figures. An example from the second phase of the lowest stratum (Hissar I, c.3500-c.2800 B.C.) may be seen in the chalice pictured in Fig. 25, which is now in the Archaeological Museum at Teheran. At the top is a feline, perhaps a leopard, which is apparently stalking an ibex from behind a rock.

Turang Tepe or "Pheasant Mound" is also in northern Iran, about twelve miles northeast of Astarabad or Gurgan. The site is shown in Fig. 23 where the truncated, partly conical, partly·pyramidal shape of the main mound may be clearly seen. Test excavations have been made here by Frederick R. Wulsin,[6] and the findings have revealed

[3] André Godard, *Les bronzes du Luristan* (Ars Asiatica, xvii). 1931; René Dussaud in PSPA I, pp.254-277; Ernst Herzfeld and Sir Arthur Keith in PSPA I, pp.46-51.

[4] G. Contenau and R. Ghirshman, *Fouilles du Tépé-Giyan près de Néhavend 1931 et 1932*. 1935.

[5] Erich F. Schmidt, *Excavations at Tepe Hissar, Damghan*. 1937; M. Rogers Warren in PSPA I, pp.151-162.

[6] Frederick R. Wulsin in *Supplement to the Bulletin of the American Institute for Persian Art and Archaeology*. II, 1 bis (March 1932); and in PSPA I, pp.163-167. For related discoveries at Shah Tepe, see T. J. Arne in *Acta Archaeologica*, 6 (1935), pp.1-48.

a Bronze Age culture of considerable importance, dating probably around 2200 to 1200 B.C. The numerous graves contained offerings, usually of pottery, but also of stone, bronze or copper, silver and lead. The most plentiful pottery was a burnished gray ware. A number of human figurines were likewise unearthed, prominent among which were representations of a goddess of fertility.[7]

From the end of the Stone Age to the end of the Bronze Age, then, the peoples of the Iranian plateau remained mostly at the stage of village life. To the west of the plateau the city of Susa of course continued its development, and a series of Elamite kingdoms came into existence there, most of which were, however, under the domination of Mesopotamia. Likewise in the northwestern part of the plateau around Lake Urmia the transition from village to urban life was made relatively early, and by the beginning of the first millennium B.C. the kingdoms of Man and Urartu (Biblical Minni and Ararat, Jeremiah 51:27) were developing into importance. It was the Aryan immigration, however, which introduced a distinctively new period of cultural development on the Iranian plateau proper, and resulted in the foundation of the large and famous cities like Ecbatana, Pasargadae and Persepolis.[8]

THE ARYANS

It was probably around or shortly after the middle of the second millennium B.C. that the Aryans first entered Iran. Those who came at this time seem to have passed on through the land. One large body went eastward into the Indus valley to take a thenceforward prominent place in the history of India. Others pressed into western Asia where they left their mark in the name of the sun god Surya, who was worshiped among the non-Aryan Kassites; and in the names of the gods Mitra, Varuna, Indra and the Nasatyas (the Twins), which appear in Hittite records from Mitanni.[9] Somewhat later, perhaps toward the end of the second millennium B.C.,[10] other Aryans came into Iran and settled permanently in the land. From them the country derived its name of Airyana or Iran, meaning "the [land] of the Aryans," a designation to which the Persian government officially returned in 1935.[11]

---

[7] Phyllis Ackerman in PSPA I, pp.198f.,212f.   [8] PSPA I, pp.52,61f.

[9] Arthur Christensen, *Die Iranier* (in Walter Otto, ed., Handbuch der Altertumswissenschaft, III, i, 3, 3, 1). 1933, p.209; V. Gordon Childe, *The Aryans, A Study of Indo-European Origins* (The History of Civilization). 1926, p.18.

[10] William F. Albright in BASOR 106 (Apr. 1947), p.19.

[11] Ernst E. Herzfeld, *Archaeological History of Iran.* 1935, p.8; PSPA I, pp.42,60.

The names of the gods just mentioned are well known also in India, and thus it is shown that the western Aryans shared a common linguistic and religious background with those who went eastward. An outstanding feature of that common heritage in religion was the worship of the great powers of nature, while even the titles which were applied to the deities were the same in the west and the east. In the course of time, however, an interesting differentiation in usage took place between Iran and India. In India the Aryans called their gods *devas* and *asuras*, but soon came to look upon the *devas* as good gods and upon the *asuras* as evil demons. In Iran the Aryans used the same two words, save that the "s" of India was "h" in their language and thus *asura* became *ahura*. The differentiation between the *devas* and the *ahuras*, moreover, was carried out in diametrical opposition. In Iran the *devas* became for the most part the evil spirits. Thus, for example, Indra was a prominent and beneficent deity in India but appears in Iran as a demon.[12] Only a few of the good gods of India, such as Mitra (Mithra) and Soma (Haoma), were the objects of equal reverence in Iran. The *ahuras*, on the other hand, were not demons as in India but "lords" or "masters" who became the real gods of Iran.[13]

The two main tribes of Aryans to settle in Iran were the Amadai (Medes) and the Parsua (Persians). Both are mentioned for the first time in the inscriptions of Shalmaneser III about 836 B.C., and they appear regularly thereafter in the annals of the Assyrian kings. Shalmaneser III writes, for example: "I received the gifts of 27 kings of the land of Parsua. From Parsua I departed. To the lands of . . . and of the Medes . . . I descended."[14]

THE MEDES

The Medes settled toward the northwestern part of the plateau and eventually occupied three provinces known as Media Magna, now Iraq-i-ajam; Media Atropatene, modern Azerbaijan; and Media Rhagiana, around present-day Teheran. The one great natural route from Mesopotamia to the Caspian plateau runs across the Zagros Mountains and through the heart of the country occupied by the Medes, and it is not surprising to learn that for centuries they suffered conquest and the exaction of tribute by the Assyrian kings.[15]

[12] HERE XII, p.604; cf. A. Christensen, *Essai sur la démonologie iranienne*. 1941.
[13] Goetz, *Epochen der indischen Kultur*, pp.27f.
[14] ARAB I, §581.
[15] Percy Sykes, *A History of Persia*. 3d ed. 1930, I, pp.115-119.

MAP 2

IRAN

0 50 100 150

Scale of miles

For at least a brief time, however, the Medes had a great empire. According to Herodotus (c.484-425 B.C.), the founder of their royal dynasty was a certain Deioces, whom the Greek historian called "a clever man."[16] The capital of Deioces was at Hagmatana, "the meeting place of many roads," a city which the Greeks knew as Ecbatana and which is now Hamadan. His kingdom appears to figure in the inscriptions of Sargon II (721-705 B.C.) under the name Bit-Daiukki, "House of Deioces."[17]

Daiukku or Deioces was succeeded by his son Fravartish, the Phraortes of the Greeks, and he in turn by his son Uvakhshatra or Cyaxares (625-585 B.C.). By this time the Medes were strong enough to war successfully against their Assyrian enemies, and in cooperation with Nabopolassar of Babylon and with the king of the Scythians, Cyaxares took and destroyed Nineveh in 612 B.C. Cyaxares' son and successor, Ishtuvegu or Astyages (585-550 B.C.) enjoyed a long and luxurious reign, but in the end was dethroned by Cyrus, as dominance among the Iranian peoples passed from the Medes to the Persians.[18]

[16] I, 96-103. tr. A. D. Godley, LCL (1920-24), I, pp.127-135.
[17] ARAB I, §23.
[18] René Grousset in PSPA I, p.63.

2. THE ACHAEMENID PERIOD, c.700-331 B.C.

THE PERSIANS

THE Persians had gone on to the southern part of the Iranian plateau and settled not far from the Elamite land Anshan or Anzan in a region which they called Parsumash or Parsamash in memory of their homeland, Parsua. Around 700 B.C. their leader was Hakhamanish or Achaemenes, from whom the kings of the Achaemenid dynasty traced their descent. Chishpish or Teispes his son extended the Persian domain to include an area east of Anshan and north of the Persian Gulf which became known as Parsa (Fars) or Persian land. After the death of Teispes, his son Cyrus I (c.640-c.600) succeeded to the throne of Parsumash, and his other son Ariaramna (c.640-c.615 B.C.) ruled in Parsa.

The kings who followed Cyrus I in Parsumash were Cambyses I (c.600-c.559 B.C.), Cyrus II the Great (c.559-530 B.C.) and Cambyses II (530-522 B.C.). As is well known, Cyrus the Great was one of the outstanding rulers of all history. Hitherto the Persians had been subservient to the Medes, but Cyrus took Ecbatana without difficulty, and from that time on Parsa was the first ranking satrapy in the land, Media the second, and Elam the third. Thereafter Cyrus extended his conquests from Asia Minor and Babylon to eastern Iran. Everywhere he proceeded with a deep understanding of men, and manifested a humane attitude which contrasted most favorably with that of other ancient oriental conquerors. His capital and eventually his tomb were at Pasargadae[19] in the land of Parsa.

When Cambyses II died the new empire almost broke up. Many of the recently annexed provinces revolted, and a Magian named Gaumata pretended to be the younger brother of Cambyses (who actually had been murdered) and attempted to usurp the throne. Then the Persian line descended from Ariaramna reentered the picture in prominence. Ariaramna had been succeeded by Arsames, whose son was Hystaspes (Vishtaspa), and whose grandson was Darius I the Great (522-486 B.C.). It was Darius who became the deliverer of the imperiled empire. As was imperishably recorded on the massive Rock of Behistun (Fig. 26), Darius seized and slew Gaumata and suppressed all rebellion. He subsequently completed a reorganization of his holdings into twenty satrapies, and administered with great efficiency and wisdom an empire which extended from

[19] cf. Ernst Herzfeld, *Archaeologische Mitteilungen aus Iran.* I (1929), pp.4-16.

Egypt and Macedonia to southern Russia and the Indus valley. His capital was at Persepolis (Fig. 27) and his tomb at Naqsh-i-Rustam (Fig. 28). After Darius I the rulers of Persia were Xerxes (486-465 B.C.), Artaxerxes I Longimanus (465-423 B.C.), Darius II (423-404 B.C.), Artaxerxes II Mnemon (404-359), Artaxerxes III Ochus (359-338), Arses (338-335), and Darius III (335-331). Then the Achaemenid empire was destroyed by Alexander the Great.[20]

[20] For more details of this history and for archeological monuments at Ecbatana, Pasargadae, Persepolis, Susa, Behistun and Naqsh-i-Rustam see FLP pp.192-205; A. T. Olmstead, *History of the Persian Empire* [*Achaemenid Period*]. 1948.

3. ZOROASTER AND THE RISE OF ZOROASTRIANISM

ZOROASTER[21] lived not later than the period to which our swift historical survey has now brought us, and at this point we turn therefore to consideration of the prophet and his religion. First it is necessary to give a brief account of the most important written sources, the scriptures of Zoroastrianism.

THE ZOROASTRIAN SCRIPTURES

The authoritative religious writings of the Zoroastrian religion are known as the Avesta. This word may mean "the original text" in contrast with the Zand (Zend) or "commentary" which was later attached to it, thus giving rise to the term Zend-Avesta. These scriptures comprised in their entirety no less than twenty-one treatises known as Nasks,[22] but of these many have now been lost. The chief portions still extant are the following: (1) the Yasna, a liturgical work; (2) the Gathas, included in the Yasna, but written in verse and containing the teachings of Zoroaster; (3) the Visparad, invocations addressed to "all the lords"; (4) the Yashts, hymns of praise; and (5) the Vendidad, a priestly code of purifications and penalties.[23] In addition, there are a number of minor texts and fragments. As to date, the Gathas may well be contemporary with Zoroaster himself, while the composition and redaction of the remaining portions of the Avesta may have extended down into the fourth century A.D. The language in which the Avesta is written is commonly referred to as "Avestan." It is an ancient Iranian language to which Old Persian, Middle Persian and Modern Persian are related. Sanskrit and "Avestan" are very similar, and these two languages together with their respective linguistic relatives form the Indo-Iranian or Aryan family of Indo-European languages. The language of the Gathas seems older than that of the rest of the Avesta, and may be said to bear to the Younger Avestan somewhat the same relation as the Vedic language in India does to the classical Sanskrit.[24]

In later times a version of the Avesta was made in Pahlavi, a form of the Middle Persian language. This version was composed perhaps

[21] Zoroaster is the Greek form of the name which appears in Avestan as Zarathushtra, in Pahlavi as Zaratusht, and in modern Persian as Zaradusht or Zardusht.

[22] Dinkard III, 8. SBE XXXVII, p.6.

[23] These works and additional fragments are translated by James Darmesteter and L. H. Mills in SBE IV, XXIII, XXXI.

[24] A. V. Williams Jackson in HERE II, p.270.

in the fourth century A.D. and revised in the sixth.[25] It not only provided a translation or paraphrase of the text, but also gave at many points an explanatory commentary. In addition to this, an extensive literature dealing with religious subjects also came into existence in the Pahlavi language. At least fifty-five works are known, of which the most important are: (1) the Bundahish or "original creation," dealing with cosmogony, mythology and history; (2) the Dinkard or "acts of religion," relating to religious doctrines, customs, traditions, history and literature; (3) the Dadistan-i Dinik or "religious opinions" of the high priest Manushkihar in response to ninety-two questions; (4) the Epistles of the same Manushkihar; (5) the Selections of Zad-sparam, written by the younger brother of Manushkihar; (6) the Shayast la-shayast or "the proper and improper," a miscellaneous compilation of laws and customs concerning sin and impurity; (7) the Dinai-i Mainog-i Khirad or "opinions of the Spirit of Wisdom" in reply to sixty-two inquiries on miscellaneous religious subjects; (8) the Shikand-gumanik Vijar or "doubt-dispelling explanation," in defense of the Zoroastrian solution of the problem of evil as opposed to Jewish, Christian, Manichean, and Muslim theories; (9) the Arda-Viraf Namak or Book of Arda-Viraf, who describes his visit to heaven and hell while in a trance.[26] Manushkihar, the author of the Dadistan-i Dinik, is known from a note in one of his epistles[27] to have lived around A.D. 881, and a ninth century date is probable for most of the Pahlavi works which have just been listed.[28]

In Fig. 29 we show a facsimile of a single leaf of the Bundahish, written probably in the first half of the fourteenth century and now in the University Library of Copenhagen. Fig. 30 reproduces a page of the Arda-Viraf Namak from a more extensive codex dating probably in the latter half of the fourteenth century and preserved in the same library.[29]

[25] E. W. West in SBE XLVII, p.xvii.

[26] For English translations of these books in whole or in part see E. W. West in SBE V, XVIII, XXIV, XXXVII, XLVII; and Martin Haug and E. W. West, The Book of Arda Viraf, The Pahlavi Text Prepared by Destur Hoshangji Jamaspji Asa, Revised and Collated with Further MSS., with an English Translation and Introduction, and an Appendix Containing the Texts and Translations of the Gosht-i Fryano, and Hadokht-Nask. 1872.

[27] Epistle III, 21. SBE XVIII, p.365.

[28] Edward G. Browne, A Literary History of Persia from the Earliest Times until Firdawsí. 1902, pp.7f.,105-107.

[29] Codices Avestici et Pahlavici Bibliothecae Universitatis Hafniensis, I, The Pahlavi Codices K20 and K20b, Containing Ardāgh Virāz-Nāmagh, Bundahishn etc., Published in Facsimile by the University Library of Copenhagen, with an Introduction by Arthur Christensen. 1931, pp.10f.,15.

THE DATE OF ZOROASTER

Although there is little doubt that Zoroaster was an actual historical personage, the date of his life is uncertain. Three chief periods have been suggested for him. The first is at a time earlier than 6000 B.C. This was the date generally accepted by the ancient Greeks. Xanthus the Lydian (c.450 B.C.) was quoted by Diogenes Laertius (A.D. c.230) as stating that there were six thousand years between Zoroaster and the invasion of Xerxes (c.480 B.C.). Hermodorus, a disciple of Plato (c.427-347 B.C.) was also quoted by Diogenes as putting Zoroaster five thousand years before the taking of Troy, an event traditionally dated about 1200 B.C. Eudoxus (c.365 B.C.) was said by Pliny the Elder (A.D. 23-79) to have placed the life of Zoroaster six thousand years before the death of Plato, and to have had in this assertion the support of Aristotle (384-322 B.C.). Hermippus (c.200 B.C.) was also cited by Pliny as dating Zoroaster five thousand years before the Trojan War. Plutarch (A.D. c.46-c.120) gave the same date of five thousand years before the Trojan War.[30] Such an extremely early date is scarcely credible, and as a matter of fact the Greek tradition rested perhaps upon a misunderstanding of the Zoroastrian belief concerning the preexistence of Zoroaster's spiritual body. According to the Dinkard,[31] the spiritual body of the prophet was framed together six millenniums before Zoroaster was born on earth, and this could easily have accounted for the rise of the idea among the Greeks that Zoroaster had lived at that remote time.[32]

A second period proposed for Zoroaster is around the tenth or ninth centuries B.C. Among those who support such a date are historians of the highest eminence, and it may well prove to be correct.[33] According to a variant reading in the text of Diogenes, Xanthus placed Zoroaster six hundred years before Xerxes, which would give a date a little earlier than 1000 B.C. This textual reading is perhaps less likely to be correct, however, than the one already cited with the figure of six thousand years, which is in agreement with the prevail-

---

[30] Carl Clemen, *Fontes historiae religionis Persicae* (Fontes historiae religionum ex auctoribus Graecis et Latinis collectos subsidiis Societatis Rhenanae Promovendis Litteris, edidit Carolus Clemen, Fasciculus I). 1920, pp.74,42,48.

[31] VII, 15f. SBE XLVII, pp.21f., cf. xxviii,xl.

[32] cf. esp. É. Benveniste, *The Persian Religion According to the Chief Greek Texts*. 1929, pp.15f.

[33] Eduard Meyer, *Ursprung und Anfänge des Christentums*. II (1921), p.58; CRW p.142; Maneckji Nusservanji Dhalla, *History of Zoroastrianism*. 1938, p.xxxi; Albright in BASOR 106 (Apr. 1947), p.19; Arthur Christensen in *Acta Orientalia*. 4 (1926), pp.90f. (he subsequently changed his position).

ing Greek tradition.[34] Other evidence of greater weight pointing back to as early as around 1000 B.C. is to be found in the fact that the Gathas are at about the same stage of linguistic development as the most ancient Vedic hymns in India.

A third epoch in which Zoroaster may have lived is the Achaemenid Period. It, too, is favored by most eminent historians. We consider this period to be the most likely, but we also believe the tenth or ninth century date to be a very strong possibility. Several approaches lead to the Achaemenid Period, although they result in considerable variation in precise dates. One is a literary study of the Yashts which finds traces in them of a Zoroastrian reworking of earlier hymns, and surmises that the Zoroastrian reformation took place around 650-600 B.C.[35] Another is an investigation of the relationships of the Achaemenid kings to the Zoroastrian religion; including the possible connection of the father of Darius with Zoroaster. One survey of this evidence concludes that Zoroaster lived from 559 to 522 or after.[36] Some facts in this field will be set forth in later sections of our own chapter. Yet another line of inquiry turns to the chronology embodied in the Zoroastrian theory of the ages of the world as given in the Bundahish. This theory is admittedly a theological and eschatological construction; nevertheless it is not impossible that it preserves some memory of when Zoroaster lived, and was made to accord with some facts in history. Despite the difficulties and ambiguities inherent in it, this theory will now be set forth briefly, both because it contains information of possible value on the date of Zoroaster and because it is of intrinsic interest for an understanding of Zoroastrian thought.

The theory of world-ages appears prominently in the Bundahish and other writings. While the Bundahish probably belongs to the ninth century A.D. it no doubt draws upon much earlier sources. As a matter of fact the idea of the ages of the world must be as old as the fifth century B.C., since belief in the preexistence of Zoroaster's spiritual body six thousand years before his birth on earth is a part of the

[34] James H. Moulton, *Early Zoroastrianism* (The Hibbert Lectures, Second Series). 1913, p.412.

[35] Christensen, *Die Iranier*, pp.214f.; based on his *Les Kayanides* (Det Kgl. Danske Videnskabernes Selskab. Historisk-filologiske Meddelelser, XIX, 2). 1931.

[36] Johannes Hertel, *Die Zeit Zoroasters* (Indo-iranische Quellen und Forschungen, 1). 1924, pp.21,47. Historians of the first rank who accept substantially this dating include C. F. Lehmann-Haupt in Jal Dastur Cursetji Pavry, ed., *Oriental Studies in Honour of Cursetji Erachji Pavry.* 1933, pp.251-280; and Olmstead, *History of the Persian Empire*, p.94; in *Review of Religion.* 4 (1939), pp.3f.

theory and since this belief had evidently become known among the Greeks by the time of Xanthus.

A concise statement of the theory may be found in Chapter xxxiv of the Bundahish,[37] and the account which follows is based primarily upon this chapter along with supplementary references in other chapters of the Bundahish and in other Zoroastrian books. Bundahish xxxiv begins with the statement that "Time was for twelve thousand years." These twelve thousand years which comprise the total extent of all time are then divided into four periods of three thousand years each. The first period of three thousand years "was the duration of the spiritual state, where the creatures were unthinking, unmoving, and intangible." Comparing Bundahish i, 8 (sbe v, p.5), we gather that it is meant that at this time the *fravashis* or spiritual prototypes of later creatures were already in existence.

The second period of three thousand years "was the duration of Gayomard, with the ox, in the world." Gayomard was the primeval man, who with the primeval ox lived undisturbed during this trimillennium. According to Dinkard vii, ii, 15f. (sbe xlvii, pp.21f.), the spiritual body of Zoroaster was framed together by the archangels at the beginning of this period; and according to Bundahish i, 22; iii, 1 (sbe v, pp.8f.,15), the evil spirit remained in impotent confusion throughout the entire three thousand years.

When the third period of three thousand years began, "the adversary rushed in, and Gayomard lived thirty years in tribulation." In Bundahish iii, 21-23 (sbe v, pp.18f.) we are told that the evil spirit was assisted by a thousand demons in his attack on Gayomard, and that during the thirty years of his existence in duress Gayomard declared, "Although the destroyer has come, mankind will be all of my race; and this one thing is good, when they perform duty and good works." The sole-created Gayomard then passed away, but from his seed grew up Mashya and Mashyoi (also called Marhaya and Marhiyoih), the first human pair, who became the progenitors of mankind (Bundahish xv. sbe v, pp.52-59; Dadistan-i Dinik xxxvii, 82. sbe xviii, p.105). Among their descendants were Hoshyang, considered to have been founder of the first Iranian dynasty (Bundahish xv, 28. sbe v, p.58), and Takhmorup and Yim, kings who also appear in the Shah Namah of Firdausi as Tahmuras and Jamshed (cf. Bundahish xxxi, 1-3. sbe v, p.130). The dynasties of these kings filled out the first thousand years of this third trimillennium.

[37] sbe v, pp.149-151.

Throughout the second thousand years of this period Dahak held sway, the reference evidently being to a foreign dynasty personified as a single king. During the first half of the third thousand years the dynasty of Fredun (Feridun in the Shah Namah) ruled, and then the second five hundred years was occupied with the following reigns: Manushkihar,[38] 120 years; Zob, 5 years; Kai-Kabad, 15 years; Kai-Kaus, "till he went to the sky,[39] 75 years, and 75 years after that, altogether 150 years"; Kai-Khusrov, 60 years; Kai-Lorasp, 120 years; Kai-Vishtasp, "till the coming of the religion, 30 years."[40]

Thus we are brought up to the beginning of the fourth trimillennium, which was inaugurated by "the coming of the religion," that is to say by the founding of Zoroastrianism. This last period of three thousand years extends yet, of course, far into the future, but its first thousand years and slightly more are covered by the chronological notices which bring Chapter xxxiv of the Bundahish to a conclusion. These notices fall into two groups: first a rather detailed list of kings or dynasties from Kai Vishtasp to Alexander "the Ruman";[41] then summary statements mentioning the Ashkanians or Arsacids who ruled for two hundred and eighty-four years, Ardashir and the Sasanians who ruled for four hundred and sixty years, and the Arabs to whom sovereignty finally passed.

Returning to the detailed list which extends from Kai-Vishtasp, the last Kayanid, to Alexander, we find that Kai-Vishtasp is said to have still held sway for ninety years after "the coming of the religion," and then to have been followed by four more rulers, apparently Achaemenids, prior to Alexander the Great. The names and years of these five kings who ruled between "the coming of the religion" and the time of Alexander the Great may be tabulated as follows:[42]

[38] This Manushkihar, a descendant of Fredun (Bundahish xxxi, 9-12. SBE v, pp.133f.) and an ancestor of Zoroaster (Bundahish, xxxii, 1f. SBE v, pp.140f.), is of course not to be confused with Manushkihar, author of the Dadistan-i Dinik and of several epistles.

[39] The reference is to the legendary attempt of Kai-Kaus to fly in a machine lifted by four eagles, each attracted upward by meat set on a spear above its head. This is narrated in the Shah Namah, 411f. tr. Warner and Warner, ii, pp.103f.; cf. *The Sacred Books and Early Literature of the East*, vii, pp.329f.

[40] The series of kings whose names begin with Kai forms a dynasty known as the Kaianid or Kayanid. cf. Clément Huart, *Ancient Persia and Iranian Civilization* (The History of Civilization). tr. M. R. Dobie. 1927, p.210.

[41] Alexander the Great was called "the Ruman" in Zoroastrian tradition because he came from Greek provinces which later were a part of the eastern Roman empire.

[42] cf. J. Hertel, *Achaemeniden und Kayaniden, Ein Beitrag zur Geschichte Irans* (Indo-iranische Quellen und Forschungen, 5). 1924, pp.16f. Vohuman is equated with

Kai-Vishtasp	90
Vohuman	112
Humai	30
Darai	12
Darai son of Darai	14
	258

A reign of fourteen years is then ascribed to Alexander "the Ruman," and since he died in 323 B.C. this chronology would seem to indicate 595 B.C. for the founding of Zoroastrianism.

Before accepting this figure, however, comparison must be made with certain other statements, and possible revision introduced. In the Book of Arda-Viraf and in the Selections of Zad-sparam it is said that Zoroastrianism remained in purity for three hundred years until Alexander the Great came to Iran and destroyed the monarchy.[43] The passage in question in the Book of Arda-Viraf stands at the opening of the work and reads as follows:

They say that once upon a time the pious Zaratusht [Zoroaster] made the religion which he had received current in the world; and till the completion of 300 years the religion was in purity and men were without doubts. But afterward the accursed evil-spirit, the wicked one, in order to make men doubtful of this religion, instigated the accursed Alexander the Ruman, who was dwelling in Egypt, so that he came to the country of Iran with severe cruelty and war and devastation; he also slew the ruler of Iran, and destroyed the metropolis and empire, and made them desolate.

And this religion, namely, all the Avesta and Zand, written upon prepared cowskins, and with gold ink, was deposited in the archives in Stakhar Papakan [Persepolis]; and the hostility of the evil-destined, wicked Ashemok, the evil-doer, brought onward Alexander the Ruman, who was dwelling in Egypt, and he burnt them up. And he killed several desturs and judges and herbads and mobads and upholders of the religion,[44] and the competent and wise of the country of Iran. And he cast hatred and strife, one with the other, amongst the nobles and householders of the country of Iran; and self-destroyed, he fled to hell.[45]

"Artahshatar" (Ardashir) in Bahman Yasht II, 17 (SBE V, pp.198f.) and Bundahish XXXI, 30 (SBE V, p.137). This must be Artaxerxes I. Darius (Darai) I Hystaspes is made the father of Darius III Codomanus. The list is thus incomplete. It is doubtful whether Kai-Vishtasp is connected with the others. cf. Christensen, Les Kayanides.

[43] West in SBE XLVII, p.xxviii; cf. A. V. Williams Jackson, Zoroaster, The Prophet of Ancient Iran. 1898, pp.159,176.

[44] These are various grades of the Zoroastrian priesthood. The destur is the high priest. The judge is also of high rank, but is distinguished from the destur. The herbad is one who has completed his theological studies. The mobad is a herbad who is chiefly engaged in the performance of ceremonies. The upholder of the religion is a student of the Avesta.

[45] I, 1-11. Haug and West, The Book of Arda Viraf, pp.141-143.

[81]

The statement in the Selections of Zad-sparam says of Zoroastrian-ism that "it exists day and night till the three-hundredth year. After-ward the religion is disturbed and the monarchy is contested."[46]

These references in the Book of Arda-Viraf and the Selections of Zad-sparam may be explained and dismissed as giving only a round number for the period of time which appears more precisely in the Bundahish as totaling 258 years.

Significantly enough, the exact figure of 258 years appears ex-plicitly in another document. This is The Chronology of Ancient Na-tions, which was written in A.D. 1000 by the Muslim scholar al-Biruni. In discussing Zoroastrian chronology, al-Biruni says, "From his [Zoro-aster's] appearance till the beginning of the Era of Alexander, they count 258 years."[47]

It appears that al-Biruni and the author of the Bundahish drew upon similar but not identical sources. Both give 258 years from Zoroaster to Alexander the Great, but in the Bundahish the 258 years bring us to a point fourteen years before the death of Alexander, while with al-Biruni the terminus ad quem is "the beginning of the Era of Alexander." Since in the Bundahish the figure of 258 years has been worked into a chronological scheme which is on the whole artificial and mystical, we may prefer the testimony of al-Biruni and believe that the original Zoroastrian tradition dated Zoroaster 258 years before the Era of Alexander.

Al-Biruni thought that the Era of Alexander began with Alexan-der's attack on Persia in the twenty-sixth year of his life (331 B.C.), but since he also says that this was the era employed by the Jews and Greeks for more than a thousand years,[48] it could in actuality have been the same as the Seleucid Era, which was the first real era in history and which prevailed for so long in western Asia.[49] In that case, since the Seleucid Era began in 312-311 B.C., the appearance of Zoroaster would be dated in 570 B.C.

We may suppose that by the "appearance" of Zoroaster, al-Biruni meant the birth of the prophet. On the other hand, the Dinkard (VII, viii, 51. SBE XLVII, p.105) reckons the first century of Zoroastrian-ism from the spiritual "conference" of Zoroaster which took place

[46] XXIII, 11f. SBE XLVII, p.166.
[47] p.14. C. Edward Sachau, ed., The Chronology of Ancient Nations, An English Ver-sion of the Arabic Text of the Athâr-ul-Bâkiya of Albîrûnî, or "Vestiges of the Past," Collected and Reduced to Writing by the Author in A.H. 390-1, A.D. 1000. 1879, p.17.
[48] p.28. ed. Sachau, pp.32f.
[49] Eduard Meyer, Geschichte des Altertums. I, i (2d ed. 1907), p.239.

when the prophet was thirty years old, and it is of course possible that this was the terminus a quo. If we accept the former hypothesis, we come at the conclusion of this line of chronological calculation to the year 570 B.C. as the date of the birth of Zoroaster.[50]

This date is here set forth, it must be remembered, not as an assured fact but only as a possibility which is to be considered seriously and which has back of it the line of reasoning we have just traced. Since it does give us a precise, though hypothetical, date, it may be of interest to indicate the other chronological points in Zoroaster's life which would follow from it if we continue to accept Zoroastrian tradition. The Dinkard states not only that Zoroaster was thirty years old at his "conference," but also that he was forty-two years old when Vishtasp was converted, and seventy-seven years old at the time of his death (VII, v, 1. SBE XLVII, pp.73f.). Counting from a birth date of 570 B.C., the "conference" would have taken place in 540 B.C., the conversion of Vishtasp in 528 B.C., and the prophet's death in 493 B.C.

VISHTASPA

As we have seen, a certain Vishtasp or Vishtaspa is named in Zoroastrian traditions as ruler at the time when Zoroaster lived, and his conversion in the forty-second year of the prophet's life was of much importance for the establishment of the new faith.

The name Vishtaspa is philologically the same as Hystaspes,[51] the name of the father of Darius I the Great (522-486 B.C.). This Hystaspes is known to us both from Herodotus and from Persian inscriptions. Herodotus says that "Hystaspes son of Arsames was an Achaemenid, and Darius was the oldest of his sons."[52] Darius declares in his own inscriptions, "I am Darius, great king, king of kings, king of lands, son of Hystaspes, the Achaemenid";[53] and Xerxes writes as

---

[50] Ernst Herzfeld, Archaeologische Mitteilungen aus Iran. II (1930), pp.39-47; in Pavry, ed., Oriental Studies in Honour of Cursetji Erachji Pavry, pp.132-136; and Zoroaster and His World. 1947, I, pp.1-30. For a severe criticism of this view see H. S. Nyberg, Die Religionen des alten Iran (Mitteilungen der Vorderasiatisch-Aegyptischen Gesellschaft [E. V.], 43). German tr. by H. H. Schaeder. 1938, pp.31-36. Nyberg himself concludes (pp.44f.) that it is impossible to determine the date of Zoroaster, except to say that he lived sometime before 485 B.C. For reviews of Herzfeld's Zoroaster and His World see Richard N. Frye in Harvard Journal of Asiatic Studies. 10 (1947), pp.440-448; Arthur D. Nock in AJA 53 (1949), pp.272-285.

[51] L. W. King and R. C. Thompson, The Sculptures and Inscription of Darius the Great on the Rock of Behistûn in Persia. 1907, p.lxi.

[52] I, 209.

[53] F. H. Weissbach, Die Keilinschriften der Achämeniden. 1911, pp.80f.; cf. King and Thompson, The Sculptures and Inscription of Darius the Great on the Rock of Behistûn in Persia, pp.1,84,85,93,152,159.

follows in an inscription recently discovered at Persepolis: "Says Xerxes the king: My father [is] Darius, Darius' father was one named Vishtaspa, Vishtaspa's father was one named Rshama. Vishtaspa as well as Rshama, both were alive when Ahuramazda, as was his will, made Darius my father king over this earth."[54]

The approximate dates of Hystaspes' life may be estimated from information provided by Ctesias and Herodotus. Ctesias was a fifth century B.C. Greek physician who was at the Persian court and who wrote a history called *Persica* which was preserved in abridged form in the *Bibliotheca* of Photius, the ninth century A.D. patriarch of Constantinople. According to Ctesias-Photius, Darius was seventy-two years old when he died (486 B.C.),[55] and thus would have been born in 558 B.C. This is in general agreement with Herodotus,[56] who says that Darius was around twenty years of age in the year Cyrus the Great died (530 B.C.). Since his oldest son Darius was born about 558 B.C., it may be estimated that Hystaspes himself was born around 580 B.C. Ctesias also tells that Hystaspes died by accident when he went to view the tomb of Darius, which that king had prepared in advance of his own death.[57] The death of Hystaspes, we may therefore estimate, took place around 500 B.C.[58]

While Hystaspes was never king in the sense of "great king," it is probable that he ruled the provinces of Bactria and Hyrcania under Cyrus the Great,[59] and the Behistun inscription shows that he suppressed rebellion in Parthia and Hyrcania under Darius the Great.[60] The Arab historian Masudi (d. A.D. c.956) states that his residence was in Balkh, which was the ancient Bactra, the capital of Bactria.[61]

If Zoroaster lived around 570-493 B.C., it would be possible to identify the Vishtaspa whom he converted with this Hystaspes, the father

[54] Ernst E. Herzfeld, *A New Inscription of Xerxes from Persepolis* (SAOC, 5). 1932, p.4.

[55] §50 (19). John Gilmore, *The Fragments of the Persika of Ktesias*. 1888, p.152. Ctesias wrongly says that Darius reigned thirty-one years instead of thirty-six.

[56] I, 209.

[57] §46 (15). ed. Gilmore, p.150.

[58] Herzfeld, *Archaeologische Mitteilungen aus Iran*. I (1929), p.123.

[59] C. F. Lehmann-Haupt in Paulys *Real-Encyclopädie der classischen Altertumswissenschaft*, ed. Georg Wissowa, Wilhelm Kroll and Kurt Witte. Zweite Reihe, II, 1 (1921), col. 85; and in Pavry, *Oriental Studies in Honour of Cursetji Erachji Pavry*, pp.252,261,268.

[60] King and Thompson, *The Sculptures and Inscription of Darius the Great on the Rock of Behistûn in Persia*, pp.40-43,125-127,184-186.

[61] Abū-l Ḥasan 'Alī ibn Ḥusain ibn 'Alī ul-Mas'ūdī, *Murûj udh-Dhahab wa Ma'ādin ul-Jawāhir*, XXI. tr. C. Barbier de Meynard and Pavet de Courteille, *Les Prairies d'Or*. 1861-77, II (2d printing, 1914), p.123.

of Darius the Great. This is nothing new but was already done by the Roman historian Ammianus Marcellinus (A.D. c.360), who said in speaking of Media, of the Magi and of magic or "holy rites": "To this science, derived from the secret lore of the Chaldeans, in ages long past the Bactrian Zoroaster made many contributions, and after him the wise king Hystaspes, the father of Darius."[62] If, on the other hand, Zoroaster lived at quite a different time, say around 1000 B.C., the identification would of course be impossible. The fact that it is possible when a date around 570-493 B.C. is assigned to Zoroaster lends some strength to the hypothesis of the later date.

THE LIFE OF ZOROASTER

Where Zoroaster lived is almost as uncertain as when. The two chief possibilities are the northeast and the northwest of Iran. Favoring the northeast are the facts that Ammianus Marcellinus called Zoroaster a Bactrian, that Vishtaspa-Hystaspes ruled in Bactria and Hyrcania, and that the geographical allusions of the Avesta give prominence to eastern Iran.[63] On the other hand the language of the Gathas has been identified as a dialect of northwestern Iran,[64] and in both Zoroastrian and Arabic traditions there are references indicating that Zoroaster was born in that region. Several of these passages may be cited:

Chapter xx of the Bundahish contains a list and description of rivers in which we read: "The Daraja River is in Airan-vej, on the bank of which was the dwelling of Porushasp, the father of Zaratusht" (xx, 32. SBE V, p.82). A little later in the same book it is explicitly stated that Zoroaster was born at this place: "The Daraja River is the chief of exalted rivers, for the dwelling of the father of Zaratusht was on its banks, and Zaratusht was born there" (xxiv, 15; SBE V, p.89). Finally it is stated that "Airan-vej is in the direction of Ataropatakan" or Azerbaijan (xxix, 12. SBE V, p.120). While any specific identification of the Daraja River is hypothetical, this sequence of passages clearly reflects the opinion that the native place of Zoroaster was in Azerbaijan.

Arab sources also state that Zoroaster came from Azerbaijan, and point specifically to the district of Shiz and the city of Urumiah (Ur-

[62] *History.* XXIII, vi, 32. tr. John C. Rolfe, LCL (1935-39) II, p.367. cf. Hertel, *Die Zeit Zoroasters*, p.21.
[63] Jackson, *Zoroaster, The Prophet of Ancient Iran*, p.218; cf. Christensen, *Die Iranier*, p.214.
[64] Grousset in PSPA I, p.68.

miah, or Urmia, now called Rizaiyeh). Yaqut, who compiled a large geography about A.D. 1224, says under the heading, Shiz: "A district of Azerbaijan. . . . It is believed that this is the native land of Zaradusht, the prophet of the fire worshipers. The chief place of the district is Urmiah"; and under the heading, Urmiah: "It is claimed that this is the city of Zaradusht and that it was founded by the fire worshipers."[65] Ibn Hurdadhbah (A.D. c.816) likewise speaks of "Urmia, the city of Zaradusht and . . . Shiz, in which last city there is the fire temple Adharjushnas, which is held in high esteem by the Magians."[66]

The Selections of Zad-sparam (XVI, 12. SBE XLVII, p.147) point to a different city for the origin of Zoroaster, and state that "Zaratusht arose from Ragh," meaning the ancient city of Ravy, Rhages, or Rai ('Pάγαι), whose ruins are near modern Teheran. A proposed explanation to reconcile the discrepancy is that the mother of Zoroaster came from this place. In the Dinkard (VII, ii, 9f. SBE XLVII, p.20) she is represented as coming to Porushasp from another district than that in which the latter lived, and the Arab writer Shahrastani (A.D. 1086-1153), who lived in Khorasan, states explicitly in regard to Zoroaster, "His father was from Azerbaijan and his mother, whose name was Dughdu, was from Rai."[67]

Perhaps a reconciliation can also be effected between the views which place Zoroaster in the northwest and in the northeast of Iran respectively, by supposing that he was indeed born in the northwest but later lived and worked in the northeast. An explicit statement to this effect is made by al-Biruni and will be quoted a little later.

As has appeared in the references already given, the traditional name of Zoroaster's father was Porushasp. In Chapter XXXII of the Bundahish (SBE V, pp.140f.) the genealogy of the prophet is traced on back to Manushkihar (cf. above p. 80). From this genealogy we need here only note that one of the ancestors was Spitaman, and that from him the family designation of Spitama was derived. According to the same source (SBE V, pp.142-144), Zoroaster himself was married to three wives and had several sons and daughters.

[65] C. Barbier de Meynard, *Dictionnaire géographique, historique et littéraire de la Perse et des contrées adjacentes extrait du Mo'djem el-Bouldan de Yaqout, et complète a l'aide de documents arabes et persans pur la plupart inédits.* 1861, pp.367,26.

[66] Quoted by Richard J. H. Gottheil in *Classical Studies in Honour of Henry Drisler.* 1894, p.44.

[67] I, ii, 2, ch.1, §3. Theodor Haarbrücker, *Abu-'l-Fath' Muh'ammad asch-Schahrastâni's Religionspartheien und Philosophen-Schulen zum ersten Male vollständig aus dem Arabischen übersetzt und mit erklärenden Anmerkungen versehen.* 1850-51, I, p.280. Bundahish XXXII, 10 (SBE V, p.144) gives Dughda as the name of Zoroaster's mother.

The first spiritual "conference" of Zoroaster is described both in the Dinkard (vii, iii, 51-62. sbe xlvii, pp.47-50) and in Chapter xxxi of the Selections of Zad-sparam (sbe xlvii, pp.154-159). Following the latter and fuller source, we learn that at the age of thirty Zoroaster crossed the Daiti River and on the far bank met the archangel Vohu Manah or Good Thought. Vohu Manah asked Zoroaster, "Who mayest thou be, and from whom of them mayest thou be? also what is mostly thy desire, and the endeavor in thy existence?" Zoroaster replied, "I am Zaratusht of the Spitamas; among the existences righteousness is more my desire, and my wish is that I may become aware of the will of the sacred beings, and may practice so much righteousness as they exhibit to me in the pure existence." Upon this reply, Vohu Manah led Zoroaster "to an assembly of the spirits," and "when he came within twenty-four feet of the archangels, he then did not see his own shadow on the ground, on account of the great brilliancy of the archangels." Zoroaster cried, "Homage to Auharmazd,"[68] and "went forward and sat down in the seat of the inquirers." Ahura Mazda then instructed Zoroaster in the doctrines of the pure religion.

Other revelations are said to have continued to come to Zoroaster during a span of ten years, and then at the end of this period he won his first convert, his own cousin Maidhyo-maungha or Medyomah. As is stated in the Selections of Zad-sparam (xxiii, 1. sbe xlvii, p.163): "On the completion of revelation, that is, at the end of the ten years, Medyomah, son of Arastai, became faithful to Zaratusht." At this time the prophet said despondently, "In ten years only one man has been attracted by me" (*ibid.*, xxiii, 2).

It was two years longer before Zoroaster won his great victory with the conversion of the ruler Vishtaspa. It is said that Zoroaster departed "alone, by the advice and command of Auharmazd, to the residence of Vishtasp," and that when he met the king "he invited Vishtasp to the religion of Auharmazd" (Dinkard vii, iv, 65f. sbe xlvii, pp.64f.). Before the conversion of the king was completed, Zoroaster experienced a "terrible combat with evil" in which he himself suffered imprisonment and was involved "in controversy about the religion with the famous learned of the realm" (Dinkard vii, iv, 69,73. sbe xlvii, pp.65-67). The king was at last won to the faith, however, and his conversion marked the beginning of the triumph of Zoroastrianism throughout the land. As the author of the Dinkard

[68] The supreme god is known as Ahura Mazda in the Avesta, as Auharmazd in the Pahlavi literature, and as Ormazd or Hormuzd in later Persian.

says, if Vishtaspa and the people of that time had not accepted the religion announced by Zoroaster, "it would not have reached unto us" (VII, iv, 63. SBE XLVII, p.64).

A concise summary, covering the essential facts thus far and suggesting the later course of events, is found in the writings of the Muslim author, al-Biruni (A.D. c.973-c.1048): "Zarathustra went forth from Adharbaijan [Azerbaijan] and preached Magism in Balkh [Bactra]. His doctrines came into favor with King Gushtasp [Vishtaspa], and his son Isfendiyad spread the new faith both in east and west, both by force and by treaties. He founded fire temples throughout his whole empire, from the frontiers of China to those of the Greek empire. The succeeding kings made their religion [i.e., Zoroastrianism] the obligatory state religion for Persis and Iraq."[69]

Vishtaspa's son Isfendiyad (Isfendiar or Asfandiyar), who is called Spento-data in Avestan and Spend-dad in Pahlavi (i.e. Darius, according to Herzfeld), played an important part in the spreading of the faith, as stated by al-Biruni. In particular he was the great hero of the holy wars which the Zoroastrians had to fight against invading Turanians. His part in achieving the victory in these conflicts, through which the faith of Zoroaster was established on a firm foundation, is narrated in stirring detail in the Shah Namah or Book of Kings, the epic history of Persia composed by Firdausi (A.D. c.940-c.1020).[70]

In these wars, however, Zoroaster himself is said to have lost his life. According to the Shah Namah, this was when the Turanians stormed Balkh and destroyed the Zoroastrian temple Nush Azar. We read:

> The host reached Balkh, the world was wrecked with sack
> And slaughter. Making for the Fane of Fire (Nush Azar),
> For hall and palace decked with gold, they gave
> Them and the Zandavasta to the flames.
> The fane had eighty priests, God's worshippers,
> And all before the Fire the Turkmans slew,
> And swept that cult away. The Fire, that erst
> Zarduhsht had litten, of their blood did die;
> Who slew that priest himself I know not I.[71]

[69] *India* I, 10. ed. Sachau, I, p.21. cf. below p.179.

[70] tr. Arthur G. Warner and Edmond Warner, *The Sháhnáma of Firdausi Done into English* (Trübner's Oriental Series. 9 vols. 1905-15). vol. v. Part of the account (1495-1553. tr. Warner and Warner, v, pp.30-87) in the Shah Namah concerning Zoroaster, Gushtasp and Isfendiar was derived according to Firdausi from his predecessor Dakiki.

[71] 1559. tr. Warner and Warner, v, p.92.

The same story is repeated a little later, and it is also told how a messenger carried to the absent Vishtaspa the news of the fall of the city, of the death of Lohrasp, the father of Vishtaspa, and of the slaying of the Master, by whom Zoroaster is meant:

> The Turkmans
> Have slain at Balkh Luhrasp, the king of kings,
> And turned our days to gloom and bitterness,
> Proceeded thence to Nush Azar and there
> Beheaded both Zarduhsht and all the archmages,
> Quenched in whose blood the radiant Fire expired.[72]

In Zoroastrian traditions the very name of the murderer of their prophet is given. In the Dinkard (v, iii, 2. SBE XLVII, p.126) the killing of Zoroaster is ascribed to Bradro-resh the Tur, and in the Dadistan-i Dinik (LXXII, 8: SBE XVIII, p.218) Tur-i Bradar-vakhsh is mentioned, "by whom the best of men [i.e. Zoroaster] was put to death." Also the exact day of Zoroaster's death is recorded in the Selections of Zad-sparam (XXIII, 9. SBE XLVII, p.165): "In the forty-seventh year Zaratusht passes away, who attains 77 years and 40 days in the month Ardavahisto on the day Khur." This was the eleventh day of the second month of the Zoroastrian year.

THE GATHAS

For an understanding of the original teachings of Zoroaster we are dependent upon the Gathas.[73] The Gathas are five in number, containing seventeen hymns in all, and are now found as a part of the Yasna. Each Gatha is named after its opening words.

As revealed in the Gathas, Zoroaster's religion was a development of the ancient *asura-ahura* conceptions, with two characteristic features: first a strong tendency toward monotheism, and second an avowed but not fully elucidated dualism. The supreme god is called Ahura Mazda, meaning the Lord, the All-knowing One. In origin Ahura Mazda is probably identical with the ancient Varuna, and he appears now as a universal being who is the creator and sustainer of the world of good. Although Mazda is the Ahura par excellence, there are also other divine beings among whom the higher ones also are occasionally called Ahuras. These other divine beings are sometimes said to be sons and daughters of Mazda, or are spoken of as created by him, but soon come to be treated as personified qualities

---

[72] 1559f. tr. Warner and Warner, v, p.93.
[73] Christensen, *Die Iranier*, pp.221-227.

of his nature. Six of these are called Amesha Spentas or Immortal Beneficent Ones. They are: Vohu Manah or Good Thought, Asha Vahishta or Best Righteousness (Right), Khshathra Vairya or Wished-for Dominion, Spenta Armaiti or Holy Piety, Haurvatat or Welfare, and Ameretat or Immortality. Along with the foregoing there is sometimes counted as a seventh, Spenta Mainyu or Holy Spirit, who is probably the same as Mazda himself in his character as opponent of the spirit of evil. Yet other spiritual beings include Sraosha or Obedience, Ashi or Reward, and the strange figure of the Ox-soul which evidently represents the realm of animal life as entrusted to the diligent husbandman.

Over against the good world of the Ahuras stands the evil world of the Devas. As the idea of Asha or Righteousness makes clear the essence of the world of good, so the conception of the Druj or Lie, in the sense of antagonism to religious truth and order, expresses the nature of the world of evil. Sometimes the Druj or Lie appears personified as a feminine demon. Other spiritual personalities of the evil world include Aeshma or Fury, Aka Manah or Evil Thought who opposes Vohu Manah or Good Thought, and Angra Mainyu (Ahriman) or Evil Spirit who contends against Spenta Mainyu or Holy Spirit.

As long as this cosmic conflict continues man must choose his side and take his part in the struggle. By good thoughts, good deeds and good words, man assists the cause of Ahura Mazda. As George Foot Moore put it, "There is no place for saints who flee from the world; the saint is he who overcomes the evil in the world."[74]

A dualism of good and evil thus appears clearly in the Gathas. It is, however, a dualism which is limited in time, and the ultimate triumph of Ahura Mazda and of good is definitely envisaged. At death every soul must approach the Cinvat Bridge or Bridge of the Separator. There the righteous pass over to blessedness while the adherents of the Lie are turned back to punishment. At the end of the world, moreover, there will be a fiery test of all things when a flood of molten metal is poured out in which all evil will be burned up, but the good be left unharmed.

We may now turn directly to the Gathic texts.[75] The first Gatha is called Ahunavaiti, and consists of seven hymns found in Chapters

---

[74] MHR I, p.394.

[75] For translations of the Gathas see L. H. Mills, SBE XXXI, pp.1-194; James H. Moulton, *Early Zoroastrianism*, pp.343-390; and *Early Religious Poetry of Persia* (The Cambridge Manuals of Science and Literature). 1911, pp.80-118. Quotations here are from the translation by Moulton in *Early Zoroastrianism*.

28 to 34 of the Yasna. It opens with this prayer of Zoroaster (Yasna 28:1-4,7):

With outspread hands in petition for that help, O Mazda, first of all things I will pray for the works of the holy spirit, O thou the Right, whereby I may please the will of Good Thought and the Ox-soul.

I who would serve you, O Mazda Ahura and Good Thought—do ye give through the Right the blessings of both worlds, the bodily and that of Thought, which set the faithful in felicity.

I who would praise you, as never before, Right, and Good Thought, and Mazda Ahura, and those for whom Piety makes an imperishable Dominion grow; come ye to my help at my call.

I who have set my heart on watching over the soul, in union with Good Thought, and as knowing the rewards of Mazda Ahura for our works, will, while I have power and strength, teach men to seek after Right. . . .

Grant, O thou the Right, the reward, the blessings of Good Thought; O Piety, give our desire to Vishtaspa and to me; O thou, Mazda and Sovran, grant that your Prophet may perform the word of hearing.

The second hymn (Yasna 29) consists of a dialogue in heaven, in which the Ox-soul complains that the cattle on earth are treated with violence, and in which Vohu Manah names Zarathushtra Spitama to protect them. The Ox-soul however laments, "That I must be content with the ineffectual word of an impotent man for my protector." Zoroaster then prays earnestly for strength for his task, and the Ox-soul is satisfied and says,"O Ahura, now is help ours."

The third hymn is one of the central expositions of the creed of the prophet. It runs as follows (Yasna 30):

Now will I proclaim to those who will hear the things that the understanding man should remember. . . .

Hear with your ears the best things; look upon them with clear-seeing thought, for decision between the two Beliefs, each man for himself before the Great Consummation. . . .

Now the two primal Spirits, who revealed themselves in vision as Twins, are the Better and the Bad in thought and word and action. And between these two the wise once chose aright, the foolish not so.

And when these twain spirits came together in the beginning, they established Life and Not-Life, and that at the last the Worst Existence shall be to the followers of the Lie, but the Best Thought to him that follows Right.

Of these twain Spirits he that followed the Lie chose doing the worst things; the holiest Spirit chose Right, he that clothes him with the massy heavens as a garment. So likewise they that are fain to please Ahura Mazda by dutiful actions.

Between these twain the demons also chose not aright, for infatuation came upon them as they took counsel together, so that they chose the

Worst Thought. Then they rushed together to Violence, that they might enfeeble the world of man.

And to him [mankind] came Dominion, Good Thought, and Right; and Piety gave continued life of their bodies and indestructibility, so that by thy retributions through the [molten] metal he may gain the prize over those others.

So when there cometh the punishment of these evil ones, then, O Mazda, at thy command shall Good Thought establish the Dominion in the Consummation, for those who deliver the Lie, O Ahura, into the hands of Right.

So may we be those that make this world advance! O Mazda, and ye other Ahuras, gather together the Assembly, and thou too the Right, that thoughts may meet where Wisdom is at home.

Then truly on the Lie shall come the destruction of delight; but they that get them good name shall be partakers in the promised reward in the fair abode of Good Thought, of Mazda, and of Right.

If, O ye mortals, ye mark those commandments that Mazda hath ordained—of happiness and pain, the long punishment for the liars, and blessings for the righteous—then hereafter shall ye have bliss.

The long fourth hymn contains the following exalted passage (Yasna 31:7f.), in which the idea of the opening sentence has been compared to the thought of the two parts of the nineteenth Psalm and to the saying of Immanuel Kant about the starry heavens above and the moral law within.[76]

He that in the beginning thus thought, "Let the blessed realms be filled with lights," he it is that by his wisdom created Right. Those realms that the Best Thought shall possess thou dost prosper, Mazda, by thy spirit, which, O Ahura, is ever the same.

I conceived of thee, O Mazda, in my thought that thou, the First, art also the Last—that thou art Father of Good Thought, for thus I apprehended thee with mine eye—that thou didst truly create Right, and art the Lord to judge the actions of life.

The fifth hymn (Yasna 32) is a dialogue in which Zoroaster denounces the Devas; and the sixth contains the saying (Yasna 33:14), "As an offering Zarathushtra brings the life of his own body," which has been compared with Romans 12:1. The seventh hymn contains the words (Yasna 34:4), "Of thy Fire, O Ahura, that is mighty through Right, promised and powerful, we desire that it may be for the faithful man with manifested delight, but for the enemy with visible torment"; and then concludes with the supplication (Yasna 34:15), "O Mazda, make known to me the best teachings and actions, these, O Good Thought, and, O Right, the due of praise.

76 Moulton, *Early Religious Poetry of Persia*, p.85.

Through your Dominion, O Ahura, assure us that mankind shall be capable according to thy will."

The second Gatha is called Ushtavaiti and contains four hymns (Yasna 43-46). We quote from the passage in which the prophet muses on the mystery of nature (Yasna 44:3-5,7):

This I ask thee, tell me truly, Ahura. Who is by generation the Father of Right, at the first? Who determined the path of sun and stars? Who is it by whom the moon waxes and wanes again? This, O Mazda, and yet more, I am fain to know.

This I ask thee, tell me truly, Ahura. Who upheld the earth beneath and the firmament from falling? Who the waters and the plants? Who yoked swiftness to winds and clouds? Who is, O Mazda, creator of Good Thought?

This I ask thee, tell me truly, Ahura. What artist made light and darkness? What artist made sleep and waking? Who made morning, noon, and night, that call the understanding man to his duty? . . .

This I ask thee, tell me truly, Ahura. Who created together with Dominion the precious Piety? Who made by wisdom the son obedient to his father? I strive to recognize by these things thee, O Mazda, creator of all things through the holy spirit.

The third Gatha (Yasna 47-50) is known as Spenta Mainyu since it opens with the name of the Holy Spirit:

By his holy Spirit and by Best Thought, deed, and word, in accordance with Right, Mazda Ahura with Dominion and Piety shall give us Welfare and Immortality.

This verse appears to be a sort of Zoroastrian creed, including as it does mention of all seven of the Amesha Spentas together with Ahura Mazda.

The fourth and fifth Gathas contain but a single hymn each. In the fourth, named Vohu Khshathra, we read of "Ahura Mazda, who through his Dominion appoints what is better than good to him that is attentive to his will, but what is worse than evil to him that obeys him not, at the last end of life" (Yasna 51:6). In the fifth, called Vahishto Ishti, it is stated (Yasna 53:1): "The best possession known is that of Zarathushtra Spitama, which is that Mazda Ahura will give him through the Right the glories of blessed life unto all time, and likewise to them that practise and learn the words and actions of his Good Religion."

ACHAEMENID INSCRIPTIONS

Since Zoroaster lived not later than the Achaemenid Period and perhaps at the very height of that period, it will be of interest now to inquire whether any reflection of his religion appears in the inscriptions of the Achaemenid kings.

It is possible, as we have seen, to identify the Vishtaspa whom Zoroaster converted with Hystaspes. Since the latter exercised authority under Cyrus II the Great, it may be further supposed that Cyrus had some knowledge of the prophet and perhaps even manifested a favorable attitude toward the new religious teaching.[77] For this supposition there is, however, no direct inscriptional evidence. In his Akkadian cylinder inscription telling of the fall of Babylon (539 B.C.) Cyrus mentions Marduk, chief god of that city,[78] and according to the Old Testament he spoke of Yahweh in his proclamation concerning the rebuilding of the Jewish temple.[79] In view of the diplomatic purpose of Cyrus, these references are natural and do not contradict the hypothesis of acquaintance by Cyrus with Zoroastrianism or even espousal of it. That hypothesis remains at present, therefore, without positive proof or disproof.

Darius I the Great (522-486 B.C.) also makes reference to the deity worshiped by the Jews as "the God of heaven" in his decree furthering the rebuilding of their temple,[80] and in the Behistun inscription mentions "the other gods, [all] that there are."[81] Nevertheless almost all of his inscriptions emphasize his devotion to Ahura Mazda. In the great trilingual inscription on the Rock of Behistun Darius tells how he put down the widespread revolt initiated by Gaumata. He begins with mention of himself and his lineage, and then acknowledges that it is "by the grace of Ahuramazda" that he is king over the twenty-three provinces of the Persian empire. Coming to the account of the revolt, he introduces it with the statement that "the Lie multiplied in the land." Telling of his suppression of the rebellion he says first of all, "I prayed to Ahuramazda; Ahuramazda brought me help."[82] Throughout the inscription he speaks constantly of "the grace of Ahuramazda" and ascribes his victory and his possession of the kingdom to the help of that god.[83] So continuous is the emphasis upon the help of Ahura Mazda and so explicit is the reference to the connection of the revolutionists with the Lie, that it seems possible

[77] Lehmann-Haupt in Pavry, *Oriental Studies in Honour of Cursetji Erachji Pavry*, p.279.

[78] F. H. Weissbach, *Die Keilinschriften der Achämeniden*. 1911, pp.2f.; FLP p.191.

[79] II Chronicles 36:23 = Ezra 1:2.

[80] Ezra 6:6-12.

[81] King and Thompson, *The Sculptures and Inscription of Darius the Great on the Rock of Behistûn in Persia*, p.71.

[82] *ibid.*, pp.3,7,11.   [83] *ibid.*, p.3, etc.

to suppose that Zoroastrianism was at that time the newly adopted national religion and that the Magians were representatives of the old faith of "the Lie," whose rebellion had been motivated at least in part by religious reasons.[84]

After the Behistun inscription, the next longest inscription of Darius I is that on his tomb at Naqsh-i-Rustam. Here the great king presents not only a statement of some of his achievements but also an evaluation of his own character. In it all Darius acknowledges the favor of Ahura Mazda through which he has received his endowments. Darius says:

A great god is Ahuramazda, who created this excellent work which is seen, who created happiness for man, who bestowed wisdom and activity upon Darius the king.

Says Darius the king: By the favor of Ahuramazda I am of such a sort that I am a friend to right, I am not a friend to wrong; it is not my desire that the weak man should have wrong done to him by the mighty; nor is that my desire, that the mighty man should have wrong done to him by the weak.

What is right, that is my desire. I am not a friend to the man who is a Lie-follower. I am not hot-tempered. What things develop in my anger, I hold firmly under control by my will-power. I am firmly ruling over my own [impulses].

The man who co-operates, him according to his co-operative action, thus him do I reward. Who does harm, him according to the damage thus I punish. It is not my desire that a man should do harm; nor indeed is that my desire, if he should do harm, he should not be punished. . . .

Of such a sort is my understanding and my command: when what has been done by me thou shalt see or hear of, both in the city and in the war-camp, this is my activity over my will-power and my understanding.

This indeed is my activity: as far as my body has the strength, as a battle-fighter I am a good battle-fighter. . . .

Trained am I both with hands and with feet. As a horseman I am a good horseman. As a bowman I am a good bowman both afoot and on horseback. As a spearman I am a good spearman both afoot and on horseback.

And the [physical] skillfulnesses which Ahuramazda has bestowed upon me and I have had the strength to use them—by the favor of Ahuramazda, what has been done by me I have done it with those skillfulnesses which Ahuramazda has bestowed upon me.[85]

[84] Ernst Herzfeld in *Revue de l'histoire des religions.* 1936, pp.21f.; H. R. Hall, *The Ancient History of the Near East from the Earliest Times to the Battle of Salamis.* 7th ed. 1927, p.556; and in CAH III, p.313; Lehmann-Haupt in Pavry, *Oriental Studies in Honour of Cursetji Erachji Pavry,* pp.253,271f. Benveniste, *The Persian Religion According to the Chief Greek Texts,* denied that Zoroastrianism ever became the religion of the Achaemenids. Christensen, *Die Iranier,* p.215 favors that position.

[85] Roland G. Kent in JNES 4 (1945), pp.41f.

The third longest inscription we have from Darius concerns his construction of a palace at Susa, a work of about 517-516 B.C. As the words of Darius show, the palace was completed while his father Hystaspes was still living. Like the records just mentioned and like most of the Achaemenid inscriptions, this, too, is written in Old Persian, Elamite and Akkadian. The reverse side of the beautiful but damaged baked clay tablet containing the Old Persian inscription is shown in Fig. 31. It need not be quoted at length since it is largely concerned with details of the work and workers on the palace, but we may note that it begins, "A great god is Ahuramazda, who has created that heaven, who has created man, who has created good things for man, who has made Darius king, sole king of many, sole commander of many. I am Darius, great king, king of kings, king of lands, king of this earth, son of Hystaspes, the Achaemenid"; and that it concludes, "King Darius says: By the grace of Ahuramazda I constructed a magnificent [palace] in Susa. May Ahuramazda protect me and my . . . my father and my country against injury."[86]

As in the case of the palace at Susa so, too, in the case of the canal which Darius constructed from the Nile River to the Red Sea, the king gave praise to Ahura Mazda in his commemorative inscription:

A great god [is] Ahuramazda, who created yonder sky, who this earth created, who created man, who created welfare for man, who made Darius king, who bestowed upon Darius the King the kingdom, great, rich in horses, rich in men. I [am] Darius the Great King, King of Kings, King of countries containing all [kinds of] men, King in this great earth far and wide, son of Hystaspes, an Achaemenian. Saith Darius the King: I am a Persian; from Persia I seized Egypt; I ordered this canal to dig, from the river by name Nile, which flows in Egypt, to the sea which goes from Persia. Afterwards this canal was dug thus as I commanded, and ships went from Egypt through this canal to Persia thus as was my desire.[87]

From the numerous other inscriptions of the same king we quote one more: "I am Darius, great king, king of kings, king of lands, son of Hystaspes, the Achaemenid. King Darius says: Mine is Ahuramazda, Ahuramazda I reverence! May Ahuramazda bring me help!"[88]

[86] V. Scheil, *Inscriptions des Achéménides à Suse* (Mémoires de la Mission Archéologique de Perse, XXI). 1929, pp.17,21, Pl. IX; J. M. Unvala in PSPA I, p.339; Herzfeld in *Archaeologische Mitteilungen aus Iran.* 3 (1931), pp.29-124; Roland G. Kent in JAOS 51 (1931), pp.189-240.

[87] Roland G. Kent in JNES 1 (1942), p.419.

[88] Scheil, *Inscriptions des Achéménides à Suse*, p.50; cf. F. H. Weissbach in *Archiv für Orientforschung, Internationale Zeitschrift für die Wissenschaft vom Vorderen Orient.* 7 (1931-32), p.45.

Like Darius his father, Xerxes (486-465 B.C.) also regularly begins his inscriptions with some such affirmation as, "A great god [is] Ahuramazda, who created this earth, who created yonder heaven, who created man, who created good things for man, who made Xerxes king, sole king of many, sole commander of many," and frequently refers to "the grace of Ahuramazda" through which he has been able to accomplish what he has done.[89]

In a long inscription of Xerxes discovered at Persepolis, it is revealed that he, too, had to contend with uprisings, and that in part at least these took place in lands where previously the Devas were worshiped. Xerxes states, "Then by Ahuramazda's will of such temples of the Daivas I sapped the foundations, and I ordained: the Daivas shall not be worshiped. Where the Daivas had been worshiped before, there I worshiped Ahuramazda with Arta the exalted; and whatever else had been done wrongfully, that I righted. This which I did, I did it all by the will of Ahuramazda; Ahuramazda helped me until I had completed the task." Xerxes then includes in the same inscription this exhortation: "Thou who art of an after age, if thou thinkest, 'I wish to be happy in life, and in death I wish to belong to Arta,' abide in those laws which Ahuramazda has established and worship Ahuramazda together with Arta the exalted. The man who abides in the laws which Ahuramazda has established and worships Ahuramazda together with Arta the exalted, that one shall be happy in life, and in death he shall belong to Arta." Finally the king concludes with the supplication, "May Ahuramazda guard from evil me and my house and this land. This I implore of Ahuramazda; this may Ahuramazda grant me."[90]

It may be noted that Arta, who is mentioned so prominently along with Ahura Mazda in the foregoing passages, is probably the same as Asha or Right. The name of Xerxes (Persian, Khshayarsha) himself is probably related to the Avestan Khshathra or Dominion, and his son's name, Artaxerxes, corresponds to Asha Khshathra and means, "One whose Dominion is according to Right."[91]

Like his predecessors, Artaxerxes I Longimanus (465-423 B.C.) says in an inscription at Persepolis:

[89] F. H. Weissbach, *Die Keilinschriften der Achämeniden.* 1911, p.107; Unvala in PSPA I, pp.342f.

[90] Erich F. Schmidt, *The Treasury of Persepolis and Other Discoveries in the Homeland of the Achaemenians.* OIC 21 (1939), pp.14f.

[91] Moulton, *Early Zoroastrianism,* p.109.

A great god is Ahuramazda, who created this earth, who created yonder sky, who created man, who created happiness for man, who made Artaxerxes king, one king of many, one lord of many.

I [am] Artaxerxes the Great King, King of Kings, King of Countries containing all [kinds of] men, King in this great earth far and wide, son of Xerxes the King, grandson of Darius, an Achaemenian.

Saith Artaxerxes the Great King: By the favor of Ahuramazda, this palace Xerxes the King, my father, previously [built]; afterwards I built [it to completion]. Me may Ahuramazda along with the gods protect, and my kingdom, and what was built by me.[92]

When we come to Artaxerxes II Mnemon (404-359 B.C.), we find new elements entering the inscriptions. Concerning his reconstruction of the Apadana or Hall of Columns built by Darius I at Susa, he states:

Says Artaxerxes, great king, king of kings, king of lands, king of this earth . . . : This hall of columns (*apadana*) Darius [I] my great-grand-father[92a] had constructed. Later on, during the reign of my grandfather Artaxerxes [I] had burnt it down. By the grace of Ahuramazda, and Anahita, and Mithra, I reconstructed this hall of columns. May Ahuramazda, Anahita and Mithra protect me from all injury, and may they neither injure nor destroy this [hall of columns] which I have constructed.[93]

We observe that Anahita and Mithra are now mentioned along with Ahura Mazda as if they formed a triad of deities. The goddess Anahita appears also in the Yashts. In the fifth or Aban Yasht (SBE XXIII, pp.52-84), which means the Yasht of the Waters, there is a long hymn of praise in her honor. Here she is called Ardvi Sura Anahita, meaning the High, Powerful, Undefiled, and is described as a river-goddess and bringer of fertility. At the opening of the Yasht (v, i, 3) she seems to be a spring-fed river itself, which pours down from a western mountain to the earth-surrounding ocean: "Ahura Mazda spake unto Spitama Zarathushtra, saying: 'Offer up a sacrifice, O Spitama Zarathushtra! unto this spring of mine, Ardvi Sura Anahita, the wide-expanding and health-giving, who hates the Devas and obeys the laws of Ahura, who is worthy of sacrifice in the material world, worthy of prayer in the material world; the life-increasing and holy, the herd-increasing and holy, the fold-increasing and holy, the wealth-increasing and holy, the country-increasing and

---

[92] Roland G. Kent in JNES 4 (1945), p.230.

[92a] Literally "father of the father of my father"—an unprecise way of referring to one who was really his great-great-grandfather, since the sequence of kings was Darius I, Xerxes, Artaxerxes I, Darius II, Artaxerxes II.

[93] Weissbach, *Die Keilinschriften der Achämeniden*, pp.123-125; Unvala in PSPA I, p.344.

holy. . . . The large river, known afar, that is as large as the whole of the waters that run along the earth; that runs powerfully f.om the height Hukairya down to the sea Vouru-Kasha.' "

At the end of the same Yasht (v, 126), however, the mystical river is fully personified, and Anahita appears "in the shape of a maid, fair of body, most strong, tall-formed, high-girded, pure, nobly born of a glorious race."

Anahita later became widely known abroad, and was assimilated with goddesses like Ma, Cybele, Ishtar and Aphrodite.[94]

Mithra is the same as Mitra, the sky god who appears in the Vedic literature of India. In the Avesta, Mithra is the object of worship and praise throughout the long tenth or Mihir Yasht (SBE XXIII, pp.119-158). In this Yasht he appears as a god of light, closely connected but not yet identical with the sun. He is the one "who first of the heavenly gods reaches over the Hara,[95] before the undying, swift-horsed sun; who, foremost in a golden array, takes hold of the beautiful summits, and from thence looks over the abode of the Aryans with a beneficent eye" (Yasht x, 13). He is also the great protagonist of the good, who drives forward in his chariot to smite the forces of evil (Yasht x, 124f.,130,133-135):

With his arms lifted up toward Immortality, Mithra, the lord of wide pastures, drives forward from the shining Garo-nmana [Paradise], in a beautiful chariot that drives on, ever-swift, adorned with all sorts of ornaments, and made of gold. Four stallions draw that chariot, all of the same white color, living on heavenly food and undying. The hoofs of their fore-feet are shod with gold, the hoofs of their hind-feet are shod with silver; all are yoked to the same pole. . . . On a side of the chariot of Mithra, the lord of wide pastures, stand a thousand spears well-made and sharp-piercing. They go through the heavenly space, they fall through the heavenly space upon the skulls of the Devas. . . . After he has smitten the Devas, after he has smitten down the men who lied unto Mithra, Mithra, the lord of wide pastures, drives forward. . . . Angra Mainyu, who is all death, flees away in fear. . . . O, may we never fall across the rush of Mithra, the lord of wide pastures, when in anger! May Mithra, the lord of wide pastures, never smite us in his anger; he who stands up upon this earth as the strongest of all gods, the most valiant of all gods, the most energetic of all gods, the swiftest of all gods, the most fiend-smiting of all gods, he, Mithra, the lord of wide pastures.

Later Mithra was identified with the Semitic sun god, Shamash, and his worship spread into the west, where as *deus Sol invictus Mithras*

[94] Franz Cumont, *The Oriental Religions in Roman Paganism.* 1911, pp.54,65,146.
[95] The mountain where the sun rises.

he was prominently known throughout the Roman empire in the early centuries of the Christian era.[96]

As in the inscriptions of Artaxerxes II, so, too, in those of Artaxerxes III Ochus (359-338 B.C.), Mithra is linked with Ahura Mazda. In his building inscriptions this king says: "May Ahura Mazda and Mithra protect from all evil that which I have constructed"; "May Ahura Mazda and god Mithra protect me and this country and that which has been constructed by me."[97]

Because of the prominence of Anahita and Mithra in these last inscriptions we may conclude that, from the time of Artaxerxes II on, the old Iranian nature religion, as advocated no doubt by the Magians, was regaining its strength and finding an increasingly large place within the framework of Zoroastrianism.[98]

ACHAEMENID ARCHITECTURE AND SCULPTURE

We may now ask whether there are any marks of the Zoroastrian religion in the architectural and sculptural monuments of the Achaemenid Period. A well-known statement of Herodotus[99] might lead us to expect a complete lack of anything of this sort. The Greek historian declared that the Persians had no images of the gods, no temples and no altars, and that they considered the use of such things to be a sign of folly. When they worshiped, he said, they went up on the summits of the loftiest mountains and sacrificed to Jupiter, meaning the firmament, and to the sun and moon, to the earth, to fire, to water and to the winds. On the other hand we have the explicit statement of Darius the Great in the Behistun inscription: "The temples which Gaumata, the Magian, had destroyed I restored for the people."[100] The solution of the apparent contradiction probably lies in the fact that Herodotus was describing the old popular cult which was practiced on the high hills beneath the open

[96] Franz Cumont, *The Mysteries of Mithra.* 2d ed. tr. Thomas J. McCormack, 1903; H. Stuart Jones in HERE VIII, pp.752-759.

[97] Scheil, *Inscriptions des Achéménides à Suse,* p.100; Weissbach, *Die Keilinschriften der Achämeniden,* p.129; Unvala in PSPA I, p.345.

[98] Herzfeld, *Archaeological History of Iran,* p.40. Magian influence is probably also to be recognized in the eventual adoption by Zoroastrianism of the practice of exposure of the bodies of the dead, a custom of the Magi which is attested by Herodotus (I, 140) and Strabo (*Geography,* xv, iii, 20). Moulton, *Early Zoroastrianism,* pp.202-204; Benveniste, *Les mages dans l'ancien Iran.* 1938.

[99] I, 131.

[100] King and Thompson, *The Sculptures and Inscription of Darius the Great on the Rock of Behistûn in Persia,* p.13.

sky, while with the adoption of Zoroastrianism by the Achaemenid kings and under their patronage actual temples were erected.[101]

The characteristic temple of Zoroastrianism was the fire sanctuary. Fire was a natural symbol of Ahura Mazda, who was expected to destroy the wicked in a flood of molten metal at the end of the world (cf. pp. 90,92); and in the Vendidad (viii, 80 [246]. sbe iv, p.112). Fire was personified as the son of Ahura Mazda. According to Arab writers like Shahrastani,[102] there were places of fire worship in Iran even before the time of Zoroaster, but the prophet built new fire temples and so did Vishtaspa and other Zoroastrian kings. Actually we now know that the veneration of fire goes back to the earliest times in Central Asia. Archeological excavation in Khorezm, in the delta of the Amu Darya (Oxus) east of the Caspian Sea, has uncovered the communal houses of a neolithic people of the fourth and third millenniums b.c. In the center of each house was a sacred hearth in which a fire was kept burning continuously; and thus we have a primitive anticipation of the inextinguishable fires of the later faith.[103]

It is possible that such a fire temple of the Achaemenid Period is to be recognized in the famous Ka'bah-i-Zardusht ("Cube of Zoroaster") at Naqsh-i-Rustam. This is a rectangular stone structure in the shape of a sort of tower house. It stands in front of the cliff at Naqsh-i-Rustam, directly over against the rock-hewn tomb of Darius I the Great, and may be clearly seen in the photograph of that place in Fig. 28. One interpretation of the building is that it is a tomb of Achaemenid times, possibly of Zoroaster as its popular designation would suggest, or more probably of some Achaemenid king.[104] In 1936, however, some excavation was done around the lower part of the structure, and a hitherto unknown Pahlavi inscription of thirty-four lines was uncovered. Decipherment of the inscription[105] finds that it was written in the third century a.d. and has to do with the enthronement of a Sasanian monarch. Mention is also explicitly made of the fire of Anahita, and the supposition is thereby raised that at least in Sasanian times the building was a fire temple. As the great

[101] Ernst Diez, *Iranische Kunst*. 1944, p.59.

[102] i, ii, 2, ch.1. tr. Haarbrücker, pp.298f.

[103] V. Altman in jaos 67 (1947), p.83.

[104] Herzfeld, *Archaeological History of Iran*, pp.35,37,60; *Iran in the Ancient East*, p.213.

[105] Martin Sprengling in *The American Journal of Semitic Languages and Literatures*. 53 (Oct. 1936-July 1937), pp.126-144; A. T. Olmstead in *Classical Philology*. 37 (1942), pp.241-262,398-420; cf. R. Ghirshman in *Syria*. 24 (1944-45), pp.174-193.

temple near the capital it was the sacred center for the crowning of the kings, and also probably the place where the crown jewels were stored.

If the immediately foregoing interpretation is correct, then perhaps the Ka'bah-i-Zardusht was a fire temple from the very beginning. Its location agrees with this, for it is so placed that the shadows of the cliffs would prevent the sun from entering the door and falling upon the sacred fire, a provision which is in accord with Zoroastrian usage. Since the structure is directly opposite the tomb of Darius the Great it may have been erected by that ruler.[106]

Turning now to the tomb of Darius itself, we find that its façade is a cruciform recess in the face of the cliff.[107] The doorway opening into the inner chamber is in the long horizontal panel, while in the panel above there is a large sculptured picture. This shows a platform supported by twenty-eight men arranged in two rows and doubtless representing the countries of the Persian empire. On this platform there is a pedestal of three steps on which the king is standing. In his left hand he holds a bow, while his right hand is uplifted toward an altar on which a fire is burning. Above, hovers a symbolic winged figure, concerning which we will shortly say more, while in the upper right hand corner is also a crescent moon shown upon a full moon disk.[108]

The description just given is also applicable to the tombs of the successors of Darius, for they were patterned in both plan and sculptures after the grave of this great king. Those of Xerxes (486-465 B.C.), Artaxerxes I (465-423), and Darius II (423-404) are in the same cliff at Naqsh-i-Rustam, while those of Artaxerxes II Mnemon (404-359) and Artaxerxes III Ochus (359-338), and the unfinished tomb of Darius III Codomannus (335-331) are in the rocks near Persepolis.[109] The sculptured panel of the grave of Artaxerxes III at Persepolis, corresponding in detail to that of the tomb of Darius the Great, is pictured in Fig. 33.[110]

The winged symbol which occupies the place of honor in these panels appears frequently in other Achaemenid sculptures. It is used

106 Diez, *Iranische Kunst*, p.61.   107 FLP Fig. 91.

108 F. H. Weissbach in *Berichte über die Verhandlungen der Konigl. Sächsischen Gesellschaft der Wissenschaften zu Leipzig*. Philologisch-historische Klasse. 62 (1910), p.4.

109 Friedrich Sarre, *Die Kunst des alten Persien* (in William Cohn, ed., Die Kunst des Ostens, v). 1923, p.14.

110 Friedrich Sarre and Ernst Herzfeld, *Iranische Felsreliefs, Aufnahmen und Untersuchungen von Denkmälern aus alt- und mittelpersischer Zeit*. 1910, Fig. 5.

at Persepolis, for example, on the eastern gate of the Tripylon above the figures of Darius I and Xerxes;[111] on the palace of Xerxes;[112] and on the Hall of One Hundred Columns.[113] It is also prominent on the sculptured panel at the Rock of Behistun, from which place we reproduce the close-up photograph in Fig. 32.[114]

The symbol consists essentially of a winged ring or disk from which an anthropomorphic form arises, attired in robe and tiara like a king. At Behistun the headdress is cylindrical and is surmounted by a solar disk with eight rays.[115] The lower part of the body ends in feathers which spread out beneath the disk, while scrolls depend on either side. One hand is extended as if in blessing, and the other holds forth an object like a ring.[116]

This type of representation probably came originally from Egypt, where the winged sun disk appears as early as the Middle Kingdom and is frequent in the time of the New Kingdom. From Egypt it had made its way by the middle of the second millennium B.C. also to Assyria, where ere long the feathered tail became a characteristic part of the composition. Typical examples appear on the monuments of Tukulti-Ninurta II (890-884 B.C.), Ashur-nasir-pal II (883-859 B.C.), and Shalmaneser III (858-824 B.C.). This symbol in Assyria is usually taken to represent the national god Ashur, but it is also possible that it may have stood for Ninurta.[117]

In Persia on the Achaemenid monuments of which we have just been speaking there is no doubt that the winged symbol represents the god Ahura Mazda, of whom the kings so frequently speak in their accompanying inscriptions. Hovering over the royal figures, the symbol expresses the divine protection of that deity for which prayer is so earnestly made.

As far as actual images or idols of the deities are concerned, we have an interesting statement by Berossos, who was a priest of Marduk at Babylon in the time of Antiochus I (281-261 B.C.), and who was quoted on this point by Clement of Alexandria (A.D. c.200) in

[111] FLP Fig. 93.

[112] PSPA IV, Pl. 86,C; Sarre and Herzfeld, *Iranische Felsreliefs*, Pl. XXIII.

[113] PSPA IV, Pl. 89,B; Sarre and Herzfeld, *Iranische Felsreliefs*, Pl. XXV.

[114] King and Thompson, *The Sculptures and Inscription of Darius the Great on the Rock of Behistûn in Persia*, Pl. VIII.

[115] *ibid.*, pp.xxii-xxiii.

[116] Georges Perrot and Charles Chipiez, *Histoire de l'art dans l'antiquité*. v (1890), pp.813f.

[117] Birger Pering in *Archiv für Orientforschung, Internationale Zeitschrift für die Wissenschaft vom Vorderen Orient*. 8 (1932-33), pp.281-296.

his *Exhortation to the Greeks.*[118] According to Berossos, idolatry was introduced by Artaxerxes II (404-359 B.C.), who set up images of Anahita in various cities, a fact which we can well credit remembering the prominence of the mention of the goddess in the inscriptions of this king. The passage runs as follows: "It was not, however, till many ages had passed that they began to worship statues in human form, as Berosus shows in his third book of *Chaldaean History*; for this custom was introduced by Artaxerxes the son of Darius and father of Ochus, who was the first to set up the statue of Aphrodite Anaitis in Babylon, Susa and Ecbatana, and to enjoin this worship upon Persians and Bactrians, upon Damascus and Sardis." Such idols of Anahita as Berossos mentions are not now extant, but we do have representations of this goddess from the Achaemenid Period on gold intaglio seals. There Anahita is shown richly costumed, wearing a crown or a high headdress, and holding a flower and wreath, or a branch and bird.[119]

[118] v. tr. G. W. Butterworth, LCL (1919), pp.147-149.
[119] Ackerman in PSPA I, p.214; IV, Pl. 124,w,Y.

4. ALEXANDER THE GREAT AND THE SELEUCID KINGS, 331-c.250 B.C.

ALEXANDER the Great conquered Persia in 331 B.C. He did such damage to Zoroastrianism that in the traditions of the religion he was ever after remembered as "the accursed Sikander (or Iskander)." In an act evidently intended to symbolize the end of Achaemenid power, Alexander burned the royal capital at Persepolis, and in this conflagration an original copy of the Zoroastrian scriptures perished. In a brief notice the Dinkard (v, iii, 4. SBE XLVII, p.127) states that the Avesta and Zand were written upon oxhides with gold, "and kept in the royal treasury," and in a fuller passage in the last chapter of the third book (SBE XXXVII, p.xxxi) declares that it was Kai-Vishtasp who commanded the Zoroastrian scriptures to be written down, and that "he ordered them to deliver the original to the treasury of Shapigan, and to distribute copies provided. And, after that, he sends a copy to the fortress of documents, to keep the information also there. And during the ruin that happened to the country of Iran, and in the monarchy, owing to the evil-destined villain Alexander, that which was in the fortress of documents came to be burnt, and that in the treasury of Shapigan into the hands of the Arumans, and was translated by him even into the Greek language, as information which was connected with the ancients."

The "fortress of documents" just mentioned in the Dinkard, where one copy of the Zoroastrian writings was kept, must have been at Persepolis, since this copy is said to have been burnt by Alexander. It will be remembered (p.81) that the Book of Arda Viraf also states that the Avesta and Zand were written with gold ink on prepared cowskins, deposited in the archives at Stakhar Papakan, and there burned by Alexander. Likewise the Arab historian Tabari (A.D. 838-923) and Tha'alibi (A.D. 961-1038) record that an original copy of the Zoroastrian scriptures was kept at Persepolis. Speaking of Bishtasp or Vishtaspa, Tabari writes: "It is said that he built in Persia the city of Pasa or Fasa, and in India and other places temples for the fires, and placed over them the fire priests. . . . Zaradusht, the son of Aspiman, appeared in the thirtieth year of his reign. He laid claim to the gift of prophecy. Now he wished that the king should receive his faith; but he refused. But afterward he believed in him and accepted that to which Zaradusht had invited him. He brought the king part of a book, which he claimed to be an inspiration. It was written upon the hides of twelve thousand oxen—the writing cut into the hide and covered with gold. Bishtasp sent this to a place in Istakhr called Darbisht."[120] On Tabari's authority, Tha'alibi says that Zoroaster's book was written on twelve thousand cowhides and deposited "in the citadel of Istakhr."[121] Istakhr, it may be explained, was the name of the later capital which replaced Persepolis. The actual site of Istakhr is about three miles from Persepolis, and the city mound is shown in an air view in Fig. 34.

The "treasury of Shapigan," mentioned in the Dinkard as the repository of another copy of the Zoroastrian scriptures, may have been in Samarkand. A ninth century Pahlavi treatise called Shatroiha-i-Airan or "The Cities of Iran" states that Samarkand was founded by Kai-Kaus and completed by his son Siavakhsh, and that a splendid fire temple was built there by his grandson Kai-Khusrov. Then the treatise continues: "In the end, Zoroaster brought the religion and by the order of king Vishtasp wrote 1,200 chapters of religious writings on golden tablets and deposited them in the treasury of that fire temple. At last the accursed Sikander [Alexander] burnt and threw into the river the [collection of the] religious writings of seven kings."[122] We know that Samarkand, anciently called Maracanda, was destroyed by Alexander the Great in 329 B.C., but the statement of the present treatise that Alexander burned the Zoroastrian books here too, may be due to a confusion with what happened at Persepolis. As we have seen, the Dinkard only claims that at the treasury of Shapigan the books fell into the hands of the Arumans, that is the Greeks from what was later a part of the Roman empire, and that they had translations of them made into Greek.

Although Alexander the Great was remembered by the Zoroastrians as an archenemy of their faith, our understanding of his purposes in general would lead us to suppose that he really desired not to destroy any single religion but rather to cause all the religions of both east and west to be mingled in the united world of which he dreamed.[123] As an illustration of the outworking of this Hellenistic idea which Alexander so powerfully furthered, we may cite the temple which, after his conquest, was built at the foot of the terrace of

---

[120] Quoted by Gottheil in *Classical Studies in Honour of Henry Drisler*, p.37.

[121] H. Zotenberg, *Histoire des rois des Perses par Aboû Mansoûr 'Abd al-Malik ibn Mohammad ibn Ismâ'il al-Tha'âlibi, Texte arabe publié et traduit.* 1900, p.257.

[122] Jivanji Jamshedji Modi, *Asiatic Papers, Papers Read before the Bombay Branch of the Royal Asiatic Society.* 1 (1905), p.153.

[123] cf. W. W. Tarn in CAH VI, pp.434-437.

Persepolis. This was used for the worship of the old gods of Persia, but now their names were written in Greek: Zeus Megistos for Ahura Mazda; Apollo and Helios in the place of Mithra; and Artemis and Queen Athena instead of Anahita.[124]

Alexander's successors in the east were the Seleucids,[125] whose cultural and religious interests were also thoroughly Hellenistic. Among the cities which they founded and which were centers of Hellenistic influence were Seleucia on the Tigris, which was founded by Seleucus I Nicator (312-281 B.C.) shortly after the beginning of his official reign in 312 B.C.; and Hecatompylos, the "Town of a Hundred Gates," a city in Parthia the exact site of which has not yet been located.[126]

As we shall see later (pp.142), Seleucus I sent his ambassador Megasthenes to the court of Chandragupta Maurya, and in the next century or two Greek influence bore rather strongly upon India. Indeed from there it even made itself felt in farthest East Asia.[127] The Seleucids, however, turned their interests more and more away from the east and toward the west. Their capital was first at Babylon, then at Seleucia on the Tigris, and finally at Antioch in Syria.[128] In the east their possessions soon fell into the hands of the Greco-Bactrians and the Parthians.

It was around 250 B.C. that a satrap of Bactria named Diodotus rebelled and was able to establish a Greco-Bactrian kingdom which included Bactria, Sogdiana and Margiana, and which later was extended to Arachosia, the Indus and the Punjab. This kingdom endured until around 135 B.C.,[129] when it gave way to nomadic invaders from central Asia, the Sakas who passed on to settle in Sistan (which derived its name from them) and Sind. In India, however, Greek rulers maintained themselves longer, and of these the best known was Menander (Milinda), who may be dated in the first century B.C.[130]

[124] Herzfeld, Iran in the Ancient East, p.274.

[125] Edwyn R. Bevan, The House of Seleucus. 2 vols. 1902.

[126] Erich F. Schmidt, Flights Over Ancient Cities of Iran (Special Publication of the Oriental Institute of the University of Chicago). 1940, pp.34f.

[127] Christensen, Die Iranier, p.303.

[128] Huart, Ancient Persia and Iranian Civilization, pp.103f.

[129] The kings were: Diodotus I, c.250-c.240; Diodotus II, c.240-c.225; Euthydemos of Magnesia, c.225-c.200; Demetrios, c.200-c.175; Eukradites, c.175-c.165; Heliokles Dikaios, c.160-c.135. Grousset in PSPA I, p.70; W. W. Tarn, The Greeks in Bactria and India. 1938.

[130] Christensen, Die Iranier, pp.303f.

5. THE PARTHIAN PERIOD, c. 250 B.C.-A.D. c.229

ARSACES

THE success of the Greco-Bactrians encouraged the Parthians also to rise against the Seleucids. The Parthians were a people who had come into northern Iran, and whose leader at this time was Arsaces, whom the Roman historian Trogus Pompeius (A.D. c.10) described as "a man of uncertain origin but of undisputed bravery."[131] Arsaces was joined in the leadership of the revolt by his brother Tiridates, and the two brothers became the first two kings of the Parthian dynasty, Arsaces being on the throne c. 250-c.248 B.C. and Tiridates I following him c.248-c.211 B.C. The Parthian era is taken as beginning in 247 B.C. All the successors of Arsaces used his name as a title,[132] and the Arsacid dynasty comprised in all some thirty-nine kings who reigned until A.D. c.229.[133]

By progressive steps, and particularly through the successful campaigns of Mithradates I (c.171-138/137 B.C.), most of Persia and Mesopotamia now came into the hands of the Parthians. Early in the first century B.C., prior to the coming of the Yueh-chi, Parthian power was also for a time extended into India. The ruling dynasty there is often called "Pahlava" to distinguish it from the contemporary royal family of Parthia.[134] The greatest of the Pahlava kings was Gondophares..In the west the Parthians came into conflict with the Romans, and carried on intermittent warfare for some three hundred years.

After the achievements of Mithradates I the Arsacid rulers, although really foreigners, set themselves up as heirs of the Achaeme-

[131] As quoted in the abridgement of his work by the later Roman historian, Justin, XLI, 4. tr. John S. Watson, *Justin, Cornelius Nepos, and Eutropius*. 1876, p.275.

[132] Justin XLI, 5. tr. Watson, p.276.

[133] These kings were: Arsaces, c.250-c.248; Tiridates I, c.248-c.211; Artabanus I, c.211-c.191; Priapatius, c.191-c.176; Phraates I, c.176-c.171; Mithradates I, c.171-138/137; Phraates II, 138/137-c.128; Artabanus II, c.128-124/123; Mithradates II, c.123-88/87; Gotarzes I, 91-81/80; Orodes I, 80-76/75; Sinatruces, 76/75-70 or 69; Phraates III, 70 or 69-58/57; Mithradates III, 58/57-55; Orodes II, c.57-37/36; Pacorus I, died in 38; Phraates IV, c.38-2; Tiridates II, c.30-c.25; Phraataces (Phraates V), 2 B.C.-A.D. 4; Orodes III, A.D. 4-c.6/7; Vonones I, 7/8-12; Artabanus III, 12-c.38; Tiridates III, c.36; Cinnamus, c.37; Gotarzes II, c.38-51; Vardanes, c.39-47/48; Vonones II, c.51; Vologases I, 51/52-79/80; Pacorus II, 78-115/116?; Artabanus IV, 80-81; Osroes, c.109/110-128/129; Parthamaspates, c.117; Vologases II, 105/106?-147; Mithradates IV, 128/129?-147?; Vologases III, 148-192; Vologases IV, 191-207/208; Vologases V, 207/208-222/223; Artabanus V, c.213-227; Artavasdes, c.227-228/229?. Neilson C. Debevoise, *A Political History of Parthia*. 1938, p.270; Richard A. Parker and Waldo H. Dubberstein, *Babylonian Chronology 626 B.C.-A.D. 45*. SAOC 24, 1942, p.22.

[134] Debevoise, *A Political History of Parthia*, p.65.

nids, and took the old title "king of kings."[135] At first their capital was at Hecatompylos, but in the first half of the second century B.C. they transferred the seat of their rule to Ctesiphon, a city which they built on the left bank of the Tigris opposite Seleucia.[136] The official Parthian language was Pahlavi, which is Persian written in Aramaic characters.[137]

The spirit of Hellenism still prevailed in this time. On their coins the Arsacid kings regularly called themselves "Philhellenes,"[138] and in religion they were doubtless broadly eclectic. Despite the damage it had suffered under Alexander, and the syncretistic influences to which it had been exposed under the Seleucids, the religion of Zoroaster yet lived on, however, and in the Parthian Period seems gradually to have regained some of its strength.

Isidore of Charax, a Greek author who probably lived in Charax Spasini at the head of the Persian Gulf around the end of the first century B.C., says that Arsaces, doubtless meaning the first ruler of that name, was proclaimed king in the city of Asaak, and that "an everlasting fire is guarded there."[139] The mention of the fire at this city is doubtless an indication of the existence of Zoroastrianism in the Parthian territory at the time. Isidore of Charax also attests the worship of Anahita, for in connection with Ecbatana he mentions "a temple, sacred to Anaitis," and says, "they sacrifice there always."[140] The ruins of this very temple are believed to have been discovered at Kangavar, which is some distance from Hamadan or the ancient Ecbatana. The structure found here was built of stone, and had an enormous columnar hall over six hundred and sixty feet square, portions of some of the columns of which are still standing.[141]

Mithra, likewise, was prominent in the Parthian Period. Mithradates I was the first of several Arsacid monarchs whose name honored this god, and the tenth Yasht in praise of Mithra (p.99) is believed to date from the last years of his reign.[142]

[135] Grousset in PSPA I, p.72.

[136] Maximilian Streck, Seleucia und Ktesiphon (in Der alte Orient, 16 [1916-17], 3/4). 1917, pp.17f.

[137] Debevoise, A Political History of Parthia, pp.xxvi,27.

[138] E. T. Newell in PSPA I, pp.475-492.

[139] Wilfred H. Schoff, Parthian Stations by Isidore of Charax, An Account of the Overland Trade Route between the Levant and India in the First Century B.C., The Greek Text, with a Translation and Commentary. 1914. §11, p.9.

[140] ibid., §6, p.7.

[141] Oscar Reuther in PSPA I, p.413.

[142] A. T. Olmstead in JAOS 56 (1936), p.253 n.40; Debevoise, A Political History of Parthia, p.27.

Mithradates II (c.123-88/87 B.C.), "to whom," as Trogus Pompeius wrote, "his achievements procured the surname of Great; for . . . he carried on many wars, with great bravery, against his neighbors, and added many provinces to the Parthian kingdom,"[143] and Gotarzes II (A.D. c.38-51) have left us two badly damaged carvings on the Rock of Behistun near the monument of Darius I. In the first, Mithradates is seen with three officials including "Gotarzes, the satrap of satraps," who as Gotarzes I (91-81/80 B.C.) became his co-regent and successor; and in the second, "Gotarzes, the son of Gew," or Gotarzes II, is charging an enemy, while a winged Victory hovers overhead to crown him with a wreath.[144]

VOLOGASES I

Vologases I (A.D. 51/52-79/80) is of special interest to us because he is probably the king called Valkhash in Dinkard IV, 24 (SBE XXXVII, p.413).[145] This passage reads: "Valkhash, descendant of Ashkan, in each district, just as he had come forth, ordered the careful preservation, and making of memoranda for the royal city, of the Avesta and Zand as it had purely come unto them, and also of whatever instruction, due to it, had remained written about, as well as deliverable by the tongue through a high-priest, in a scattered state in the country of Iran, owing to the ravages and devastation of Alexander and the cavalry and infantry of the Arumans."[146] According to this statement, then, Vologases I was responsible for first undertaking to have the remnants of the scattered Zoroastrian scriptures gathered together again. It is entirely credible to picture the king in this role, especially inasmuch as his brother Tiridates is definitely known to have been a Zoroastrian. Tacitus (A.D. c.55-c.117) says that Tiridates was a priest,[147] and Pliny (A.D. 23-79) calls him a Magian and relates that he was so scrupulous in the observance of the regulations of his faith that on a journey to Rome he went all the way by land in order to avoid defiling the sea.[148]

[143] Justin XLII, 2. tr. Watson, p.278.

[144] Ernst E. Herzfeld, Am Tor von Asien, Felsdenkmale aus Irans Heldenzeit. 1920, pp.39f.

[145] Neilson C. Debevoise in The American Journal of Semitic Languages and Literatures. 47 (1930-31), p.81.

[146] cf. also Dinkard VII, 3 (SBE XLVII, p.82): "Even after the devastation which happened owing to Alexander, those who were rulers after him brought back much to the collection from a scattered state; and there are some who have ordered the keeping of it in the treasury of Shapan."

[147] Annals XV, 24. tr. John Jackson, LCL (1931-37) IV, p.253.

[148] Natural History XXX, 6. tr. John Bostock and H. T. Riley (Bohn's Classical Library), V (1856), p.428.

KUH-I-KHWAJA

While relatively few Parthian ruins are yet known on the Iranian plateau proper, there is an interesting and impressive monument of the first century A.D. in the east in Sistan which should be mentioned before leaving this period. This is at the Kuh-i-Khwaja, the "Mount of the Lord," where a broad flat-topped hill stands in a lake. The place may well have been sacred in very ancient times,[149] and it has even been surmised that it was here that Vishtaspa gave a safe refuge to Zoroaster against Gaumata.[150] On the southern slope of the mount are the ruins of a palace and temple, probably dating in their original form from the first century A.D. and then having been restored in the third century. The palace was built around a large court, while the temple stood upon a higher platform. The temple had an inner room with a cupola over it supported on four corner-piers, and around this inner room ran a narrow closed passageway. There was also a monumental entrance. In the room under the cupola the foundation of a stone fire altar was still preserved and the altar itself was fallen not far away. Such, then, was a first century fire temple.

As for the palace, the walls of many of its rooms were originally painted. Besides ornamental compositions, there was a scene on the back wall of the gallery showing a king and queen standing under something like a canopy, and there was a representation on the window wall of the gallery of a series of gods. The gods were portrayed in Greek style and with Greek garments, but their emblems and attributes are half Greek and half oriental. One wears a winged helmet. In purely Greek art there would have been two wings and the god would have been Hermes. Here there are three wings and the god is Vrthragna, a deity of the sun and of war, closely associated with Mithra, and fully described in his ten avatars in the fourteenth or Bahram Yasht (SBE XXIII, pp.231-248). Another god holds a trident, which in Greek symbolism would indicate Poseidon; here it is the mark of Śiva, the god of India. It was thus a far-reaching syncretism which prevailed at this place, in which Zoroastrianism was mingled with elements from both Greece and India.[151]

[149] Phyllis Ackerman in PSPA I, pp.874-877.

[150] Herzfeld, *Archaeological History of Iran*, p.62.

[151] Herzfeld, *Archaeological History of Iran*, pp.58-74; *Iran in the Ancient East*, pp.291-297.

6. THE SASANIAN PERIOD, A.D. c.229-651

THE revolt which put an end to the empire of the Parthians began in the province of Fars, or, as the Greeks called it, Persis. Here at the beginning of the third century A.D. the Sasanian family rose to power. Their name was derived from a certain Sasan, who had been a priest in the fire temple of Anahita at Istakhr.[152] In this city, Ardashir, son of Papak, son of Sasan, was recognized as king. Under his leadership the rebellion against the authority of the Parthians went forward swiftly. In the fighting which broke out, the Parthian king Vologases V was evidently killed (A.D. c.222/223), and about A.D. 227 Artabanus V also suffered defeat and death. The Parthian forces fled to the mountains and endeavored to continue the struggle under Artavasdes, but he, too, was finally captured and executed in Ctesiphon (A.D. c.229). Ardashir I thereby became master of all Iran, and the empire which he founded, endured until the victory of the Arabs in A.D. 651.[153]

Throughout most of its history the Sasanian empire was engaged in conflict with the Roman and the Byzantine empires. This was a continuation of the Greco-Persian and the Roman-Parthian wars, and was mutually destructive to both the east and the west. Nevertheless, under the Sasanian kings Persia enjoyed a period of great cultural brilliance and made outstanding achievements in architecture, sculpture, painting, metalwork and textiles. The Sasanian capitals were at Istakhr and Ctesiphon.[154]

ARDASHIR I

Ardashir I assumed the title, "King of the kings of the Iranians," and as this suggests the rise of the Sasanian empire represented a revival of national Iranian or Persian feeling. For this reason the

[152] Schmidt, *Flights over Ancient Cities of Iran*, p.12.

[153] The Sasanid kings were: Ardashir I, c.229-241; Shapur I, 241-272; Hormuzd I, 272-273; Bahram I, 273-276; Bahram II, 276-293; Bahram III, 293; Narseh (Narses), 293-302; Hormuzd II, 302-310; Shapur II, 310-379; Ardashir II, 379-383; Shapur III, 383-388; Bahram IV, 388-399; Yazdegerd I, 399-420; Bahram V Gor, 420-438; Yazdegerd II, 438-457; Hormuzd III, 457-459; Peroz, 459-484; Balash, 484-488; Kavadh I, 488-531; Djamasp, 496-498; Chosroes (Khusrov or Khusrau) I Anushirvan, 531-579; Hormuzd IV, 579-590; Chosroes II Parvez, 590-628; Bahram VI Cobin, Bistam, 590-596; Kavadh II Sheroe, 628; Ardashir III, 628-630; Shahrbaraz, 630; Boran and others, 630-632; Yazdegerd III, 632-651. Theodor Nöldeke, *Geschichte der Perser und Araber zur Zeit der Sasaniden, aus der arabischen Chronik des Tabari übersetzt und mit ausführlichen Erläuterungen und Ergänzungen versehn.* 1879, p.435; Eduard Meyer in EB XVII, p.583.

[154] Grousset in PSPA I, p.74.

empire is also known as Neo-Persian, and its kings consciously and vigorously continued the traditions of their Achaemenid predecessors. In this reawakening of Iranian sentiment the Zoroastrian faith played an important part. Ardashir I took the designation "Mazdayasnian," and the Mazdean cult became the religion of state.[155]

According to the Dinkard (IV, 25f. SBE XXXVII, p.414), the first two Sasanian kings, Ardashir I and Shapur I, were responsible for carrying forward the collection of the Zoroastrian writings which Vologases I had begun: "That Artakhshatar [Ardashir I], king of kings, who was son of Papak, summoned Tosar, and also all that scattered instruction, as true authority, to the capital; Tosar having arrived, him alone he approved, and, dismissing the rest of the high-priests, he also gave this command, namely: 'For us every other exposition of the Mazda-worshiping religion becomes removed, because even now there is no information or knowledge of it below.' Shahpuhar [Shapur I], king of kings and son of Artakhshatar, again brought together also the writings which were distinct from religion, about the investigation of medicine and astronomy, time, place, and quality, creation, existence, and destruction, the submission of a wild beast, evidence, and other records and resources that were scattered among the Hindus, and in Arum[156] and other lands; and he ordered their collocation again with the Avesta, and the presentation of a correct copy of each to the treasury of Shapigan; and the settlement of all the erring upon the Mazda-worshiping religion, for proper consideration, was effected."

FIRUZABAD

As one of the first marks of his defiance of the Parthians, Ardashir I had built in southern Fars the city of Ardashir-Khurra ("Ardashir's Glory") or Gur, which is now known as Firuzabad. As may be seen in the air view in Fig. 35, the city was surrounded with great circular defenses which are about three-quarters of a mile in diameter. Exactly in the center of the circle one structure still remains standing above ground. This is a tapering pyramidal tower, on which traces of steep stairways can still be seen. It is thought that this may have been a tower to bear the everlasting fire of the Zoroastrian faith.[157]

At the edge of the Firuzabad valley are the impressive, domed

---

[155] Eduard Meyer in EB XVII, p.580; Arthur Christensen, *L'Iran sous les Sassanides.* 1936, p.136.
[156] The eastern empire of the Romans.
[157] Schmidt, *Flights over Ancient Cities of Iran,* p.20.

ruins of the palace of Ardashir I, as shown in the air view in Fig. 36.[158] Not far away, where a rocky gorge opens into the plain of Firuzabad, is a rock carving symbolizing the victory of Ardashir I over the Arsacids.[159] Three tournaments are shown between three pairs of horsemen. At the right Ardashir I is engaged in combat with Artabanus V; in the center his son Shapur is slaying the vizier of Artabanus; and at the left a page of Ardashir is dragging an antagonist from the saddle. Yet farther up the gorge a second rock sculpture portrays the divine investiture of Ardashir I.[160] The same theme is also the subject of rock carvings of Ardashir I at Naqsh-i-Rajab[161] and Naqsh-i-Rustam. Of the three scenes of investiture just mentioned, that at Naqsh-i-Rustam is the finest and is probably the masterpiece of early Sasanian rock sculpture. A photograph of this monument is shown in Fig. 37.[162] Here Ardashir and the god Hormuzd, as Ahura Mazda was now called, face each other on horseback, and the king receives from the god the ribboned circlet which was the symbol of power. The composition is in perfect symmetry. The flowing cloak of the god is balanced by the figure of an attendant behind the king, and the prostrate form of the evil being Ahriman beneath the steed of Hormuzd is matched by the body of Artabanus V under the horse of Ardashir. The portrayal of the enemy as fallen beneath the feet of the conqueror is a frequent motif in the Sasanian rock reliefs, and evidently has a magical import, the desire being to make the triumph permanent.[163] In this aspect, then, these reliefs may be compared with the rock pictures of prehistoric and primitive man. An inscription in three languages, Arsacidan and Sasanian Pahlavi and Greek, accompanies the investiture scene and reads: "This represents the servant of Hormuzd, the divine Ardashir, king of kings of Iran, scion of a divine family, son of the divine Papak, of the kings."[164]

SHAPUR I

Shapur I (A.D. 241-272) was the son of Ardashir I, and he did a number of things which paralleled the work of his father. As we have seen (p.113), the Dinkard states that he, too, was interested in the

---

[158] Sarre and Herzfeld, *Iranische Felsreliefs*, p.128.

[159] Herzfeld, *Iran in the Ancient East*, Pl. CIX.

[160] *ibid.*, Pl. CVIII,upper.   [161] *ibid.*, Pl. XVIII,lower.   [162] PSPA IV, Pl. 154,A.

[163] Herzfeld, *Archaeological History of Iran*, pp.81f.,84,86; *Am Tor von Asien*, p.154 n.102.

[164] Friedrich Sarre in PSPA I, p.594.

collecting of the Zoroastrian writings. Like his father also he built a new city. It was located some distance southwest of Istakhr, and bore the king's own name, Shapur.[165] As shown in the air view in Fig. 38, the site is between a curving river and a broad, deep moat which appears in the upper part of the picture. At the left on a rocky spur is the citadel of the town. Yet farther to the left where the stream flows out of a rocky gorge are a number of rock sculptures some of which belong to Shapur I and some to his successors.[166] They include representations of the victory of Shapur I over the Roman emperor Valerian (A.D. 260), a scene which Shapur portrayed repeatedly and of which the finest example is at Naqsh-i-Rustam.[167] Shapur I further followed the pattern set by his father in that he had his own investiture by Hormuzd represented in a rock sculpture at Naqsh-i-Rajab which is very similar to that of Ardashir I at Naqsh-i-Rustam.[168]

Bahram I, who was the younger son of Shapur I and who reigned A.D. 273-276, likewise followed the example of his father and grandfather in the portrayal of his investiture. At Shapur there is a fine panel (Fig. 39) which is almost a copy of the sculptures of Ardashir I and Shapur I. The king, at the right, receives the symbol of authority from Hormuzd, at the left. Both king and god are mounted upon horses which are sculptured with superior artistic skill.[169]

It was during the reigns of Shapur I, Hormuzd I and Bahram I that the remarkable prophet Mani lived and worked. His teachings, which were a combination of Mazdean, Jewish, Christian, Gnostic and Buddhist elements, were first promulgated in public on the coronation day of Shapur I, and met with some favor on the part of that monarch. The Zoroastrian priests opposed him strongly, however, and he soon went into a long exile during which he preached in the Far East. Returning with royal favor under Hormuzd I, he was soon thereafter (A.D. c.274) given up to a horrible death at the hands of the Mazdean clergy by Bahram I.[170]

Going on to the time of King Narseh (A.D. 293-302), we find at Naqsh-i-Rustam an investiture scene (Fig. 40) where all the partici-

[165] Georges Salles and R. Ghirshman in *Revue des arts asiatiques.* 10 (1936), pp.117-129; 12 (1938), pp.12-19.

[166] Sarre and Herzfeld, *Iranische Felsreliefs*, pp.213-223.

[167] FLP p.198.

[168] Sarre and Herzfeld, *Iranische Felsreliefs*, p.97.

[169] Sarre in PSPA I, p.597.

[170] A. V. Williams Jackson, *Researches in Manichaeism with Special Reference to the Turfan Fragments.* 1932, p.6.

pants are standing and where Narseh, in the center, receives the symbol of authority from the goddess Anahita, at the right. The figure at the left is that of an attendant.[171]

TAQ-I-BUSTAN

Thus far in Sasanian history the most important rock sculptures have been at Naqsh-i-Rustam and Shapur, but by the last part of the fourth century A.D. yet a third place came into prominence. This was at Taq-i-Bustan near Kermanshah. Here springs pour forth from a great rocky hill into what is now an artificial lake (Fig. 41).[172] At the right near the modern building is a rock panel with a relief of Ardashir II (A.D. 379-383). This may be seen in greater detail in Fig. 42.[173] The king stands in the center and receives in outstretched hand the usual emblem of authority which is extended to him by the god Hormuzd. Participating in the investiture, at the left, is the god Mithra, distinguished by the radiant sun rays. Mithra stands upon a lotus, a motif probably reflecting influence from India, while Ardashir II and Hormuzd tread upon the prostrate form of an enemy.

Some distance to the left of this relief is a small grotto which was probably constructed by Shapur III (A.D. 383-388) to serve as a resting place from the hunt. It was adorned by the same king with figures of himself and of Shapur II, and with inscriptions describing both of them as "Mazda-worshiping" kings. The much larger grotto to the left is the Taq-i-Bustan or "Grotto of the Garden" proper, which gives its name to the entire place. Since it probably dates from two centuries later under Chosroes II Parvez it will be mentioned again below in its chronological order (p.119).[174]

SHIZ

Bahram V Gor reigned from A.D. 420 to 438. The Arab historian Tabari tells how, early in his reign, Bahram Gor fought victoriously against the Turanians. On his way home the king passed through Azerbaijan, and sent to the fire temple in Shiz the treasures he had taken from the Turanian leader, as well as the latter's queen herself whom he made to serve as a priestess in that temple. Tabari's account reads: "Bahram's route, on returning from that campaign, lay

---

[171] Sarre and Herzfeld, *Iranische Felsreliefs*, pp.84-88.
[172] Herzfeld, *Am Tor von Asien*, Pl. XXVIII.
[173] *ibid.*, Pl. XXIX.   [174] *ibid.*, pp.57-71.

through Azerbaijan. Accordingly he sent to the fire temple in Shiz the rubies and other jewels which were in the crown of the [vanquished] Khakan, and also his own sword, inlaid with pearls and jewels, as well as many other ornaments. The Khatun, the wife of the Khakan, he made a servant in the temple."[175] Ibn Hurdadhbah, it will be remembered (p.86), also referred to "the fire temple Adharjushnas" in the city of Shiz; and in the geography of Yaqut there is furthermore an extended description of the same city and fire temple. The passage in Yaqut, which cites the poet Mis'ar ibn Muhalhal (A.D. c.940) and another unnamed author, runs as follows: "Here is what Mis'ar ibn Muhalhal says about Shiz: 'This town is situated . . . in the midst of mountains containing mines of gold, quicksilver, lead, silver, orpiment, and amethysts. . . . Walls enclose the city, and at the center of it is a lake whose depth is not known. . . . I sounded it to a depth of more than 14,000 cubits, without the plumb line coming to a rest. . . . There is also at Shiz a fire temple, which is for the inhabitants the object of great veneration. From it are lighted all the sacred fires of the Gabars from the East to the West. The dome is surmounted by a silver crescent, which is considered a talisman, and which many rulers have tried in vain to remove from its foundation. One of the remarkable things in regard to the temple is that the fire has been kept burning in it for 700 years, and has not left any ashes and has not gone out once.' Yaqut, the humble author of this book, adds: 'This whole story comes from Abu Dulaf Mis'ar ibn Muhalhal, the poet, and I cannot be responsible for its authenticity, for he tells things which are exaggerated and untrue. I have simply transcribed it as I found it. Allah knows the truth.' Another author states that at Shiz there is the fire temple of Adharakhsh which is highly celebrated among the Magians, and that it was customary for the kings of Persia, when they ascended the throne, to make a pilgrimage thither on foot. The inhabitants of Maragha call the place Gazna."[176]

In the passages just quoted the fire temple at Shiz was called Adharakhsh or Adharjushnas. This is evidently the same as the Atur Gushnasp (Gushasp) which is mentioned in the Bundahish (xvii, 7. SBE v, p.63) as one of the famous fires of Zoroastrianism.[177] It is ex-

[175] Nöldeke, Geschichte der Perser und Araber zur Zeit der Sasaniden, aus der arabischen Chronik des Tabari, p.104, cf. pp.100,102.

[176] de Meynard, Dictionnaire géographique, historique et littéraire de la Perse et des contrées adjacentes extrait du Mo'djem el-Bouldan de Yaqout, pp.367-370; A. V. Williams Jackson, Persia Past and Present, pp.132f.

[177] Jackson, Zoroaster, The Prophet of Ancient Iran, p.100.

tremely interesting that the site of the city of Shiz and the ruins of
the fire temple of Atur Gushnasp have been identified with much
probability. Shiz was located, it is believed, at the place now called
Takht-i-Sulaiman or "Throne of Solomon." This site, with its well-
preserved city wall, and the lake within the city, is shown in an air
view in Fig. 43. Also visible to the left of the lake are the ruins of
the ancient, domed fire temple.[178]

A vizier of Bahram V Gor named Mihrnarseh is said by Tabari to
have built four villages in the valley of Gira and to have provided
each with a fire temple.[179] The ruins of four fire temples, two large
and two small, have actually been found in the Gira valley, which is
between Firuzabad and Kazerun, and their identification with those
founded by Mihrnarseh is most probable. In each case the central
part of the temple consists of a square room roofed with a dome.
Around this room runs a corridor which is roofed on the sides with
vaults and at the corners with four small domes. The architectural
plan is perfectly symmetrical, and appears to be a development from
the simple, corridor-surrounded, square room of the fire temple at
Kuh-i-Khwaja (p.111).[180]

Under Kavadh I (A.D. 488-531), the leader of a Manichean sect,
Mazdak, preached a doctrine of radical communism and nonviolence,
but suffered death together with many of his followers at the hands
of Kavadh's son, Chosroes.[181] Chosroes or Khusrau I, surnamed Anushirvan ("of the Immortal Soul"), reigned from A.D. 531 to 579, and
was one of the most illustrious of the Sasanian monarchs. He conducted economic reforms, and manifested a spirit of free thought
and liberalism in religion. In his time orthodox Zoroastrianism suffered decadence.[182]

CHOSROES II PARVEZ

Chosroes II, who received the name of Parvez ("the Victorious"),
reigned from A.D. 590 to 628. He was famed for the splendor of his

[178] Christensen, L'Iran sous les Sassanides, p.161; Schmidt, Flights over Ancient
Cities of Iran, p.73, Pl. 89.

[179] Nöldeke, Geschichte der Perser und Araber zur Zeit der Sasaniden, aus der
arabischen Chronik des Tabari übersetzt, pp.111f.

[180] Herzfeld, Archaeological History of Iran, pp.91-93; Ugo Monneret de Villard in
Bulletin of the American Institute for Persian Art and Archaeology. 4 (1935-36),
p.176.

[181] Arthur Christensen in Det. Kgl. Danske Videnskabernes Selskab. Historish-filo-
logiske Meddelelser. IX, 6 (1925).

[182] Christensen, L'Iran sous les Sassanides, p.429.

oriental court, and legend busied itself with his remarkable possessions which included a rich golden throne, a very swift Roman horse called Shabdez, and a large and beautifully ornamented carpet known as "the Spring of Chosroes" which was spread in the palace at Ctesiphon and gave the illusion of spring even in the midst of winter.[183]

It was probably in the time of Chosroes II that the large grotto at Taq-i-Bustan was constructed (p.116). The walls of this grotto are covered with sculptures. On the side walls are fine, lively scenes of boar and deer hunting. On the back wall there are two scenes. In the lower panel, sculptured in very high relief, is a colossal figure of Chosroes II on his famous horse Shabdez (Fig. 44);[184] in the upper panel is an investiture scene where Chosroes II stands between Hormuzd at the right and Anahita at the left, both of whom are extending to him the symbols of authority (Fig. 45).[185]

Beneath the outward splendor of the reign of Chosroes II, however, Persia was growing weaker. In the last years of this king's reign the East Roman emperor Heraclius (A.D. 610-641) successfully invaded Persia and burned the fire temple at Shiz, or Ganzaca as the Byzantines called it.[186] Thereafter, virtual anarchy ensued and various kings and pretenders followed one another. The last Sasanid king was Yazdegerd III who occupied the throne from A.D. 632 to 651. In the year of his coronation the first Arab cohorts entered Persia, and in A.D. 651 Yazdegerd III was assassinated and the entire land fell to the Muslims.

While the official Muslim policy was that of toleration of Zoroastrianism,[187] there was actual persecution and controversy,[188] and the Dinkard (SBE XXXVII, p.xxxi) speaks of "the ruin and devastation that came from the Arabs." Under these circumstances the ancient Persian faith gradually almost disappeared from the land.

Only a remnant of Zoroastrians remained in Iran. Known as the Gabars, they number today less than ten thousand.[189] The others made their way in the seventh and eighth centuries to India, where, as the descendants and survivors of the ancient Persians, they are called the

[183] Jivanji Jamshedji Modi, *Asiatic Papers.* 4 (1929), pp.19-45.
[184] PSPA IV, Pl. 161,A.
[185] PSPA IV, Pl. 160,B; Herzfeld, *Am Tor von Asien*, pp.71-103.
[186] Georgius Cedrenus (A.D. c.1100), *Historiarum Compendium.* I, 721f. (Jacques Paul Migne, *Patrologiae cursus completus. . . . Series Graeca.* 121 [1894], cols. 789f.).
[187] C. H. Becker in EI, I, p.1051.
[188] Eduard Meyer in EB XVII, p.586.
[189] D. Menant in HERE VI, pp.147-156.

Parsis.[190] Settling largely on the western coast, particularly in Bombay, they formed a distinct community which now contains some one hundred thousand persons. It was among the Parsis that Anquetil du Perron in the eighteenth century found and learned to read the ancient manuscripts of the Avesta, and thus inaugurated the modern western study of the religion of Zoroaster.[191]

[190] D. Menant in HERE IX, pp.640-650. For their funeral customs see also Nathan Söderblom and Louis H. Gray in HERE IV, pp.502-505; Jackson, *Persia Past and Present*, pp.387-400; Jivanji Jamshedji Modi, *The Funeral Ceremonies of the Parsees, Their Origin and Explanation*. 3d ed. 1923.

[191] Robert W. Rogers, *A History of Ancient Persia, from Its Earliest Beginnings to the Death of Alexander the Great*. 1929, pp.28-30; John W. Waterhouse, *Zoroastrianism*, pp.42f.

CHAPTER III

Hinduism

Hinduism is the inclusive name for the native religion and social system of India, a faith and society to which some 245,-000,000 persons belong.

The words Hinduism and Hindu as well as India are derived ultimately from the Sanskrit *sindhu* meaning river, a term which was applied preeminently to the Indus River. The corresponding Persian form of the Sanskrit word was *hindu,* and the Achaemenian kings designated the area beside the Indus as Hinduka. The Greeks used forms based on Persian usage but in borrowing them omitted the *h* and made such words as Indos and India. While the former was the name of the river, the latter was applied to the whole country. Our names come from the Greek by way of Latin.

The land occupied by the nations of India and Pakistan is a vast quadrangle extending from the rampart of the Himalayas to a point only eight degrees from the equator. From east to west across its greatest breadth it stretches for some two thousand miles, and from north to south its length is nearly the same. Three regions distinguish themselves within the land. The first is that of the stupendous mountain wall which curves like a scimitar along the northern frontier. The peaks of the Himalayas and the adjacent Karakoram range are the highest in the world, and separate the subcontinent from the remainder of Asia with a formidable barrier. The wall of mountains continues in the extreme northwest with the Hindu Kush, and runs down all the way to the sea with such subsidiary but not insignificant ranges as the Sulaiman, named for the Biblical Solomon.[1] Here, however, there are ways through, and the Kabul River, and the Khyber, Bolan and other passes, provide gateways between India and Afghanistan.

The second division of the land is made up of the plains which curve across the north from the Arabian Sea to the Bay of Bengal. These flat and fertile regions are traversed by three important river systems. The first is that of the Indus. Its main sources are north of the Himalayas and it flows through Kashmir, then curves to the

[1] The legend is that Solomon visited India to marry Balkis, and returning tarried on these hills to allow his bride to look back on her beloved land. EB XXI, p.536.

southwest and empties at last into the Arabian Sea below Karachi. The Indus has five main tributaries, the Jhelum, Chenab, Ravi, Beas, and Sutlej, and the region traversed by the rivers is known as the Punjab or "five waters." The alluvial plain built up and watered by the Indus in the last three hundred and fifty miles of its journey to the sea is called Sind.

The Ganges forms the second river system. With its numerous tributaries, it drains the whole southern slope of the Himalayas. So level are the plains it flows across on its way to the sea, that nearly a thousand miles from its mouth it is only five hundred feet above sea level. The third system is the Brahmaputra (Son of Brahma), which rises beyond the Himalayas not far from the sources of the Indus but flows in the opposite direction, crossing southern Tibet under the name of the Tsangpo or "purifier," then pouring through mountain gorges and finally coming down across Assam to join the Ganges and flow with it into the Bay of Bengal.

The third main geographical division is the plateau which covers most of the southern or peninsular part of the land and is known as the Deccan. On the east and west this tableland falls off toward the coasts in hills and slopes known as the Eastern and Western Ghats.

As elsewhere in the world, so also in India prehistoric man made his appearance within the Pleistocene epoch. The stone tools of his Paleolithic culture are found all the way from Madras in the southeast to the Punjab in the northwest.[2] A group of hand axes and other implements from Paleolithic times which were found in the Soan valley in the Punjab is shown in Fig. 46.[3] Neolithic tools also are found at various places, and the discovery of the Late Stone Age sites at Sukkur and Rohri on the lower Indus in Upper Sind is particularly important. These sites are near Mohenjo-daro, which is one of the chief places where remains of India's first known civilization are found, and suggest that that civilization was the result of an indigenous development as well as of influence from abroad.[4]

[2] H. de Terra and T. T. Paterson, *Studies on the Ice Age in India and Associated Human Cultures* (Carnegie Institution of Washington Publication No. 493). 1939, pp.301-312,327-330; Hallam L. Movius, Jr., *Early Man and Pleistocene Stratigraphy in Southern and Eastern Asia* (Papers of the Peabody Museum of American Archaeology and Ethnology, Harvard University, xix, 3). 1944, Fig. 45, p.105; V. D. Krishnaswami in *Ancient India, Bulletin of the Archaeological Survey of India.* 3 (Jan. 1947), pp.11-57.

[3] De Terra and Paterson, *Studies on the Ice Age in India and Associated Human Cultures*, Pl. xxxi.

[4] *ibid.*, pp.331-336.

1. THE PRE-ARYAN PERIOD

THE civilization just referred to emerged in the Chalcolithic Age, when the use of stone for implements was gradually being supplanted by the employment of metals, and continued in the Bronze Age. At the same time civilization was also advancing notably in the valleys of the Tigris and Euphrates and of the Nile, and there is clear evidence of the cultural interrelationship of all three areas.[5] While the Indian civilization was thus related to a wider Afrasian culture, it was nevertheless a particular focus of that culture and had its own distinctive character. Its most important known centers were at Harappa, Mohenjo-daro and Chanhu-daro, and it probably flourished from about 2500 to about 1500 B.C.[6]

HARAPPA, MOHENJO-DARO AND CHANHU-DARO

From the area of its general distribution this is often called the Indus valley civilization;[7] from the type site where its distinctive elements were first recognized it is more precisely designated the Harappa civilization. Harappa is on the Ravi River in the Punjab, fifteen miles southwest of Montgomery, and its mounds have long been a prominent landmark.[8] In 1853 and 1856 the site was visited by Alexander Cunningham, who became the first director general of the Archaeological Survey of India. In the twenties and thirties of the present century, eleven years of intensive explorations were conducted here;[9] again in 1946 another season of work was devoted to further excavation.[10]

Mohenjo-daro, "the Place of the Dead," is four hundred miles from Harappa, on the lower Indus, twenty-five miles south of Larkana in Sind. In 1922 Mr. R. D. Banerji was studying a second century Buddhist stupa which stands at this place, and discovered that

[5] FLP pp.19,75.

[6] For other prehistoric sites and their cultural sequences see W. Norman Brown in JAOS Supplement 4 (1939), pp.35f.; Stuart Piggot in Ancient India. 1 (Jan. 1946), pp.8-26; and Prehistoric India to 1000 B.C. 1950.

[7] Ernest Mackay, Early Indus Civilization. 2d ed. rev. by Dorothy Mackay. 1948.

[8] India's Past, A Survey of Her Literatures, Religions, Languages and Antiquities. 1927, p.9.

[9] Madho Sarup Vats, in Annual Bibliography of Indian Archaeology (Kern Institute—Leyden). 12 (1937), pp.1-9; and Excavations at Harappā, Being an Account of Archaeological Excavations at Harappā Carried Out between the Years 1920-21 and 1933-34. 2 vols. 1940.

[10] R. E. M. Wheeler in Ancient India. 3 (Jan. 1947), pp.58-130.

beneath the ground was a buried ancient city.[11] In that and the following years the site was extensively and carefully excavated, although the subterranean water level had risen to such a point that it was no longer possible to reach the lowest strata.[12]

Chanhu-daro too, is in the lower Indus valley, eighty miles south of Mohenjo-daro. Once directly on the river, the site is now twelve miles from it, the Indus having shifted its course that far to the west. In 1931 Mr. N. G. Majumdar examined the mounds at this place and recognized their ancient date and importance. In 1935-1936 excavations were conducted there by the first American Archaeological Expedition to India.[13]

Harappa and Mohenjo-daro were large cities, Chanhu-daro a much smaller town, but all three represent what was essentially a complex urban civilization. The cities were well built and carefully planned; there must have been a strong central government.[14]

At Mohenjo-daro the main street was thirty-three feet in width, and all the streets ran due north and south or east and west, intersecting at right angles. The houses of the ordinary townspeople were extraordinarily commodious and substantial. Usually built of burnt brick, many had excellent bathrooms, as well as elaborate drainage systems and rubbish chutes for the disposal of refuse. The most prominent public buildings were a large bath at Mohenjo-daro and a great granary at Harappa. No large palaces or temples were found.

Both agriculture and trade were sources of wealth. Wheat, barley and the date palm were cultivated. The short-horned bull, humped zebu or Brahmany bull, elephant, buffalo, camel, sheep, pig and dog were domesticated. Interchange of goods may have extended indirectly to Burma or China on the east; it certainly reached to Mesopotamia on the west.[15]

Copper and bronze were employed for weapons and utensils, while

[11] John Cumming, ed., *Revealing India's Past, A Co-operative Record of Archaeological Conservation and Exploration in India and Beyond, by Twenty-two Authorities, British, Indian and Continental.* 1939, pp.99f.

[12] John Marshall, ed., *Mohenjo-daro and the Indus Civilization, Being an Official Account of Archaeological Excavations at Mohenjo-daro Carried Out by the Government of India between the Years 1922 and 1927.* 3 vols. 1931; E. J. H. Mackay, *Further Excavations at Mohenjo-daro, Being an Official Account of Archaeological Excavations at Mohenjo-daro Carried Out by the Government of India between the Years 1927 and 1931.* 2 vols. 1937-38.

[13] E. J. H. Mackay, *Chanhu-daro Excavations 1935-36* (American Oriental Series, 20). 1943.

[14] V. Gordon Childe, *What Happened in History.* 1942. p.120.

[15] V. Gordon Childe, *New Light on the Most Ancient East.* 1935, p.210.

gold and silver were used for ornaments, as were also amazonite, lapis lazuli, ivory and shells. Fine pottery was made on a fast wheel and often decorated very beautifully, black painting on a red slip being perhaps most characteristic. Several examples of painted pottery from Mohenjo-daro are shown in Fig. 47.[16]

That a high degree of proficiency was attained in sculpturing is indicated by a number of finds. The finest piece of statuary unearthed at Mohenjo-daro is pictured in Fig. 48.[17] It is a steatite statue now seven inches high, possibly representing one of the ancient inhabitants of the city. The figure is shown with an elaborately decorated shawl over the left shoulder and under the right arm. A short beard and close-cut mustache are worn, and the hair is parted in the middle. The eyes are narrow and straight, and the nose prominent and well formed. Several other facial types are reflected by other statuettes and figurines found at Mohenjo-daro. One, with thick lips and coarse nose, has been said to be comparable to the surviving aboriginal tribes of south India, and another is claimed to be Mongoloid in character.[18]

Among the most numerous and distinctive products of art were the seals. These were of both the cylinder and the stamp variety. The latter, consisting of square tablets of steatite with a boss on the back and engraving on the face, is by far the more common. These vary in size from about one-half inch square to two and one-half inches square. They have a perforated boss on the back which suggests that they may have been carried as amulets. The intaglio engravings are very beautifully executed. They usually show some animal such as the "unicorn," bull, zebu, elephant, rhinoceros, tiger, buffalo, crocodile, antelope, or a hybrid creature, and also have a brief inscription in a pictographic script. This script has not yet been deciphered.

RELIGION OF THE PRE-ARYANS

From the archeological remains of the Harappa civilization it is possible to learn something of the religion which prevailed in this pre-Aryan period. A very large number of human figurines has been unearthed at Harappa, Mohenjo-daro and Chanhu-daro, the majority of which are female. Some of these, like the figure of a woman kneading dough or holding a dish of cakes in her arms, may have been

[16] Marshall, ed., *Mohenjo-daro and the Indus Civilization*, III, Pl. LXXXVII.
[17] *ibid.*, III, Pl. XCVIII,3.
[18] Childe, *New Light on the Most Ancient East*, pp.208f.

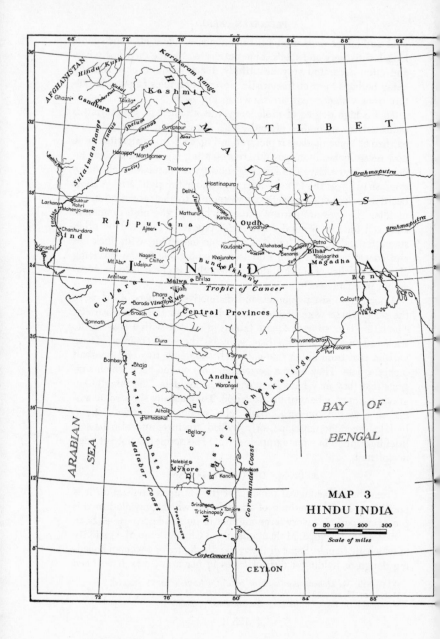

MAP 3
HINDU INDIA

0 50 100   200   300
Scale of miles

toys or dolls for children. Others, however, holding children or obviously pregnant, may have been intended as aids toward procuring offspring; while many which were standing, almost nude figures, comparable to similar objects found in Mesopotamia, Palestine and Egypt, must have been effigies of a mother goddess. Such figurines are a link, then, between the dynamistic statuettes of the Old Stone Age (p.30) and the legion village goddesses to which many people in India still look as the authoresses of fertility and the givers of life and all things. They may also foreshadow the form of worship known in historic Hinduism as Śaktism. Here the object of veneration is a personification of the female energy (*śakti*).

In addition to the mother goddess, a male god was also an object of worship. A striking portrayal of this deity appears on the roughly carved seal shown in Fig. 49, which was uncovered at Mohenjo-daro.[19] A three-faced personage is seated on a low platform, with his legs bent double beneath him, and feet placed heel to heel with toes turned down. His extended arms are encased in bangles, and more ornaments cover his chest. His head is crowned with a tall headdress from which long horns project. At his right hand are an elephant and a tiger, at his left a rhinoceros and a buffalo, and beneath the throne are two deer. At the top of the seal is an inscription of seven characters.

The identification of this personage as the prototype of Śiva, one of the supreme deities in later Hinduism, is a plausible guess. His three faces accord with the representation of Śiva as often having three, four or five faces, and usually three eyes supposed to denote insight into the past, present and future. His posture is that of a yogi, and Śiva is regarded as the typical ascetic and prince of all yogis. He is accompanied by wild animals, and Śiva is called the lord of beasts. His horned headdress is comparable to the trisul or trident later used as royal insignia, a religious symbol in early Buddhist sculpture, and often specially associated in Hinduism with Śiva.

There appears to have been much animism in the religion of the early Indus civilization, and there is evidence for the worship of trees and animals, as well as for cults of baetylic and phallic stones. But the figure just considered may also show that the conception of higher deities in personal form already existed. If both a mother goddess and a prototypal Śiva were worshiped, then the people of the Indus valley had already advanced from dynamistic and ani-

[19] Marshall, ed., *Mohenjo-daro and the Indus Civilization*, i, Pl. xii,17.

mistic foundations to the creation of distinctive aspects of India's historical polytheism. "Their religion," says Sir John Marshall, speaking of the Indus peoples, "is so characteristically Indian as hardly to be distinguishable from still living Hinduism or at least from that aspect of it which is bound up with animism and the cults of Śiva and the Mother Goddess—still the two most potent forces in popular worship."[20] It is also interesting that in this ancient civilization there appear symbols, such as the swastika, which likewise have a religious significance in historic India.

[20] *ibid.,* I, p.vii.

2. THE VEDIC PERIOD

It was probably in the second half of the second millennium, some-time between 1500 and 1200 B.C., that a new people poured into India. They were the Aryans, who came from the northwest and settled in the Punjab, whence they later moved on eastward. Their language belongs to the same family as that embracing Greek, Latin, Celtic, Teutonic and Slavic. Our knowledge concerning them comes from the Vedas, which are collections of ancient religious hymns and other writings.[21] The language of these compositions is simply called Vedic, and is an early type of the Sanskrit language which was given its classical formulation by the Hindu grammarians, especially Panini in probably the fourth century B.C. The word *veda* is a Sanskrit noun meaning "knowledge,"[22] and is applied to these works as the preeminent compilation of religious knowledge.

THE FOUR VEDAS

In its wider use the word Veda includes a very large number of texts—hymns, exegesis, liturgy, speculation—and in its narrower usage the term refers particularly to the four Vedas. Of these the Rig-Veda is the oldest and most important.[23] It comprises over a thousand hymns to the gods, arranged in ten books called *mandalas* or circles. Six of these are known as family books, and are ascribed to different families of *rishis* or inspired poets. Fig. 50 shows the opening hymn to Agni in a manuscript of the Rig-Veda belonging to the Preussische Staatsbibliothek in Berlin.[24] The Yajur-Veda contains formulas in verse and prose with exegesis for use in the ritual of worship.[25] The Sama-Veda presents hymns for chanting often

---

[21] For this and other literature of India see Arthur A. Macdonell, *A History of Sanskrit Literature.* 1900; M. Winternitz, *Geschichte der indischen Litteratur* (Die Litteraturen des Ostens in Einzeldarstellungen). 3 vols. (I, 2d ed.), 1907-20; Helmuth von Glasenapp, *Die Literaturen Indiens von ihren Anfängen bis zur Gegenwart* (Handbuch der Literaturwissenschaft). 1929.

[22] It is derived from the root *vid*, "know," which is akin to the roots in Greek οἶδα, Latin *videre*, German *wissen*, and archaic English *wit*, "to know."

[23] tr. Ralph T. H. Griffith, *The Hymns of the Rigveda, Translated with a Popular Commentary.* 4 vols. 1896f. 3d ed. 2 vols. 1920-26. There are complete German translations by H. Grassmann (1876f.) and A. Ludwig (1876ff.). Selected hymns are translated by F. Max Müller in SBE XXXII and by Hermann Oldenberg in SBE XLVI.

[24] Von Glasenapp, *Die Literaturen Indiens von ihren Anfängen bis zur Gegenwart*, Fig. 26.

[25] tr. Ralph T. H. Griffith, *The Texts of the White Yajurveda, Translated with a Popular Commentary.* 1899.

accompanied by musical notations.[26] The Atharva-Veda is made up of hymns and magical charms.[27] The hymns of the Rig-Veda are generally believed to go back to the time from about 1500 to 1000 B.C.,[28] and they come down to us in a text which has been transmitted without substantial variation at least since the sixth or fifth century B.C., when the authors of the so-called Pratisakhya conducted important critical researches.[29] In this connection it must be remembered that it was long the custom to transmit the sacred texts by memorization and recital. Interesting illustrations occur later, when two pupils of the poet Valmiki recited the twenty-four thousand stanzas of the Ramayana in twenty-five days;[30] and when S. Pandit edited the Atharva-Veda using reciters of the text as well as manuscripts.

The geographical allusions which they contain make it evident that the hymns of the Rig-Veda were composed in India, and in particular there are many references to the rivers of the Indus system. The people of whom we learn in the Rig-Veda name themselves Aryas, from the Sanskrit *arya,* meaning "noble." They are in conflict with dark-skinned, flat-nosed inhabitants of the land, whom they call Dasas, using the word (*dasa*) which in Sanskrit came to mean "slave." The Dasas are presumably to be identified with speakers of Dravidian languages, some of whose descendants are possibly the submerged stratum in the north and a large mass of the population in the south of India, where Dravidian languages are current. If, as is also presumable, the Dasas were once among the inhabitants of Mohenjo-daro and Harappa, they had a background of higher civilization than would be suspected from the character of the references to them in the Rig-Veda.[31]

The Aryans themselves appear still to have been a pastoral people, whose wealth was derived mainly from their cattle and their agriculture. They were organized in tribes, each ruled by its king.

[26] tr. Ralph T. H. Griffith, *The Hymns of the Samaveda, Translated with a Popular Commentary.* 1907.

[27] tr. Ralph T. H. Griffith, *The Hymns of the Atharva-veda, Translated with a Popular Commentary.* 2 vols. 1895-96; Maurice Bloomfield in SBE XLII.

[28] CSHI p.6; cf. von Glasenapp, *Die Literaturen Indiens von ihren Anfängen bis zur Gegenwart,* p.47.

[29] F. Max Müller in SBE XXXII, pp.xliv-xlv.

[30] Ramayana VII. tr. Romesh C. Dutt, *The Ramayana and the Mahabharata Condensed into English Verse* (Everyman's Library, 403). 1910, pp.171-176.

[31] Hermann Goetz, *Epochen der indischen Kultur.* 1929, pp.24-28.

RELIGION OF THE VEDAS

As revealed in the Vedas,[32] the religion of the Aryans emphasized a worship of natural phenomena, particularly the sky and the powers associated with it. The deities are in the main conceived as human, but as A. Berriedale Keith remarks, "it is seldom difficult to doubt that the anthropomorphic forms but faintly veil phenomena of nature."[33] The name for the gods appears in Sanskrit as *deva*, meaning the "heavenly one," a word which is closely related to the Latin *deus*.[34] Another designation for deity in the Rig-Veda is *asura*, but in the Yajur-Veda, the Atharva-Veda and the subsequent Vedic literature the *asuras* have become the enemies of the gods and are thought of as evil spirits or demons.[35]

The gods are usually stated to be thirty-three in number and are ideally divided into three groups of eleven each, distributed in sky, atmosphere and earth.[36] Among these deities are the following:

Varuna, probably originally a sky god and possibly related to the Greek Ouranos or "Heaven," is the sustainer of the natural order and the upholder of the moral law. The prayers to him are the most exalted in the entire Rig-Veda.

> Varuna, true to holy law, sits down among his people; he,
> Most wise, sits there to govern all.
>
> From thence perceiving, he beholds all wondrous things,
>   both what hath been
> And what hereafter will be done.
>
> Varuna, hear this call of mine, be gracious unto us this day,
> Longing for help I cry to thee.
>
> Thou, O wise god, art lord of all, thou art the king
>   of earth and heaven;
> Hear, as thou goest on thy way.[37]

Other deities of the celestial regions are Mitra, the frequent companion of Varuna, and identical with the Persian Mithra; Dyaus, the bright sky, whose name is the same as the Greek Zeus; Surya, the sun, etymologically related to the Greek Helios; and Ushas, the goddess of the dawn, who is the Greek Eos. Possibly also a sun god in

---

[32] A. Berriedale Keith, *The Religion and Philosophy of the Veda and Upanishads* (Harvard Oriental Series, 31, 32). 2 vols. 1925.

[33] *ibid.*, p.58.

[34] *ibid.*, pp.75f.; Otto Schrader in HERE II, p.33.

[35] Keith, *The Religion and Philosophy of the Veda and Upanishads*, p.231.

[36] *ibid.*, p.86; A. A. Macdonell in HERE XII, p.602.

[37] Rig-Veda I, xxv, 10f., 19f. tr. Nicol Macnicol, *Hindu Scriptures* (Everyman's Library, 944). 1938, pp.4f.

origin is Vishnu, who occupies only a subordinate place in the Rig-Veda but was destined to achieve great importance later. An indeterminate number of these gods and sometimes all of them are styled *Adityas*, sons of Aditi. This name is appropriate to their character as deities of the light of heaven and suggests that they are bright and shining, pure and holy.

In the realm of the atmosphere or the waters of the air, Indra is the most important god, and he is indeed the most prominent deity of the Rig-Veda. Strong and mighty, the wielder of the thunderbolt, he contends in battles both atmospheric and terrestrial on behalf of his people. Closely associated with him is a troop of lesser storm gods, the Maruts. The father of the Maruts is the formidable archer Rudra. Known also as the ruler of the world and its father, Rudra is deemed on this side of his nature to be beneficent, gracious and auspicious (*śiva*), the last epithet providing the name by which he is known in late Vedic times. Other aerial deities include Vayu and Vata, the wind gods, and Parjanya, the god of the thundercloud.

In the terrestrial realm, the most notable deities are Soma and Agni. Soma is the god of an intoxicating beverage made from the Soma plant, which was used as a libation to the gods and a drink for the worshipers. Agni is the personification of fire in all its forms and particularly of the altar fire used in sacrifice. Since fire was also regularly employed for the cremation of the dead, Agni was likewise the conductor of souls into the other world. There the Fathers, or spirits of the dead, dwell in the blessed abode ruled by Yama, who was the first to die. The earth herself is also worshiped in the form of the goddess Prthivi, while the rivers too, especially the Sarasvati, a small stream in the Punjab,[38] are objects of devotion.

In addition to the great gods of the celestial, aerial and terrestrial regions, we learn in the Vedas of various minor gods of nature and of certain abstract deities. Among the minor nature deities are the Gandharvas and the Apsarases. The Gandharva is a masculine creature of the heaven, a guardian of Soma, and also connected with water. The Apsaras is a water nymph, whose very name means "the goer in the water." In the Atharva-Veda the Gandharvas and Apsarases are described as dwelling in banyan and fig trees and engaging in play, song and dance to the accompaniment of the lute and cymbal.

[38] Keith, *The Religion and Philosophy of the Veda and Upanishads*, p.173.

The gods which Keith calls "abstract"[39] are ones for which a basis does not appear in some particular phenomenon of nature; rather, they personify functions or activities or faculties. Tvastr is one of these. As his name suggests, he is the great Fashioner. It was he who forged the bolt of Indra, and it was his daughter Saranyu, wife of Vivasvant, of whom were born the twins, Yama and Yami, whence came the human race. Prajapati, too, appears. The "lord of offspring," as his name means, he is a creator god. Aditi, mother of the Adityas, may also be mentioned here. Her name suggests unbinding, or freedom from bonds, and she is invoked for release from sin. A number of times spoken of as a cow, she was evidently, at least upon occasion, conceived in theriomorphic fashion.

Opposed to the gods are their enemies the demons, for whom in the later Vedas the designation *asuras* is, as we have seen, reserved. Of these the first in rank is Vritra, the "Encloser," a terrible dragon or serpent. His mother is Danu, and he bears the appellation Danava, "offspring of Danu," as do also his kinsmen, the other enemies of the gods.

While the mythology of the Vedas is far from explicit, it is possible to reconstruct the underlying stories, at least partially, by careful study of many scattered references. By such investigation, W. Norman Brown has been able to set forth an account of the creation myth of the Rig-Veda.[40] Here we find that the universe is conceived to have two parts. The first, called Sat, "the Existent," is that in which gods and men live. It includes the three divisions which have already been mentioned, the earth, the sky and the atmosphere between. The second part of the universe is Asat, "the Nonexistent."[41] It lies below the earth, separated from us by a great chasm. This is the home of the demons.

The creation myth undertakes to explain how this entire universe came into being. In the beginning, it seems, there existed the Cosmic Waters. There, too, was the great Fashioner, the god Tvastr. He made the divine pair, Dyaus or Sky, and Prthivi or Earth, and they became the parents of the gods. Among the divine beings there ensued an epic quarrel. The Danavas or descendants of Danu, led by Vritra, represented the forces of inertia and destruction; the Adityas, sprung from their mother Aditi, with Varuna as their chief, repre-

[39] *ibid.*, p.203.
[40] W. Norman Brown in JAOS 62 (1942), pp.85-98.
[41] W. Norman Brown in JAOS 61 (1941), pp.76-80.

sented the forces of growth and liberation. For the time being the conservative forces were greater than those of expansion. In fact the Cosmic Waters themselves were at this time held back, as if within a shell, by Vritra and his cohorts, while the force of expansion, in the person of Varuna and his associates, was impotent to accomplish a liberation. Then Indra came into being as the champion of the gods, himself perhaps the son of Dyaus and Prthivi. By drinking Soma he became strong and undertook battle with Vritra. Although wounded in the fierce struggle, Indra was victorious. Forcing Heaven and Earth apart, and himself filling the space between as the atmosphere, he released the Cosmic Waters. Coming forth, they gave birth to the sun and themselves flowed into the atmospheric ocean. By his mighty deed, Indra separated Sat and Asat, and this constituted creation. After that, Varuna organized all things and prescribed the laws by which they should operate. Man himself was created to support the gods. The demons were relegated to their place beneath the earth, whence they still emerge at night to endanger human beings.

Such was the great accomplishment of which Indra sang to his companions:

> I slew Vritra, O Maruts, with might, having grown
> powerful through my own vigor.
> I, who hold the thunderbolt in my arms, have made these
> all-brilliant waters to flow freely for man.[42]

THE BRAHMANAS

Each of the four Vedas came in the course of time to have a body of prose writings attached to it, the chief purpose of which was to describe and explain the sacrificial rites with which the Vedic texts were connected. These commentaries are known as the Brahmanas[43] and they probably cover approximately the period of the first half of the first millennium B.C.[44] The name is derived from the Sanskrit *brahma*, which variously means magical spell, sacred rite or universal spirit, and is obviously applicable to expositions of religious texts and ceremonies. The priests who knew the efficacious formulas and conducted the all-important sacrifices were called Brahmans, and were at this time emerging into a position of supreme power and

[42] Rig-Veda I, clxv, 8. SBE XXXII, p.180.
[43] The Satapatha-Brahmana is translated by Julius Eggeling in SBE XII, XXVI, XLI, XLIII, XLIV.
[44] CSHI p.10.

privilege in society. The cult, over which they presided, surpassed in the complexity of its ritual detail anything the world has elsewhere known.[45]

From the geographical references in the Brahmanas and other literature dealing with this period it may be seen that the center of Aryan culture had now moved eastward into the Middle Country between the Jumna and the Ganges River. Here lived such important peoples as the Kurus and the Panchalas, while farther east and destined to greater importance later were the kingdoms of Kosala, corresponding roughly to the modern district of Oudh, and Videha, in what is now northern Bihar. Among the important cities were not only Taxila in the northwest, but also Asandivat or Hastinapura on the upper Ganges, Kauśambi on the Jumna, and Kaśi which is the later Benares.[46]

Already in the Rig-Veda there is discernible a certain tendency for the various gods to merge into one another, and in the Brahmanas there are indications of an attempt to discover some deeper ground of being which underlies all the gods and all phenomena. The word Brahman appears now in the sense of divine spirit, and it is declared that "Brahman is the ultimate thing of this universe."[47]

THE UPANISHADS

Appended to and later than the Brahmanas are the Aranyakas or Forest Books, which were either composed in the forests by hermits dwelling there or were intended to be studied in the seclusion of such surroundings. In turn, attached to the Aranyakas or sometimes even incorporated in them, and thus forming a late part of the Vedic literature, are the famous Upanishads.[48]

The Sanskrit word *upanishad* probably had the original meaning of "session," and referred to a session of pupils gathered about their teacher.[49] Hence it was an appropriate name for these writings, which are usually in the form of a dialogue between an inquirer who is seeking the way of knowledge and a wise person who is already possessed of the true understanding. The Upanishads come from varying environments and advance differing, sometimes even con-

[45] Macdonell in HERE XII, p.601.
[46] CSHI pp.10-12.
[47] Śatapatha-Brahmana XIII, vi, 2, v.7. SBE XLIV, p.409.
[48] tr. F. Max Müller in SBE I; Robert E. Hume, *The Thirteen Principal Upanishads Translated from the Sanskrit*. 1931; Dhan Gopal Mukerji, *Devotional Passages from the Hindu Bible Adapted into English*. 1929.
[49] F. Max Müller in SBE I, p.lxxxi.

tradictory, points of view. The oldest or classical Upanishads are a dozen in number, and are believed to have been composed in the period of approximately the eighth to the sixth centuries B.C.[50] The extant manuscripts of the Upanishads, as of the Vedas as a whole, are later than A.D. 1300 in date. It is possible, however, to use the commentaries of Śankara, who lived probably in the eighth century A.D., for the determination of their text.[51]

PHILOSOPHICAL RELIGION

Whereas the Vedas had reflected primarily a worship of nature, and the Brahmanas a priestly system of sacrifices, the Upanishads represent the essential philosophical development in Indian thought.[52] This philosophy is rooted in the striving, already noted, to find a single underlying reality beneath the multiplicity of the gods, and it is now proclaimed that neither worship nor sacrifice but rather meditation is the way to knowledge of that reality. In general, the Upanishads tend toward a monistic answer to the problems of metaphysics, though dualistic and theistic ideas also get support.

"Let a man meditate on the syllable Om," begins the Chandogya-Upanishad. Om was a sacred syllable, originally denoting assent, which had to be pronounced at the beginning of the reading of a Veda or of the recitation of a Vedic hymn. Here the repetition of this syllable is intended to accomplish the concentration of the mind on a higher object of thought, of which it is the symbol. Since Om is the symbol of the Veda, and since the Veda may be taken to signify all speech and life, the syllable really stands for the spirit of life in man. Furthermore, the spirit in man may be identified with the spirit in nature, and thus one rises at last to the conception that all reality is ultimately one. Such is the pathway of meditation which is recommended in the Upanishads as alone leading to true knowledge and salvation.[53]

BRAHMAN AND ATMAN

The name of the spirit or soul of the world is Brahman. Akin at

[50] A. S. Geden in HERE XII, p.540.
[51] Müller in SBE I, p.lxxi; xv, p.xii; V. S. Ghats in HERE XI, pp.185f.
[52] Walter Ruben, *Die Philosophen der Upanishaden.* 1947.
[53] Chandogya-Upanishad I, 1-3. SBE I, pp.xxiii-xxv, 1-10; cf. J. J. Boeles in *India Antiqua, A Volume of Oriental Studies Presented to His Friends and Pupils to Jean Philippe Vogel, C.I.E., on the Occasion of the Fiftieth Anniversary of His Doctorate* (Kern Institute—Leyden). 1947, pp.40-56.

one time perhaps in significance to *mana*,[54] Brahman has become the essence of everything, the all-encompassing absolute. Since to attribute personality would be to imply limitation, Brahman is deemed superpersonal and neuter, and is commonly referred to as "it" or "that." Indeed it is scarcely possible to define Brahman except with negatives (*neti neti*).[55] Nevertheless, all sorts of figures of speech are employed to give an intimation of the nature of that which is fundamentally indescribable. Thus, for one example, Brahman is likened unto the fig tree "whose roots grow upward and whose branches grow downward."[56] "That," it is said, "is called Brahman. . . . All worlds are contained in it, and no one goes beyond."[57] Another passage declares: "All this is Brahman. Let a man meditate on that [visible world] as beginning, ending and breathing in it."[58] Again we read: "That from whence these beings are born, that by which, when born, they live, that into which they enter at their death, try to know that. That is Brahman."[59] "That on which the worlds are founded and their inhabitants, that is the indestructible Brahman."[60]

The name of the spirit or soul of man is Atman. The great understanding toward which the upanishadic meditations chiefly are directed is that Brahman and Atman are identical. Since Brahman is in all things, Brahman is in man and man is in Brahman. The self of the world is the same as the self of man. In the famous phrase of the Upanishads, *Tat twam asi*, "That art thou." As it is written in the Kaivalya-Upanishad, "The highest Brahman, the soul of all, the great mainstay of the universe, . . . the eternal Being, that art thou."[61]

A notable dialogue, further illustrative of this conception, is found in the sixth book of the Chandogya-Upanishad. In the dialogue a father is conversing with his son, Svetaketu, and leading him toward an understanding of man's true relation to ultimate reality. In order to show that the universal self is diffused throughout the world and yet present within the individual, the father instructs Svetaketu to

---

[54] Archer, *Faiths Men Live By*, p.200.

[55] Geden in HERE XII, p.546.

[56] This is explained as referring to a tree which sends its branches down so that they take root in the ground and form new stems, and thus one tree grows into a veritable forest.

[57] Katha-Upanishad II, vi, 1. SBE XV, p.21.

[58] Chandogya-Upanishad III, xiv, 1. SBE I, p.48.

[59] Taittiriyaka-Upanishad III, 1. SBE XV, p.64.

[60] Mundaka-Upanishad II, ii, 2. SBE XV, p.36.

[61] vi. Quoted in Albert Schweitzer, *Indian Thought and Its Development*. tr. Mrs. Charles E. B. Russell, 1936, p.35.

place some salt in a container of water and then to return in the morning.

The son did as he was commanded.

The father said to him: "Bring me the salt, which you placed in the water last night."

The son having looked for it, found it not, for, of course, it was melted.

The father said: "Taste it from the surface of the water. How is it?"

The son replied: "It is salt."

"Taste it from the middle. How is it?"

The son replied: "It is salt."

"Taste it from the bottom. How is it?"

The son replied: "It is salt."

The father said: "Throw it away and then wait on me."

He did so; but salt exists for ever.[62]

Then the father said: "Here also, in this body, forsooth, you do not perceive the True, my son; but there indeed it is.

"That which is the subtle essence, in it all that exists has its self. It is the True. It is the Self (Atman). And that art thou, Svetaketu!"[63]

It is of course within the inmost heart that this vision of the truth may best be attained, for that is where Brahman dwells. "Manifest, near, moving in the cave [of the heart] is the great Being."[64] "He is my self within the heart, smaller than a corn of rice, smaller than a corn of barley, smaller than a mustard seed, smaller than a canary seed or the kernel of a canary seed. He also is my self within the heart, greater than the earth, greater than the sky, greater than heaven, greater than all these worlds. He from whom all works, all desires, all sweet odors and tastes proceed, who embraces all this, who never speaks and who is never surprised, he my self within the heart, is that Brahman. When I shall have departed from hence, I shall obtain him. He who has this faith has no doubt."[65] As Professor Otto Strauss has said in comment on the passage just quoted, "Whoever reads these words, which are among the oldest of the kind that have come down to us, will at once feel that they disclose a vision that fills and gladdens the whole heart. We feel the original experience of the man to whom this came. . . . To have a vision of the Absolute, to *be* the Absolute—that is the central experience."[66]

[62] The translation of these two lines is disputed.
[63] Chandogya-Upanishad VI, xiii. SBE I, pp.104f.
[64] Mundaka-Upanishad II, ii, 1. SBE XV, p.36.
[65] Chandogya-Upanishad III, xiv, 3f. SBE I, p.48.
[66] Strauss in CRW p.101.

SAMSARA AND KARMA

There also emerges in the Upanishads the idea of the reincarnation of souls. According to monistic doctrine, souls are like sparks which come forth from a fire only to fall back into it again.[67] It is thus the inherent destiny of every soul, whether of man, animal or plant, to return into the universal soul whence it came forth. According to the doctrine of reincarnation, the soul is a prisoner within its body and is destined upon death to be reborn within another earthly body. This rebirth may be in a lower or in a higher form of life depending upon the evil or good done in the previous existence. If the soul is to attain the highest form of existence and to become capable of union with the universal soul, it must, as it were, earn its own redemption.[68]

The endless cycle of births and deaths through which the soul transmigrates from one body to another is known in the Sanskrit as *samsara*, while the consequences of one's deeds which determine one's future lot are called *karma*. The outworking of this inexorable system of human destiny through rebirth is not explicitly mentioned but appears to be summarized in the Brihadaranyaka-Upanishad in the sentence: "Now as a man is like this or like that, according as he acts and according as he behaves, so will he be:—a man of good acts will become good, a man of bad acts, bad."[69] "Those whose conduct has been good," it is affirmed in the Chandogya-Upanishad, "will quickly attain some good birth, the birth of a Brahman, or a Kshatriya, or a Vaisya" (these being members respectively of the priestly, warrior or kingly, and mercantile or agricultural, castes). "But those whose conduct has been evil, will quickly attain an evil birth, the birth of a dog, or a hog, or a Candala" (the last being an outcaste son of a Brahman mother and a Sudra or laboring caste father).[70] It is also possible for the soul to pass into inorganic matter,[71] or to be born again as rice, corn, an herb, a tree,[72] a worm, an insect, a fish, a bird, a lion, a boar, a serpent, or a tiger.[73] He who is impure, thoughtless and without understanding is bound inextricably within this round of births, "but he who has understanding, who is

[67] Mundaka-Upanishad II, i, 1. SBE xv, p.34; Brihadaranyaka-Upanishad II, i, 20. SBE xv, p.105.
[68] Schweitzer, *Indian Thought and Its Development*, pp.47-53.
[69] IV, iv, 5. SBE xv, p.176.   [70] V, x, 7. SBE I, p.82; cf. xv, p.169 n.3.
[71] Katha-Upanishad II, v, 7. SBE xv, p.19.
[72] Chandogya-Upanishad v, x, 6. SBE I, p.81.
[73] Kaushitaki-Upanishad I, 2. SBE I, p.274.

mindful and always pure, reaches indeed that place, from whence he is not born again."[74] "He who forms desires in his mind, is born again," but he who strives with strength, earnestness, and right meditation to overcome desire, is able to attain a state of passionless tranquility. "When all desires which once entered his heart are undone, then does the mortal become immortal, then he obtains Brahman. And as the slough of a snake lies on an ant hill, dead and cast away, thus lies this body; but that disembodied immortal spirit is Brahman only, is only light." Or, to change the figure of speech, "As the flowing rivers disappear in the sea, losing their name and their form, thus a wise man, freed from name and form, goes to the divine Person, who is greater than the great."[75]

[74] Katha-Upanishad I, iii, 7f. SBE XV, p.13.
[75] Mundaka-Upanishad III, ii. SBE XV, pp.40f.; Brihadaranyaka-Upanishad IV, iv. SBE XV, pp.176f.

3. THE ŚIŚUNAGA AND NANDA PERIODS, c.642-c.322 B.C.[76]

INDIAN history first becomes known to us in a more definite and detailed way in the Śiśunaga Period. At this time a number of large states existed in northern India. Among these the kingdom of Magadha was rising in importance and was destined to obtain supremacy. The territory of Magadha lay along the Ganges River in what is today southern Bihar. A dynasty was founded here by Śiśunaga which endured from c.642 to c.413 B.C. The best-known kings in this line were Bimbisara and Ajataśatru. They will come before us again in the chapters on Jainism and Buddhism for they were contemporaries of Mahavira and the Buddha. Bimbisara, known to the Jains as Śrenika, ruled around 540-490 B.C. His capital was at Rajagriha, a new city which he built near the Ganges. Ajataśatru (or Kunika) reigned c.490-c.460 B.C. His son Udaya founded a new capital at Pataliputra (near the site of modern Patna), a city which was to be for centuries the most important in India. Around 413 B.C. the line of Śiśunaga gave way to the Nanda dynasty which lasted until c.322 B.C.

In 326 B.C. Alexander the Great reached the banks of the Beas (Hyphasis) River, an upper tributary of the Sutlej, the most advanced point of his penetration of India, and had to turn back when his soldiers would go no farther.[77]

[76] For most of the dates in Indian history see CSHI.

[77] The Beas was attained in the vicinity of the modern village of Gurdaspur. For the entire expedition of Alexander the Great in central Asia see Robert Fazy in *Mitteilungen der schweizerischen Gesellschaft der Freunde ostasiatischer Kultur (Bulletin de la Société Suisse des amis de l'Extrême-Orient).* 4 (1942), pp.3-26.

4. THE MAURYA PERIOD, c.322-c.185 b.c.

At about this time a man of the Maurya family, named Chandragupta (c.322-c.298 b.c.), obtained the throne of Magadha. After the
withdrawal and death of Alexander the Great, Chandragupta was
able to drive the remaining Macedonian garrisons back across the
Indus, and to establish his own power throughout northern India.
He also concluded a treaty with Seleucus I Nicator (312-281 b.c.),
who became master of Alexander's eastern provinces, whereby the
Hindu Kush was established as the western frontier of his kingdom.

MEGASTHENES

An ambassador named Megasthenes was sent by Seleucus to the
court of Chandragupta Maurya at Pataliputra. Megasthenes lived in
India for a number of years, and wrote an account of the land. Although the original is lost, this account is cited frequently by Strabo
(c.63 b.c.-after a.d. 21) in his description of India, and also by Arrian
(a.d. c.96-c.180) in the "special monograph" on India which he appended to his account of the campaigns of Alexander the Great. According to Megasthenes, as quoted by both Strabo and Arrian, Pataliputra (which they called Palibothra or Palimbothra) was situated
at the confluence of the Erannoboas (now the Son) and the Ganges
Rivers. The city was built in the form of a large parallelogram,
roughly nine miles long and two miles wide. It was surrounded by
both a moat and a wooden wall. King Sandrocottus, as the Greeks
called Chandragupta, evidently lived in great state, but not without
fear of his life since he changed his sleeping place from time to time
because of the plots against him.

Further citing Megasthenes, Strabo and Arrian report that the
population of India was divided into seven castes, including philosophers, farmers, shepherds and hunters, artisans and tradesmen, soldiers, government overseers, and royal councilors. An individual's
place within this system was rigidly fixed. "It is not legal for a man
either to marry a wife from another caste or to change one's pursuit
or work from one to another."

The philosophers were divided into two classes, Strabo reports on
the authority of Megasthenes: one called Brachmanes or Brahmans,
the other Garmanes or Śramanas. The Brahmans "converse more
about death than anything else, for they believe . . . that death, to

those who have devoted themselves to philosophy, is birth into the true life, that is, the happy life." They also believe "that the universe was created and is destructible, . . . and that it is spherical in shape, and that the god who made it and regulates it pervades the whole of it; . . . and that the earth is situated in the center of the universe." The Śramanas are ascetics who live in the forest or go about begging, and they are accustomed to "practice such endurance, both in toils and in perseverance, that they stay in one posture all day long without moving."

The Indian people in general were said by Strabo to live a simple life, but to love beauty and personal adornment. "They wear apparel embroidered with gold, and use ornaments set with precious stones, and wear gay-colored linen garments, and are accompanied with sun-shades." As for their religion "the Indians worship Zeus and the Ganges River and the local deities." "Their funerals are simple," Strabo says, "and their mounds small." In the Indus region at least, cremation was practiced, "and wives are burned up with their deceased husbands." There, too, they had the custom that "the dead are thrown out to be devoured by vultures."[78]

Chandragupta Maurya was succeeded by his son Bindusara, and then by his grandson, the famous Aśoka. Known also as Aśoka Maurya and as Aśoka-vardhana, this king succeeded to the throne around 274 or 273 B.C. and ruled until about 232 B.C.[79] In the days of his father's reign, Aśoka had already served successfully as governor of Taxila and of Ujjain, and upon accession to the throne his great abilities became fully manifest. His capital was at Pataliputra, the ancient center of Magadhan culture, and from here he ruled the already widely extended empire of Magadha. In addition he conquered the kingdom of Kalinga to the southeast in a sanguinary campaign and thenceforth held sway over almost the whole of India except the extreme south. Since Aśoka was converted to Buddhism and became the great patron of that faith, more detailed mention of his work and monuments will be given in the chapter on Buddhism.

While Buddhism and Jainism were very important and influential at this time, the classical Brahmanism of the Vedas and Upanishads

---

[78] Strabo, *Geography.* ii, i, 9; xv, i, 30,36,39-49,53-55,59f.,62,69. tr. H. L. Jones, LCL (1917-32) i, p.265; vii, pp.53,63,67-83,87-89,91,99-105,109,121; Arrian, *Anabasis of Alexander.* v, v, 1; viii (*Indica*), x-xii. tr. E. Iliff Robson, LCL (1929-33) ii, pp.17,335-341.

[79] CSHI pp.45,53.

still lived on. Furthermore, it is possible to show that a fusion was taking place between Aryan conceptions and other ideas deriving probably from early Dravidian backgrounds.[80] The religion which resulted from this mingling, and which has lived on in India from the first centuries B.C. to the present, is properly called Hinduism.[81]

SECTARIAN HINDUISM

In the Vedas the gods were largely the many elemental forces of nature personified, and in the Upanishads the ultimate reality was most often an impersonal Absolute with which the human soul was to realize its identity. Even in Brahmanism, however, a more theistic type of thought sometimes occurred, as for example in the Śvetaś-vatara-Upanishad. Now, in the Hinduism which more and more appealed to the popular mind, there was an increasing tendency to regard some one god as supreme among the many (not of course to the denial of the others), and to conceive the divine beings as personal and worthy of personal worship. As an adorable or worship-ful being a god is a *bhagavat*, his devotee is a *bhagavata*, and the personal love and devotion which he has elicited is *bhakti*.[82]

Two great gods attained the highest importance, and around each a large sectarian movement formed. The two gods were Vishnu and Śiva, and their respective sects were those of Vaishnavism and Śaivism, each with its own numerous subdivisions.[83] Both deities had already been known in the Vedic literature but had hitherto been relatively unimportant. In the present and succeeding periods they came to play a very prominent role, while around each a multitude of other gods, many of local or aboriginal origin and all regarded as manifestations of the supreme god, was gathered. The two sects "are thus actually vast amorphous conglomerates of the most hetero-geneous elements; monotheistic in essence, multifarious and gro-tesque polytheisms in semblance, with pantheism for a harmonising principle."[84]

THE SHRINE AT NAGARI

A Vaishnavite shrine is known to us from archeological evidence at about this time. It was devoted to the worship of the god Vasu-deva, perhaps originally the divine leader of a non-Aryan clan in the

[80] CHIIA p.16.   [81] Strauss in CRW p.108.
[82] Nicol Macnicol, *The Living Religions of the Indian People.* 1934, pp.39f.
[83] Sten Konow in SLR II, pp.154f.,172f.   [84] MHR I, p.329.

northwest,[85] and now probably regarded as a manifestation of Vishnu.[86] The site is at Nagari, eight miles north of Chitor in the region of Rajputana. There is a village named Ghosundi about four miles northeast of Nagari, where a number of carved stones have been found which probably were brought from Nagari. One of these was an inscribed slab which had been put up within the entrance to the village well at Ghosundi, and which now has been transferred to the Victoria Museum at Udaipur. It is ascribed to the period between 350 and 250 B.C., and is thought to be the earliest extant inscription in which the Sanskrit language is used. It records the erection of a stone enclosure in connection with the worship of Vasudeva and another divinity called Samkarshana. The site of this shrine is referred to as Narayana-vata, suggesting that Vasudeva was already identified with Narayana, who is well known later as an incarnation of Vishnu.

In the course of archeological investigations at Nagari, moreover, an actual large enclosure was studied which had been built of massive blocks of laminiferous stone. Since the Ghosundi well inscription had originally formed part of a similar block, it is a convincing supposition that this is the actual enclosure to which it referred. A much later inscription, probably of the seventh century A.D., was also found on one of the stones of this wall indicating that at that time a temple of Vishnu was standing there. Thus the worship of Vasudeva-Vishnu is evidently attested at this place from the fourth century B.C. to the seventh century A.D.[87]

YAKSHAS

The Maurya Period also provides us with an actual statue probably portraying one of the popular divinities of the time. The statue, shown in Fig. 51, was found at Parkham, near Baroda, and is now in the Archaeological Museum at Muttra (Mathura). Made of sandstone, and of very large size, standing to a height of eight feet eight inches, it is the oldest known Indian stone sculpture in the round. It is believed to represent a Yaksha. The Sanskrit word *yaksha* (feminine *yakshi*) was perhaps originally a non-Aryan or at any rate a popular designation signifying practically the same as the Aryan *deva*. The Yakshas seem to have been indigenous non-Aryan deities,

[85] A. Eustace Haydon, *Biography of the Gods.* 1941, pp.105f.

[86] Konow in SLR II, p.149.

[87] D. R. Bhandarkar, *The Archaeological Remains and Excavations at Nagari* (MASI, 4). 1920, pp.118f.,128-133.

which were especially associated with waters, and which were looked to as the beneficent bestowers of fertility and wealth.[88] They were natural objects, therefore, of the bhakti cult. The present statue conveys an impression of mass and force, and has been called "a statement of an ideal concept in a technique that is still primitive."[89] The standing position remains typical for cult statues in early Indian art, and where these are complete they usually have the right hand raised and the left on the hip.

[88] Ananda K. Coomaraswamy, *Yakṣas* (Smithsonian Institution Publication 2926). 1928; *Yakṣas* II (Smithsonian Institution Publication 3059). 1931.

[89] A. K. Coomaraswamy in EB XII, p.213.

5. THE ŚUNGA, ANDHRA, INDO-GREEK AND INDO-PARTHIAN PERIODS, c.185 B.C.-A.D. c.50

AFTER the splendid reign of Aśoka, the Maurya empire disintegrated rapidly. We know little more than that Aśoka's grandson, Daśaratha, ruled for a time and that the last king of the line, Brihadratha, was assassinated about 185 B.C.

The Śunga Dynasty (c.185-c.80 B.C.), whose first king was Pushya-mitra the slayer of Brihadratha, now ruled the central part of what had been Aśoka's empire. In the southeast and south the kingdoms of Kalinga and Andhra were independent, and the latter in particular maintained itself until about the middle of the third century A.D. In the northwest, the Greeks who had been settled in Bactria since the time of Alexander the Great, pressed on into the Punjab, and their most celebrated king, Menander or Milinda (c.161-c.145 B.C.), prob-ably invaded Magadha and may have reached Pataliputra. In the first century B.C. the Greeks gave way to new invaders, the Sakas and the Pahlavas. These were Scythians and Parthians, and their most famous king was the Parthian Gondophares who ruled at Taxila around A.D. 19-48.[90]

THE BESNAGAR INSCRIPTIONS

The prevalence of Vaishnavite worship in this time also is attested by two interesting inscriptions. From the type of their characters, they are probably to be dated in the second century B.C. The first is on a column at Besnagar, an important site near Bhilsa in central India. It is a votive inscription, and reads as follows: "This Garuda[91] column of Vasudeva the god of gods (*devadeva*) was erected here by Heliodorus, a Bhagavata, the son of Dion, and an inhabitant of Taxila, who came as Greek ambassador from Maharaja Antialkidas to King Kasiputra Bhagabhadra." These words are specially sig-nificant also as showing that, contrary to later practice, an alien could at this time be accepted as a devoted worshiper within the fold of Hindu society. The second inscription is on the fragment of another column which was found in a narrow street in Bhilsa, but which probably came from Besnagar, and is now in the Besnagar Museum.

[90] W. W. Tarn, *The Greeks in Bactria and India.* 1938, pp.133f.,225-269,312-350.
[91] The Sanskrit word Garuda is the name of a supernatural being who appears specially as the vehicle or bearer of Vishnu.

It also was a Garuda column, and it refers to "the excellent temple" of Vishnu.[92]

THE BHAJA RELIEFS

At the same time the nature deities of the ancient Vedic hymns lived on in the beliefs of the people and were the subjects of realistic and awe-inspiring portrayals in art. Illustration may be seen in certain reliefs which adorn the veranda of a cave at Bhaja near Poona in the Western Ghats. These sculptures date probably from the second or first century B.C. The cave evidently served as a monastery (*vihara*) and must have been Buddhist, but the sculptures under consideration were certainly from a non-Buddhist background. The reliefs are at the west end of the veranda, on either side of a doorway leading into a cell (Fig. 52). In the panel at the left we see a royal person, accompanied by two women, driving a four-horse chariot across the backs of two female demons who seem to float in the air. This is identified as Surya, the sun, driving with his two wives across the sky. On the other side of the doorway is another royal person who rides on a huge elephant and is accompanied by an attendant holding a trident standard. The elephant brandishes in his trunk an uprooted tree, and strides forward across a landscape filled with lesser figures. This is probably the storm god Indra, riding forth upon his cloud-elephant Airavata.[93]

TAXILA

The ancient city of Taxila was an important center of the Bactrian Greeks and Scytho-Parthians. At this site no less than three distinct buried cities are recognized. The most southerly is the Bhir mound which covers the older Hindu city (fifth to second centuries B.C.) where Panini taught and Aśoka served as governor. Hoards of jewelry and coins dating around 300 B.C., discovered in the Bhir mound in 1924 and 1945, provide decisive evidence of the date of these ruins.[94] To the north of the Bhir mound is that of Sirkap, which represents the city founded by the Greeks from Bactria. This was the capital of the Parthian dynasty of which Gondophares was the most illustrious member. Yet farther to the north is Sirsukh, which represents the Taxila of the later Kushan empire.

[92] Ramaprasad Chanda, *Archaeology and Vaishnava Tradition* (MASI, 5). 1920, pp.151-154.
[93] CHIIA pp.24-27.
[94] G. M. Young in *Ancient India*. 1 (Jan. 1946), pp.27-36.

The excavation of the mound of Sirkap by Sir John Marshall has laid bare a large part of Scytho-Parthian Taxila.[95] The ruins are an intricate complex of fortifications, streets, houses and shrines. Most of the shrines were Buddhist and possibly Jaina, while some distance outside the northern gate was a large temple which may have belonged to the Zoroastrian religion. Within the city the royal palace has been identified and found to consist of a series of apartments arranged around central courts. The entire complex measured over 350 by 250 feet, and was substantially built, yet not really pretentious or sumptuous. Among numerous coins unearthed in the palace were those of Gondophares and the Kushan king Kadphises I. Many of the excavated houses in the city were likewise constructed around open quadrangles, and often had two stories. The rooms of the lower story, however, did not communicate directly with the interior court or with the street, and apparently were entered only from the rooms above. Many of the houses were so extensive as to occasion the surmise that they were residences of Hindu teachers whose students were expected to live with their masters. The first century Greek philosopher Apollonius of Tyana is said to have visited Taxila, and his *Life*, written by Philostratus, gives an account of the city which is substantially in accord with the archeological findings. In particular the relative simplicity of the king's palace and the unusual character of the two-storied private houses are commented on in the Greek source.[96]

THOMAS

It is an interesting fact that until the modern discovery of his coins and inscriptions, the great king Gondophares had remained unknown to history save for the mention of his name in the apocryphal *Acts of Thomas*. This book, which was probably written at Edessa around A.D. 200, relates how the apostle Thomas journeyed to India[97] and preached the Christian message at the court of King Gundaphorus or Gondophares. The story is that Gondophares gave money to Thomas, who was taken for a carpenter, to build him a

---

[95] John Marshall, *A Guide to Taxila.* 2d ed. 1921, pp.67-87.

[96] Philostratus (A.D. c.170-c.245), *The Life of Apollonius of Tyana.* II, 23,25. tr. F. C. Conybeare, LCL (1912) I, pp.181,183.

[97] Parthia is named as the place of the labors of Thomas in Eusebius, *Church History.* III, i, 1; *Recognitions of Clement.* IX, 29; Socrates, *Church History.* I, 19. This may be explained, however, by the fact that in the time of Thomas north India was a part of the Scytho-Parthian empire and was ruled by a Parthian king.

palace. Thomas distributed the money to the poor and afflicted, and told the king that he was building a palace for him in heaven. Gad (or Guda), the king's brother, died and saw this palace in heaven. Being restored to life, Gad was converted to Christianity along with the king himself. After other remarkable adventures, Thomas met martyrdom in the land of another king who is referred to as Misdaeus, or the "Mazdaean."[98]

The tradition preserved in the Syrian Church of Travancore is that Thomas labored for the last twenty years of his life in south India, first on the west coast, and then on the east coast where he was martyred around A.D. 72. He is supposed to have been buried at Mylapore near Madras, where his martyr shrine, rebuilt by the Portuguese in 1547, still stands on Mount St. Thomas.[99] It is held that sometime in the century after his death, the bones of Thomas were brought back to Edessa, where a memorial church was dedicated to him.[100]

Although much of the legendary has gathered about the story of Thomas, the main facts of his work in north and south India may possibly be historical, and certainly the knowledge of, and contact with, India on the part of early Christianity is attested.[101]

[98] *Acts of Thomas.* 17-27,159-170. M. R. James, *The Apocryphal New Testament.* 1924, pp.371-376,434-438.

[99] F. C. Burkitt in EB XXII, p.143.

[100] Socrates, *Ch. Hist.* IV, 18.

[101] J. N. Farquhar in *Bulletin of the John Rylands Library, Manchester.* 10 (1926), pp.80-111; 11 (1927), pp.20-50; cf. A. Mingana, *ibid.*, 10 (1926), pp.435-514.

6. THE KUSHAN PERIOD, A.D. C.50-C.320

THE Kushans were the leading tribe among the Yueh-chi people who came out of central Asia, settled in Bactria, and in the first century A.D. pushed on into northwest India. The five principal Kushan kings were Kujala Kadphises I, Wima Kadphises II, Kanishka, Huvishka and Vasudeva. The dates of these rulers are still under debate. For Kanishka, the most important of them all, dates around A.D. 78-103, 125-150 or 144-172 have been proposed, and we may safely assume that he belongs in the second century A.D.[102]

Under Kadphises I the Kushan empire reached from the Parthian frontier to the Indus; Kadphises II extended these dominions on eastward to the Jumna and the Ganges. The latter king is well known for his gold and copper coins, on which a favorite picture is that of Śiva and his bull Nandi.[103]

Kanishka, chief of the Kushans, made his Indian capital at Purushapura (Peshawar) in the northwest, in the district known as Gandhara. The city of Mathura on the Jumna River was also of much importance at this time and was famed as a religious and artistic center. Kanishka is shown in a life-sized red sandstone statue (Fig. 53) which was found at Mat in the Mathura district. The identification of the statue is guaranteed by the inscription which it carries, but the head has been lost. The king is dressed in central Asian costume, with tunic, long open coat and high heavy boots, and makes a most imposing appearance.[104]

Kanishka was converted to Buddhism, and plays a prominent part in Buddhist traditions. On his coins, however, are found representations of Hindu, Zoroastrian and Hellenistic deities as well as of the Buddha.[105]

On the coins of Huvishka both Indian and foreign deities appear, while the coinage of Vasudeva features Śiva most prominently. After Vasudeva the Kushan empire disintegrated into small states where

[102] Tarn, *The Greeks in Bactria and India*, p.352. R. Ghirshman, *Bégram, recherches archéologiques et historiques sur les Kouchans*. 1946. reviewed by Richard N. Frye in *Artibus Asiae*. 11 (1948), p.242. Ghirshman, who proposes the date A.D. 144-172 for Kanishka, also gives A.D. 172-217 for Huvishka and A.D. 217-241 for Vasudeva. Sten Konow believes that Vasudeva was a predecessor and not a descendant of Kanishka. See *India Antiqua*, p.195.

[103] CSHI p.74.

[104] K. de B. Codrington, *Ancient India from the Earliest Times to the Guptas with Notes on the Architecture and Sculpture of the Medieval Period*. 1926, p.44.

[105] CSHI p.78.

various kings ruled in the third and fourth centuries, but gradually gave way to the rising Sasanian empire in the west and to the Guptas in India.

In the Kushan Period, probably by the end of the second century A.D., the two great epics of ancient India, the Ramayana and the Mahabharata,[106] seem to have been virtually completed. These present Hinduism in a popular form and, especially in the Bhagavad-Gita, state religion in terms of personal devotion.[107]

THE RAMAYANA

The Ramayana[108] means "the Career of Rama," and is the story of a noble character named Rama and of his devoted wife Sita. It is written in poetic form in more than 24,000 Sanskrit couplets. The epic is attributed to the poet Valmiki, and it may be supposed that he first brought into a homogeneous whole popular tales already current concerning Rama. This may have been done as early as the fourth century B.C., while the work had probably attained its present extent by the end of the second century A.D.[109]

The scene of the Ramayana is laid in northern India in the ancient kingdoms of Kosala and Videha. There by notable exploit, Prince Rama, eldest son of King Daśaratha of the Kosalas, won the hand of Sita, daughter of King Janaka of the Videhas. Shortly after the marriage, however, Rama was banished to the jungle for fourteen years, due to an unfortunate promise made earlier by Daśaratha to one of his wives. Sita faithfully followed her husband into exile, and they made their dwelling in the forest. But then Sita was carried off by the demon Ravana to an island in the ocean, probably Ceylon. Her whereabouts were discovered, however, by the monkey-leader Hanuman, and in alliance with the monkey-people Rama invaded Ceylon and recovered his wife. Thereafter, the fourteen years of exile having come to an end, Rama and Sita returned joyfully to Kosala, where Rama ascended the throne and reigned gloriously.

Thus in its essential outline the Ramayana is the story of an ideal man and woman who triumphed over great difficulties. In the form in which we have the epic, however, Rama is none other than the

---

[106] tr. Romesh C. Dutt, *The Ramayana and the Mahabharata Condensed into English Verse* (Everyman's Library, 403). 1910.

[107] Robert E. Hume, *The World's Living Religions*. 1924, p.30.

[108] tr. Ralph T. H. Griffith, *The Rámáyan of Válmíki Translated into English Verse*. 1915.

[109] A. A. Macdonell in HERE x, p.576.

incarnation (*avatara*, literally "descending") of the god Vishnu, who has consented to be born as a son of King Daśaratha in order to destroy the evil demon Ravana.

THE MAHABHARATA

The Mahabharata means the "Great Bharata" story, and deals with a famous war between the Kurus, ruled by the House of Bharata, and a closely neighboring people. Such a conflict was doubtless a historical event, and probably took place around the beginning of the first millennium B.C.[110] The composition of the epic as we have it is generally ascribed to the period from the second century B.C. to the second century A.D., although its beginnings may go back to 400 B.C. and its amplification probably continued till A.D. 400 and even later.[111] The essential tale comprises only the kernel of the entire work, around which is accumulated a vast mass of other material, moral, religious, and philosophical. In its total extent the epic comprises about one hundred thousand Sanskrit couplets.[112]

In brief outline the central story is as follows. There are two families of cousins, both descended from a great-grandfather named Kuru. The one family is that of Dhritarashtra, who has a hundred sons, called Kauravas or Kurus. The other is that of Pandu, who dies, but leaves behind him five sons, known as Pandavas. One of these sons, named Arjuna, wins Draupadi, princess of the land of Panchala, and she becomes the wife of the five brothers. The capital of the Kurus is at Hastinapura, while the Pandavas build for themselves the city of Indraprastha, supposedly near the site of modern Delhi.

Fearful of the growing power of the Pandavas, the Kurus plan to cheat them of their kingdom in a game of dice. In this they succeed, and the five brothers with Draupadi are exiled to live for twelve years in the forest and then to pass a thirteenth year among men but in disguise. After many adventures the Pandavas return from the forest, and also successfully pass the thirteenth year in disguise. At the end of this time they should have received their kingdom again, but when this is refused they prepare for war with their cousins. The battle which then takes place is exceedingly sanguinary, but after eighteen days of fighting the Kurus are destroyed, and the Pandavas

[110] Goetz, *Epochen der indischen Kultur*, p.9.

[111] E. Washburn Hopkins, *The Great Epic of India, Its Character and Origin*. 1901, pp.386-402; and in HERE VIII, p.325.

[112] tr. Pratapa Chandra Roy and Sundari Bala Roy, *The Mahabharata of Krishna-Dwaipayana Vyasa Translated into English Prose*. 10 vols. 1893-96.

come into control of the kingdom. The eldest brother, Yudhishthira, takes the throne, and performs the famous horse-sacrifice (*asva-medha*) in token of undisputed supremacy.[113] Eventually, however, the Pandavas leave their kingdom behind, retire to the Himalayas, and thence make the ascent to heaven.

THE BHAGAVAD-GITA

Appearing as an inserted section in the sixth book of the Mahabharata is the famous Bhagavad-Gita or "Song of the Blessed One,"[114] which is "probably the most important single work ever produced in India."[115] Like the Mahabharata, the period of its composition was perhaps from the second century B.C. to the second century A.D.[116]

The scene is the plain of Kuru on which the opposing forces of the Kurus and the Pandavas are drawn up. Prince Arjuna, the famed archer among the Pandavas, gazes upon his kinsmen on the other side of the battle line, and his heart fails within him. He has no desire to begin the slaughter. Then ensues a dialogue between Arjuna and his charioteer, Krishna, whose mysterious, true nature is only gradually revealed. The conversation begins as a discussion of the immediate question of the warrior's duty, and since no task could be more difficult than to slay one's own kinsmen, the solution of this problem would cast light on all lesser duties. The essential answer of the Bhagavad-Gita is that man is bound to fulfill the duties of his calling, and that such activity, rightly conducted, is indeed a way of salvation. To be sure, it is not denied that the Brahmanic way of withdrawal from the world for mystic contemplation also leads to salvation, but the greater emphasis of the Gita is upon activity.

---

[113] The Aśvamedha is described in detail in the Śatapatha-Brahmana XIII, i-v. SBE XLIV, pp.274-403; and elsewhere. See P.-E. Dumont, *L'Aśvamedha, Description du sacrifice solennel du cheval dans le culte védique d'après les textes du Yajurveda blanc* (*Vājasaneyisaṃhitā, Śatapathabrāhmaṇa, Kātyāyanaśrautasūtra*). Société Belge d'Études Orientales. 1927.

[114] The Bhagavad-Gita has been rendered into English by more than forty translators (see Robert E. Hume, *Treasure-House of the Living Religions*. 1932, pp.vii, 424-428), including Kashinath Trimbak Telang in SBE VIII, pp.1-131; Edwin Arnold in *The Harvard Classics*. 45 (1910), pp.799-884; Arthur W. Ryder, *The Bhagavad-Gita*. 1929; Franklin Edgerton, *The Bhagavad Gītā Translated and Interpreted*. 2 vols. (Harvard Oriental Series, 38, 39). 1944; Swami Prabhavananda and Christopher Isherwood, *Bhagavad-Gita, The Song of God*. 1944; and S. Radhakrishnan, *The Bhagavadgītā, with an Introductory Essay, Sanskrit Text, English Translation and Notes*. 1948.

[115] A. K. Coomaraswamy, *Hinduism and Buddhism*, p.4.

[116] R. Garbe in HERE II, p.538.

Renunciation and discipline of action
　　Both lead to supreme weal.
But of these two, rather than renunciation of action,
　　Discipline of action is superior.[117]

The proof of the necessity for activity is the simple fact that "even the maintenance of the body . . . can not succeed without action,"[118] and that if God "did not perform action," "these folk would perish."[119] The doing of one's active duty upon earth, however, must be without "attachment,"[120] that is without any trace of personal interest or desire for selfish reward. Work so done does not enchain man in bondage but on the contrary sets him free.

As the discussion in the Gita proceeds from the consideration of duty to the wider issues of religion and philosophy, the principle of loving faith and personal devotion (*bhakti*) is brought forward as the most important of all. By trust and love of God, both those who renounce the world and those who work in it, both high-caste priests and rulers, and low-caste people, women and even evil-doers, may win a sure salvation. This teaching is expressed as follows in one of the finest passages in the *Bhagavad-Gita*:

A leaf, a flower, a fruit, or water,
　　Who presents to Me with devotion,
That offering of devotion I
　　Accept from the devout-souled (giver).

Whatever thou doest, whatever thou eatest,
　　Whatever thou offerest in oblation or givest,
Whatever austerity thou performest, son of Kunti,[121]
　　That do as an offering to Me.

I am the same to all beings,
　　No one is hateful or dear to Me;
But those who revere Me with devotion,
　　They are in Me and I too am in them.

Even if a very evil doer
　　Reveres Me with single devotion,
He must be regarded as righteous in spite of all;
　　For he has the right resolution.

Quickly his soul becomes righteous,
　　And he goes to eternal peace.

---

[117] v, 2. This and the following quotations are reprinted by permission of the publishers from the *Bhagavad Gita*. Edited and Translated by Franklin Edgerton (Cambridge, Mass.: Harvard University Press, 1944).
[118] III, 8.　　　　　[119] III, 24.　　　　　[120] II, 48.
[121] Kunti was the mother of Arjuna.

Son of Kunti, make sure of this:
  No devotee of Mine is lost.

For if they take refuge in Me, son of Prtha,[122]
  Even those who may be of base origin,
Women, men of the artisan caste, and serfs too,
  Even they go to the highest goal.

How much more virtuous brahmans,
  And devout royal seers, too!
A fleeting and joyless world
  This; having attained it, devote thyself to Me.

Be Me-minded, devoted to Me;
  Worshiping Me, pay homage to Me;
Just to Me shalt thou go, having thus disciplined
  Thyself, fully intent on Me.[123]

The god toward whom this devotion is directed in the Bhagavad-Gita is of course Krishna. Like Rama in the Ramayana, Krishna appears at first in the Mahabharata as a very human hero, indeed as a less admirable one than the noble Rama.[124] But in the Gita, Krishna reveals himself to Arjuna as none other than an incarnation (*avatara*) of the supreme god. In the dialogue the deity explains that he has passed through many births, even as Arjuna also has, but that unlike Arjuna he himself has memory of them all. Whenever conditions on earth become so bad as to demand it, he creates himself again, and thus is born age after age in order to destroy evil-doers and protect the good.[125]

Upon Arjuna's request the Blessed One then allows his true form to appear, and in amazement and terror Arjuna cries:

I see the gods in Thy body, O God,
  All of them, and the hosts of various kinds of beings too,
Lord Brahma sitting on the lotus-seat,
  And the seers all, and the divine serpents.

With many arms, bellies, mouths, and eyes,
  I see Thee, infinite in form on all sides;
No end nor middle nor yet beginning of Thee
  Do I see, O All-God, All-formed!

Thou art the Imperishable, the supreme Object of Knowledge;
  Thou art the ultimate resting-place of this universe;
Thou art the immortal guardian of the eternal right,
  Thou art the everlasting Spirit, I hold.

[122] Prtha was Kunti's name, earlier in life.
[123] IX, 26f.,29-34.   [124] Hermann Jacobi in HERE VII, p.196.
[125] IV, 5-8.

Touching the sky, aflame, of many colors,
    With yawning mouths and flaming enormous eyes,
Verily seeing Thee (so), my inmost soul is shaken,
    And I find no steadiness nor peace, O Vishnu![126]

The deity then resumes human form as Krishna the charioteer, and comforts Arjuna with the assurance that his devotion is still the guarantee of his salvation.

Not by the Vedas nor by austerity,
    Nor by gifts or acts of worship,
Can I be seen in such a guise,
    As thou hast seen Me.

But by unswerving devotion can
    I in such a guise, Arjuna,
Be known and seen in very truth,
    And entered into, scorcher of the foe.

Doing My work, intent on Me,
    Devoted to Me, free from attachment,
Free from enmity to all beings,
    Who is so, goes to Me, son of Pandu.[127]

[126] xi, 15f.,18,24.
[127] xi, 53-55.

7. THE GUPTA PERIOD, A.D. C.320-C.600

THE Gupta era was inaugurated by a king who bore a name already famous in Indian history. This was Chandragupta I, the first year of whose reign began on February 26, A.D. 320.[128] He ruled at Pataliputra, and held sway over the Ganges Valley as far as Prayaga (later Allahabad) at the confluence of the Ganges and the Jumna. About A.D. 335 he was succeeded by his son Samudragupta. The latter engraved an inscription on one of Aśoka's pillars, originally set up at Kauśambi and found at Prayaga, in which extensive conquests are described. These conquests were continued particularly in the west by his son Chandragupta II, who held the throne around A.D. 385-414. Under the latter the dynasty of the imperial Guptas reached the height of its splendor. The capital was now transferred to Ayodhya, and for a time the king probably also resided at Ujjain farther to the west.

FA HIEN

At about this time a Chinese Buddhist pilgrim named Fa Hien visited India and wrote an account of his travels.[129] His trip, made around A.D. 399-414, carried him across the Gobi Desert, down into the Punjab, and then through the whole Ganges Valley, from the mouth of which he sailed for home by way of Ceylon and Java. Speaking of the middle country of India, Fa Hien says: "The people are prosperous and happy. . . . The king in his administration uses no corporal punishments. . . . Throughout the country no one kills any living thing, nor drinks wine. . . ."[130]

THE WHITE HUNS

The next kings were Kumaragupta (A.D. c.414-c.455) and Skandagupta (A.D. c.455-c.470). At this time India was threatened by new invaders from central Asia, the Hunas or White Huns. They were temporarily repelled by Skandagupta, who refers to his victory over them in an inscription which also tells of his establishment of a temple and image of Vishnu at that time.[131] Afterward, however, the White Huns poured on into India and gained control of all the western

[128] CSHI p.87.
[129] Emil Abegg in *Asiatische Studien.* 1 (1947), pp.105-128.
[130] tr. H. A. Giles, *The Travels of Fa-hsien* (399-414 A.D.), or *Record of the Buddhistic Kingdoms.* 1923, pp.20f.; Samuel Beal, *Travels of Fah-Hian and Sung-Yun, Buddhist Pilgrims from China to India* (400 A.D. and 518 A.D.). 1869, pp.54f.
[131] CSHI p.95.

and central dominions of the Guptas. Here the Huns continued to rule until the latter half of the sixth century. They established their capital at Sakala or Sialkot, and their greatest rulers were Toramana and his son Mihirakula. The reputation of Mihirakula was for cruelty and oppression, and he was especially remembered for his persecution of the Buddhists.

COSMAS INDICOPLEUSTES

Around A.D. 530 a visit was paid to India by Cosmas Indicopleustes ("the Indian navigator"), an Alexandrian merchant who subsequently became a monk. In his writings Cosmas makes reference to the White Huns, and to a ruler of theirs whom he calls Gollas. He describes this king, who may well be identified with Mihirakula, in the following words: "He is the lord of India, and oppressing the people forces them to pay tribute."[132]

While the imperial line of Guptas came to an end with the Hun invasion, another line of Guptas, probably a branch of the imperial family, maintained its rule in Magadha for some two centuries longer.

The Gupta rulers themselves were Hindus, and a Brahmanical revival took place within this period.[133] The era was also distinguished for its literary activity. Kalidasa, a dramatist and poet who flourished under Chandragupta II, has been called "the greatest name in Indian literature," and "the Indian Shakespeare."[134] The Panchatantra, which took its present form at about this time, has been said to be perhaps the best collection of stories in the world. The name of this work means "Five Books," and each book consists of a framing story, within which numerous other stories are inserted. Thus in book one, for example, the main outline is provided by the narrative of the broken friendship of the lion Rusty and the bull Lively, while some thirty inserted stories are told by two jackals, Victor and Cheek. The purpose of the Panchatantra is to provide a textbook on the wise conduct of life, and its message is that, granted security and freedom from anxiety, joy comes from the wise use of

[132] XI. tr. J. W. McCrindle, *The Christian Topography of Cosmas, an Egyptian Monk.* 1897, pp.370f.
[133] CSHI p.99.
[134] H. G. Rawlinson, *India, A Short Cultural History* (ed. C. G. Seligman). 1938, p.137; A. Berriedale Keith, *The Sanskrit Drama in Its Origin, Development, Theory and Practice.* 1924, pp.143-167.

one's active powers, from association with friends, and from the exercise of intelligence.[135]

In the realm of specifically religious literature a vast labor was performed in the collection and systematization of various teachings and lore.

THE SUTRAS

The interest in codification is especially apparent in the development of the Sutra literature. The word *sutra* means in Sanskrit "a thread," and hence is applicable to a string of rules or aphorisms. The Sutras, therefore, are systematic treatises in which a complete body of doctrine on some subject is condensed into the form of a series of concise aphoristic statements.

One large body of Sutras deals with practical matters in several different areas. The Śrauta- or Kalpa-Sutras are Books of Vedic Ritual, and give a compact description of the great sacrifices.[136] The principles involved in the Kalpa-Sutras are further discussed in the Purva Mimamsa-Sutras.[137] The Grihya-Sutras are House Books, and give the rules for the Vedic ceremonies which are to be carried out in the home.[138] The Dharma-Sutras are Law Books, and treat of both secular and religious law. Some of the older and more important Dharma-Sutras are those of Apastamba, Gautama, Vishnu, Vasishtha, and Baudhayana.[139] The Vishnu-Sutra contains this interesting and clear-cut description of the caste system: "Brahmans, Kshatriyas, Vaisyas, and Sudras are the four castes. The first three of these are [called] twice-born. . . . Their duties are: for a Brahman, to teach [the Veda]; for a Kshatriya, constant practice in arms; for a Vaisya, the tending of cattle; for a Sudra, to serve the twice-born."[140] The famous Law of Manu, which is another Dharma-Sutra still belonging to the Gupta Age, explains in its account of the creation that the four castes owe their positions to the fact of their having proceeded

[135] Franklin Edgerton, *The Panchatantra Reconstructed, An Attempt to Establish the Lost Original Sanskrit Text of the Most Famous of Indian Story-Collections on the Basis of the Principal Extant Versions, Text, Critical Apparatus, Introduction, Translation* (American Oriental Series, 2, 3). 2 vols. 1924; Arthur W. Ryder, *The Panchatantra*. 1925.

[136] F. Max Müller in SBE II, p.x, footnote.

[137] Mimamsa refers to inquiry into the connected meaning of the sacred texts, and Purva means "earlier" in distinction from the Uttara or "later" Mimamsa. George Thibaut in SBE XXXIV, pp.x-xii.

[138] Seven Grihya-Sutras are translated by Hermann Oldenberg in SBE XXIX, XXX.

[139] Translated by Georg Bühler and Julius Jolly in SBE II, VII, XIV.

[140] II, 1f.,4-8. SBE VII, p.12.

respectively from the mouth, arms, thighs and feet of the supreme god Brahman.[141] The Law of Manu also gives a detailed outline of the four stages (*ashramas*)[142] in the life of the religious man, in which he is successively a student, a married householder, a hermit in the forest, and a homeless mendicant.[143]

Another great body of Sutras is concerned not with action in practical matters, but with knowledge. The portions of the Vedic literature upon which these Sutras are based, and whose teachings they desire to systematize, are the Aranyakas and Upanishads. They are known as the Uttara Mimamsa-Sutras, or the Vedanta-Sutras, Vedanta signifying in Sanskrit the "end or final aim of the Veda." These Sutras too were probably completed before the end of the Gupta Period.[144] In form, however, they are so exceedingly condensed and abbreviated as to be almost unintelligible apart from the later commentaries of Sankara and Ramanuja which have been attached to them.[145]

THE PURANAS

The interest in compiling religious lore also gave rise in the Gupta Period to the Puranas, the oldest of which probably belong to the sixth century A.D.[146] The word *purana* means "ancient" in Sanskrit, and the Puranas are collections of Ancient Tales or Ancient Lore. They deal with many miscellaneous matters including cosmogony, theology, genealogy, and traditional history, all illustrated with numerous legends, fables and stories. Taken collectively, they have been described as "a popular encyclopaedia of ancient and mediaeval Hinduism, religious, philosophical, historical, personal, social, and political,"[147] and together with the great epics are the real Bible of the common people of India today.[148]

For a single quotation of elevated character we may give the following from the Agni Purana:

> It is the spirit of sincerity and sympathy
> That forms the backbone of virtue.

[141] I, 31. tr. George Bühler in SBE XXV, p.14. For the caste system in general see J. H. Hutton, *Caste in India, Its Nature, Function, and Origins.* 1946.

[142] Coomaraswamy, *Hinduism and Buddhism,* p.29.

[143] II, 70-246; III-V; VI, 1-32,33-97. SBE XXV, pp.43-216.

[144] HERE VIII, p.648.

[145] SBE XXXIV, XXXVIII, XLVIII.

[146] CSHI p.99; Herbert H. Gowen, *A History of Indian Literature from Vedic Times to the Present Day.* 1931, p.452.

[147] F. E. Pargiter in HERE X, p.448.

[148] J. N. Farquhar, *An Outline of the Religious Literature of India.* 1920, p.136.

And even a small cup of water presented
To the parched lips of a thirsty man,
Out of a heart-felt sympathy,
Brings immortal merit to the offerer.[149]

Many of the Vedic deities, such as Indra, Agni, Soma and Surya, appear in the Puranas, but sometimes their functions have been changed as in the case of Varuna, for example, who has now become the god of the ocean. Also, local cults are recognized, and the worship of the goddess of snakes and the veneration of the cow are mentioned. Of all the gods, however, three are the most prominent, Brahma, Vishnu and Siva. Together they make up the Trimurti or three-fold manifestation of the supreme Brahman.[150]

Brahma is "the personalized form of the impersonal Brahman,"[151] and is the creator of the world. Sometimes praised as the highest god, he is more often considered inferior to Vishnu and Siva, and in the further course of the centuries was to sink to a relatively insignificant place.[152]

Vishnu is the god who appeared in the Rig-Veda in only a minor role, but is now the gracious preserver of all things. He is usually said to have ten major incarnations, as follows: (1) as a fish when he saved Manu in the midst of the flood; (2) as a tortoise when he supported a mountain at the churning of the ocean, and the goddess Lakshmi and other precious things were produced; (3) as a boar when he raised the earth which had sunk to the bottom of the ocean; (4) as a man-lion when he destroyed a terrible demon; (5) as a dwarf when he outwitted another demon; (6) as Parasurama or Rama-with-the-ax when he rid the earth of all the Kshatriyas; (7) as Rama or Ramachandra, the hero of the Ramayana; (8) as Krishna, the figure in the Mahabharata; (9) as the historical Buddha; (10) as Kalki, a warrior who is yet to come at the end of the age to destroy the wicked and establish righteousness. In the Agni Purana, however, no less than twenty-four forms of Vishnu are enumerated, and in the Bhagavata Purana it is added that the incarnations of the deity are really innumerable.[153]

The Agni Purana is of special interest at this point because it also

---

[149] Hume, *Treasure-House of the Living Religions*, p.208. Quoted by permission of the publishers, Charles Scribner's Sons, New York.

[150] Govinda Das, *Hinduism*. 1924, p.183; J. Estlin Carpenter, *Theism in Medieval India* (Hibbert Lectures). 1926, pp.225-295.

[151] Haydon, *Biography of the Gods*, p.104.

[152] A. Hillebrandt in HERE II, p.799.

[153] Jacobi in HERE VII, pp.193f.; Pargiter in HERE X, p.452.

tells how in the sculptured representations of Vishnu each of his twenty-four forms may be differentiated.[154] The images of Vishnu usually portray him in a rather uniform way as a four-armed personage, who holds as characteristic objects a mace, a lotus, a conch and a disc. According to the Agni Purana the order in which these four objects appear in the four hands is indicative of the special aspect of the deity which is being portrayed. Thus, for example, if the lotus is in the lower right hand, the mace in the upper right, the disc in the upper left, and the conch in the lower left, the god is shown in his special form as Trivikrama, he of the three strides. The allusion is to the chief mythological feat of Vishnu, to which reference is made as early as in the Vedic hymns. There Vishnu is spoken of as "He who strode wide with his three strides across the regions of the earth";[155] and as "He within whose three wide-extended paces all living creatures have their habitation."[156] Later the Śatapatha-Brahmana explains that "by his first step he gained this same [earth], by the second this aerial expanse, and by his last [step] the sky."[157] Finally the medieval story narrates that when a demon-king was dominating the three worlds, Vishnu came to him in the form of a small dwarf and asked that he be given as much space as he could cover in three steps. When the request was granted, Vishnu strode in two paces over earth and heaven, but condescended to leave the lower world still in the demon's possession.[158] The image of Vishnu pictured in Fig. 54 is in the Indian Museum at Calcutta, and shows the god with the distinctive attributes of Trivikrama.[159]

Śiva is the god whose prototype may be recognized at Mohenjodaro, and who is now the destroyer of the world. He has several wives, who are the mother goddesses of ancient times. These include Parvati, the lovely daughter of the Himalayas, whose son is Ganesha, the elephant-headed god of wisdom; Durga "the inaccessible," a yellow woman riding on a tiger; and Kali "the black," a terrible figure dripping with blood, encircled with snakes, and adorned with skulls.

---

[154] B. B. Bidyabinod, *Varieties of the Vishnu Image* (MASI, 2). 1920. For the detailed measurements and sets of proportions according to which images are to be made, as specified in the Hindu *Agamas*, see T. A. Gopinatha Rao, *Talamana or Iconometry* (MASI, 3). 1920. The Talamana was the forerunner of the later Śilpa-Śastras.

[155] Rig-Veda I, clv, 4. SBE XXXII, p.52.

[156] Rig-Veda I, cliv, 2. Macnicol, *Hindu Scriptures*, p.12.

[157] I, ix, 3, v.9. SBE XII, p.268.

[158] K. de B. Codrington in G. T. Garratt, ed., *The Legacy of India*. 1937, p.99.

[159] Bidyabinod, *Varieties of the Vishnu Image*, Pl. VII,a.

THE TANTRAS

The Gupta Period probably witnessed at least the beginnings of yet another body of writings, the Tantras, which are generally ascribed to the sixth and seventh centuries A.D. The name of these writings is derived from a word which means, in the first place, web or warp, then an uninterrupted series, and then an orderly rule or ritual. These works also bear the name of Agamas. They comprise a number of treatises, the content of which is chiefly magical or mystical. Most distinctively they have to do with the worship of the gods of the Trimurti in their female essence (Śakti), and personal devotion is directed particularly toward the wives of Śiva.[160] With these writings we reach the fourth order of Hindu literature, the four classes in the order of inspiration and authority being: (1) *śruti*, or revealed literature, including the Vedas, Brahmanas, and Upanishads; (2) *smriti*, or traditional literature, including the Epics and Sutras; (3) *purana*; (4) *tantra*.[161]

GUPTA TEMPLES

Of the most ancient Hindu temples still standing in India some probably come from the Gupta Period. One of these is shown in Fig. 55. This is the temple known as the Lad Khan at Aihole in the Deccan. It is believed to date from around the middle of the fifth century A.D. Constructed as a low, flat building, its walls are made of stone slabs set between square pilasters, and its windows also are stone slabs perforated in various patterns. The temple has a porch, on the pillars of which are figures of river goddesses. There is furthermore a cella, with a porch of its own, built on the roof of the main temple, which forms an independent shrine of the Sun.[162]

[160] D. N. Bose, *Tantras, Their Philosophy and Occult Secrets.*
[161] Gowen, *A History of Indian Literature from Vedic Times to the Present Day*, pp.459f.; Geden in HERE XII, pp.192f.
[162] CHIIA p.79, Fig. 148.

8. THE EARLY MEDIEVAL PERIOD, A.D. C.600-C.850

HARSHA VARDHANA

AFTER the collapse of the dominion of the White Huns, a number of new dynasties arose, of which the most important was the Vardhana family of Sthanviśvara or Thanesar. A member of this family became the greatest Indian ruler of the seventh century, and the dominant force at that time in the greater part of north India. This man was named Harsha, and he ruled A.D. c.606-c.647. He united the kingdoms of Thanesar and Kanauj, and then made the city of Kanauj his capital. From there he exercised sway over an empire which extended from the mouth of the Ganges to the Sutlej.

Harsha was not only a successful warrior and administrator, but also a man of literary and religious interests. In the realm of literature, three important dramas are ascribed to him.[163] In personal religion he was a Buddhist and gave active support to that faith but also paid reverence to deities such as Śiva and Surya as well as to the Buddha.[164]

HIUEN TSANG

At this time another Chinese Buddhist pilgrim came to India. This was Hiuen Tsang who arrived about A.D. 630 and stayed for some fifteen years, over half of which were spent within Harsha's dominions. Hiuen Tsang wrote a detailed account of his experiences which is known as the Si-yu-ki or Record of Western Countries, and this is supplemented by a life of the pilgrim written by his disciple Hwui Li.[165]

The achievements and conduct of Harsha were described by Hiuen Tsang as follows: "He went from east to west subduing all who were not obedient; the elephants were not unharnessed nor the soldiers unhelmeted. After six years he had subdued the Five Indies. Having thus enlarged his territory, he increased his forces; he had 60,000 war elephants and 100,000 cavalry. After thirty years his arms reposed, and he governed everywhere in peace. He then practised

[163] Keith, *The Sanskrit Drama in Its Origin, Development, Theory and Practice*, pp.170-181.

[164] Rawlinson, *India, A Short Cultural History*, p.112.

[165] tr. Samuel Beal, *Buddhist Records of the Western World, Translated from the Chinese of Hiuen Tsiang* (A.D. 629). 2 vols. 1906; and *The Life of Hiuen-Tsiang by the Shaman Hwui Li.* 1911. See also Emil Abegg in *Asiatische Studien.* 2 (1948), pp.56-79.

to the utmost the rules of temperance, and sought to plant the tree of religious merit to such an extent that he forgot to sleep or to eat. He forbade the slaughter of any living thing or flesh as food throughout the Five Indies on pain of death without pardon."[166]

Concerning the land and people in general, Hiuen Tsang reported: "The towns and villages have inner gates; the walls are wide and high; the streets and lanes are tortuous, and the roads winding. The thoroughfares are dirty and the stalls arranged on both sides of the road with appropriate signs. Butchers, fishers, dancers, executioners, scavengers, and so on, have their abodes without the city. In coming and going these persons are bound to keep on the left side of the road till they arrive at their homes. Their houses are surrounded by low walls, and form the suburbs. The earth being soft and muddy, the walls of the towns are mostly built of brick or tiles. The towers on the walls are constructed of wood or bamboo; the houses have balconies and belvederes, which are made of wood, with a coating of lime or mortar, and covered with tiles. . . .

"Their clothing is not cut or fashioned; they mostly affect fresh white garments; they esteem little those of mixed color or ornamented. The men wind their garments round their middle, then gather them under the armpits, and let them fall down across the body, hanging to the right. The robes of the women fall down to the ground; they completely cover their shoulders. They wear a little knot of hair on their crowns, and let the rest of their hair fall loose. . . . On their heads the people wear caps, with flower-wreaths and jeweled necklets. . . .

"With respect to the division of families, there are four classifications. The first is called the Brahman, men of pure conduct. They guard themselves in religion, live purely, and observe the most correct principles. The second is called Kshatriya, the royal caste. For ages they have been the governing class: they apply themselves to virtue and kindness. The third is called Vaisyas, the merchant class: they engage in commercial exchange, and they follow profit at home and abroad. The fourth is called Sudra, the agricultural class: they labor in ploughing and tillage. . . .

"With respect to the ordinary people, although they are naturally light-minded, yet they are upright and honorable. . . . They dread the retribution of another state of existence, and make light of the things of the present world."[167]

[166] v, 1. tr. Beal, *Buddhist Records of the Western World*, i, pp.213f.
[167] ii, 5,7,11,13. tr. Beal, *ibid.*, i, pp.73-75,82f.

The capital city of Kanauj was described by Hiuen Tsang as lying near the western bank of the Ganges, and having a "dry ditch" around it, "with strong and lofty towers facing one another." On every side were flowers and woods, and "lakes and ponds, bright and pure and shining like mirrors." "The people are well off and contented," continues Hiuen Tsang. "They apply themselves much to learning, and in their travels are very much given to discussion [on religious subjects]. . . . The believers in Buddha and the heretics are about equal in number." The Hindu shrines of the place included, he said, a temple of the Sun-deva and another of Maheśvara [the god Śiva]. "The two temples are built of a blue stone of great lustre, and are ornamented with various elegant sculptures. . . . Each of these foundations has 1,000 attendants to sweep and water it; the sound of drums and of songs accompanied by music, ceases not day nor night."[168]

Concerning the important city of Benares, Hiuen Tsang wrote: "The capital borders the Ganges river. . . . Its inner gates are like a small-toothed comb; it is densely populated. The families are very rich, and in the dwellings are objects of rare value. The disposition of the people is soft and humane, and they are earnestly given to study. They are mostly unbelievers, a few reverence the law of Buddha. . . . There are a hundred or so Deva temples with about 10,000 sectaries. They honor principally Maheśvara. Some cut their hair off, others tie their hair in a knot, and go naked, without clothes; they cover their bodies with ashes, and by the practice of all sorts of austerities they seek to escape from birth and death." A copper statue of the Deva Maheśvara which Hiuen Tsang saw here was, he says, somewhat less than one hundred feet in height, and appeared grave and majestic, "as though really living."[169]

After the time of Harsha, northern India split up again into a number of small states. Meanwhile in the western Deccan the kingdom of the Chalukyas, which had arisen in the middle of the sixth century and which Harsha had been unable to conquer, maintained its existence until it was taken over by the Rashtrakutas in the middle of the eighth century. In Mysore (Maisur) the Gangas ruled from the second to the eleventh century, and in the east and south the Pallava dynasty was dominant from the fifth to the ninth century.

EARLY MEDIEVAL TEMPLES

Many fine Hindu temples belong to the Early Medieval Period,

[168] v, 1. tr. Beal, *ibid.*, I, pp.206f.,223.
[169] vII, 1. tr. Beal, *ibid.*, II, pp.44f.

of which several notable examples will be mentioned. The great brick temple of Lakshmana at Sirpur (Fig. 56) may come from the reign of Harsha himself, or may perhaps be as much later as the ninth century. While the upper part of the tower is lost, the structure is still very impressive. It was richly ornamented, and the whole was originally covered with stucco. The carving on the lintel of the stone doorway represents the Birth of Brahma.[170]

The large temple at Pattadakal now known as the Virupaksha is shown by the inscriptions upon it to have been built by a queen of the Chalukya king Vikramaditya II (A.D. c.733-c.746). A photograph of this structure, which is still in religious use, is reproduced in Fig. 57. The temple is constructed of large blocks of stone which are closely joined together without mortar. It was dedicated to Śiva, and its numerous sculptures contain many representations of this god in various forms, as well as scenes from the Ramayana and other subjects.[171]

The Kailasanatha temple at Elura[172] is one of the most magnificent architectural monuments in all India. It was doubtless the work of the Rashtrakuta ruler Krishna I (A.D. c.757-c.783), among whose achievements is said to have been the construction of a wonderful Śiva temple in "the hill Elapura." The identification of the actual temple at Elura with the one thus mentioned is further supported by the name Kannara or Krishna which was still legible in the last century in an inscription on the temple. The Elura temple appears to have been modeled after the Virupaksha at Pattadakal, but is considerably larger than the work of Vikramaditya's queen. What is most remarkable, moreover, is that the Kailasanatha at Elura was carved directly out of the solid rock as a complete monolithic shrine. A rectangular pit was quarried in the sloping hillside, 50 to 100 feet deep, 160 feet wide and 280 feet long, and the mass of rock in the middle of this excavation was sculptured into the temple itself.

The Kailasanatha displays the main architectural features which are characteristic of the Hindu temple. In Fig. 58 one sees in the foreground the massive gateway which serves as the *gopura* or entrance to the whole temple complex. Behind this and connected with

[170] CHIIA pp.93f., Fig. 186.

[171] James Fergusson, *History of Indian and Eastern Architecture.* rev. ed. by James Burgess and R. Phené Spiers. 1910, I, pp.352-355; CHIIA Fig. 188.

[172] Fergusson, *History of Indian and Eastern Architecture*, I, pp.342-348; E. B. Havell, *The Ancient and Medieval Architecture of India: A Study of Indo-Aryan Civilization.* 1915, pp.193-200.

it by a rock bridge is the two-storied porch or shrine of Nandi, the sacred bull of Śiva, for whom a place is always made in connection with a Śiva temple. On either side of the Nandi shrine are two square pillars (*dhwajastambhas*, literally banner staves), nearly fifty feet high, bearing the three-pronged emblem of Śiva. A further bridge leads on back to the main part of the temple. Here there is another *gopura*, and then a large square porch or *mandapam*, the terraced roof of which is supported by sixteen heavy columns. Behind this is the central shrine, which in a Hindu temple is called the *vimana* or "the vehicle of the gods." The *vimana* is usually a square or rectangular building with a pyramidal roof which may have one or several stories. Here at Elura the upper pyramid of the *vimana* rises to a height of ninety-six feet. The tower or its upper part is also known as a *śikhara*,[173] and is thought of as standing for Mount Meru, the dwelling place of gods and spirits, or in the case of a Śiva shrine like the Kailasanatha, as representing Mount Kailasa, which was the topmost peak of Meru and the retreat of Śiva.

Mount Kailasa also appears in the bold sculptures which adorn the temple at Elura. In a composition found on the south side of the temple and shown in Fig. 59, Śiva and Parvati are on Kailasa.[174] The demon king Ravana has been imprisoned within the mountain, because of his impious attempt to remove it to Ceylon, and now is attempting with all the strength of his twenty arms to break his way free. The very mountain quakes, and Parvati seizes Śiva's arm in fear, while her maid flees away. With undisturbed calm, however, Śiva holds everything in control beneath his foot.

Another impressive Śiva shrine which likewise dates from the seventh or eighth century is at Elephanta. Elephanta is a rocky island which overlooks the harbor at Bombay, and which was so named by the Portuguese because of a large stone elephant which once stood near the shore. The temple with which we are here concerned is a completely subterranean excavation, located in the island's western hill some two hundred and fifty feet above the high-water level. The main entrance is from the north, and there are also pillared porticoes on the east and west. The interior of the temple is an underground

---

[173] Strictly speaking, in the south it is only the dome of the tower which is called the *śikhara*, while in the north the name is applied to the entire tower. On the origin of the *śikhara* see E. B. Havell in *Commemorative Essays Presented to Sir Ramkrishna Gopal Bhandarkar*. 1917, pp.443-446.
[174] Codrington, *Ancient India from the Earliest Times to the Guptas with Notes on the Architecture and Sculpture of the Medieval Period*, Pl. 55.

hall, over ninety feet square, the roof of which is upheld by six rows of pillars finished with very fine ribbed cushion capitals. Fig. 60 shows the central aisle which leads straight from the northern portico to the rocky wall at the south.

Against the southern wall stands a colossal bust of the three-headed Śiva, one of the most imposing works of Indian art (Fig. 61). The entire carving, including the base, shoulders and triune head, is about twenty feet in height. According to the Vishnudharmottara, a manual of perhaps the seventh century on the subject of the technical details of religious art,[175] there are five faces of Śiva, each of which may be likened to one of the elements of the universe. The first is Iśana, which is compared to the invisible and omnipresent ether. This face is ordinarily not carved. The second is Tatpurusha, likened to the wind; the third, Aghora, symbolized by fire; the fourth, Vamadeva, regarded as like to water; and the fifth, Sadyojata, referred for comparison to the earth. In the Elephanta sculpture, the middle face is identified as that of Tatpurusha; the face on the spectator's left as that of Aghora, the wrathful; and the one on the right as that of Vamadeva, the blissful. The hand on the left belonging to the wrathful face has a serpent's head rising from between its fingers; the hand on the right belonging to the blissful face holds a lotus flower. All together the image represents the fully manifest Supreme Śiva.[176]

Concerning such rock and cave temples as the ones at Elura and Elephanta and others, William Rothenstein has written: "Of the individual carvers of the great rock temples we know nothing; yet the range and audacity of their achievements are astonishing. If ever there was meaning in the old idea that images lay hidden in blocks of stone, awaiting only the blows of the craftsman's mallet to be set free, then these cave carvings show the truest form of sculpture. Not from single blocks of stone or marble, but from solid hill-sides whole temples were carved. In most civilizations figures have been applied to the buildings. In India the entire fabric, with its halls and courts, its roofs and supporting shafts, its sculptured figures and enrichments, has been conceived and created from the womb of the earth itself. Building and sculpture are as the body and its organs, so

[175] III, xlviii, 1-3. tr. Stella Kramrisch, *The Vishnudharmottara (Part III), A Treatise on Indian Painting and Image-Making.* 2d ed. 1928, p.71. cf. J. V. S. Wilkinson in Richard Winstedt, ed., *Indian Art.* 1948, p.113; Stella Kramrisch in *Ancient India.* 2 (July 1946). pp.4-8, Pl. III.
[176] Stella Kramrisch in *Ancient India.* 2 (July 1946), pp.4-8.

closely united that to tear away parts would leave an open wound."[177]

This brief survey of some representative Hindu temples of the Early Medieval Period may be concluded with mention of one shrine which comes from the ancient Pallava kingdom. This is the Kailasanatha temple at Kanchi,[178] pictured in Fig. 62. It was constructed by the Pallava king Rajasimha (Narasimhavarman II), who ruled in the last quarter of the seventh century A.D. The temple is a shrine of Śiva, and is ornamented with numerous sculptures which are largely devoted to representations of Śiva and Parvati.[179]

ŚANKARA

It was in the Early Medieval Period and probably around A.D. 800 that there lived one of the greatest philosophers of Hinduism. This was Śankara, who "is regarded often as representing the standard type of Hindu thought."[180] Śankara traveled and taught throughout India from Assam to Kashmir, and from the Himalayas to Cape Comorin, and established religious centers in the four corners of the land. His purpose was the revival, explanation and inculcation of the fundamental teachings of the Upanishads. To this end he wrote numerous treatises, among which the most important are his extensive commentaries on the Upanishads and on the Vedanta-Sutras. The commentary on the Vedanta-Sutras[181] is regarded as his masterpiece both in philosophical value and in literary character. The system of the Vedanta, or "final aim of the Veda," as set forth by Śankara, is an unqualified monism. Whatever is, says Śankara, is in reality one. There is only one universal being, and that is Brahman, whose very substance is intelligence or thought. Any conceivable attribute must be denied to belong to Brahman, and the appearance

[177] Rothenstein in Codrington, *Ancient India from the Earliest Times to the Guptas with Notes on the Architecture and Sculpture of the Medieval Period*, p.5. Quoted by permission of the publishers, Ernest Benn, Ltd., London.

[178] The ancient Kanchipuram (the golden city) is the modern town of Conjeeveram.

[179] Fergusson, *History of Indian and Eastern Architecture*, I, pp.357-359; CHIIA Fig. 197.

[180] S. Radhakrishnan, *The Hindu View of Life*. 1927, p.62; cf. Paul Deussen, *Allgemeine Geschichte der Philosophie mit besonderer Berücksichtigung der Religionen*, I, 3, *Die nachvedische Philosophie der Inder*. 1908, pp.579-614; Theos Bernard, *Hindu Philosophy*. 1947, pp.7-9.

[181] tr. George Thibaut, *The Vedânta-Sûtras with the Commentary by Śankarâkârya*. SBE XXXIV, XXXVIII; Paul Deussen, *The System of the Vedanta According to Bâdarâyana's Brahma-Sûtras and Çankaras Commentary Thereon Set Forth as a Compendium of the Dogmatics of Brahmanism from the Standpoint of Çankara*. tr. Charles Johnston, 1912.

of the world itself is due to *maya* or illusion. The enlightened soul, however, is able to look through the veil of illusion and recognize itself to be Brahman. In that recognition the self gains deliverance from the influence of *maya*, and is able in the end to assert itself in its true nature as nothing other than the absolute, eternal Brahman. Such is "the summit of Indian thought"[182] as reached in Śankara.

[182] J. N. Farquhar, *The Crown of Hinduism*. 1915, pp.243f.

9. THE LATE MEDIEVAL PERIOD, A.D. c.850-c.1200

IN THE centuries immediately preceding the Muslim invasions, India was divided into many different kingdoms of which only a few can be mentioned here. In the northern part of the land there were numerous clans of Rajputs. These "Sons of Kings" were probably descended in part from peoples who had come into India from central Asia like the White Huns and the Gurjaras[183] who followed them. The legend they cherished of their origin, however, was that when Rama-with-the-ax destroyed all the Kshatriyas and left the land masterless, the gods went to Mount Abu[184] in southern Rajputana and from the sacred fire pit there produced four "fire-born clans."[185] These four clans were the Solankis, Pawars, Chauhans, and Pariharas.

The Solankis or later Chaulukyas held sway in Gujarat, with their capital at Anhilwar (Anahilavada). Their most powerful ruler was Siddharaja (A.D. 1094-1143), who was a famous builder and a patron of the Jains. The Pawars or Paramaras ruled in Malwa from the ninth to the eleventh century. Their greatest king was Bhoja, whose capital was at Dhara, and who reigned around A.D. 1010 to 1065. In addition to his exploits on the field of battle, Bhoja was celebrated as a writer and a builder, and his name has become proverbial as the ideal Hindu monarch. The Chauhans were dominant in Ajmir, and their best-known king was Prithiviraja, of whom romantic stories are told in the popular literature of Rajputana. The Pariharas or Pratiharas ruled an extensive region around Kanauj, where their capital had been established by a king known as Bhoja I or Mihira (A.D. c.840-c.890). They were superseded at the end of the eleventh century by the Gaharwars or Gahadavalas.

Other Rajput clans included the Tomaras who founded Delhi; the Palas who ruled in Bengal, until they were succeeded by the Senas about the middle of the eleventh century; and the Chandels who held sway in Jejakabhukti, the modern Bundelkhand.[186] The Chandels probably originated from the indigenous tribe of Gonds. The most famous member of their dynasty was Dhanga who reigned from

---

[183] Their name survives in the name of the modern district of Gujarat. Likewise the name Rajputana is derived from the Rajputs.

[184] A powerful Gurjara Kingdom had come into existence at Bhinmal about fifty miles from Mount Abu, and this was the historic center of the Rajput tribes.

[185] Rawlinson, *India, A Short Cultural History*, p.200.

[186] This name is derived from the Bundelas, a clan which appeared here in the fourteenth century.

A.D. 950 to 999, and who like the other Chandel kings was a great builder.

In other parts of India there were yet other kingdoms. On the southeast coast in relatively isolated Orissa, independent rulers had maintained themselves much of the time. In the eleventh century we hear of a Somavansi dynasty, and in the twelfth century princes of the Eastern Ganga dynasty ruled there. In Mysore the dominant power was now that of the Hoyśala dynasty, whose capital was at Dorasamudra, and whose kings were originally Jains but later became Vaishnavas. Yet farther south was the area ruled by the Cholas, from whose kingdom (Cholamandalam) the Coromandel Coast derives its name. This kingdom existed as early as the time of Aśoka but rose to its highest importance under the great king Rajaraja who reigned from A.D. 985 to 1012. The Chola capital was at Tanjore.

MEDIEVAL TEMPLES

The notable development of temple architecture and sculpture which was already far advanced in the Early Medieval Period now reached its climax.[187] A vast technical literature, known as the Śilpa-Śastras, provided authoritative specifications according to which the proportions and details of statues and buildings were regulated. The medieval Śilpa-Śastras, it may be added, are still in use by Indian craftsmen.[188]

In the Śilpa-Śastras three main types of temples are differentiated. The three types are designated Nagara, Vesara and Dravida, and are found respectively in northern, central and southern India.

The southern type prevails in the Madras Presidency, and is characterized by the terraced pyramidal tower, such as we have already observed in the Kailasanatha temple at Elura. For another example we may refer to the great Rajarajeśvara temple at Tanjore (Fig. 63) which was constructed by the Chola king Rajaraja by about A.D. 1012. Old Tamil inscriptions on the base of the central shrine still enumerate the gifts of gold images, vessels and ornaments which were made to the temple by Rajaraja and also by his sister and others. As may be seen in the photograph, the most impressive feature of the temple is the enormous square pyramid of the *vimana*. The tower rises in fourteen stories to its summit dome which reaches a

[187] Stella Kramrisch, *The Hindu Temple.* 2 vols. 1946.
[188] Goetz, *Epochen der indischen Kultur*, pp.232,389f.; CHIIA p.125; EB XII, p.221.

height of one hundred and ninety feet. The temple is dedicated to the worship of Śiva.[189]

The central Indian type is found in Mysore and the Deccan. The characteristic feature of this type is that it combines elements from the southern and northern styles, and adds peculiarities of its own. The temples tend to be rather widely spread out and relatively low in elevation. They are often built on a star-shaped plan. The pyramidal towers do not have the distinctive stories of the southern temples, and they carry upward the indentations which mark the shrine below. The sculptured decoration is often very elaborate. The fullest development of this style was reached in Mysore under the Hoyśala kings, and may be illustrated by the Hoyśaleśvara temple at Halebid. The village of Halebid marks the site of Dorasamudra, the capital of the Hoyśala kings, and the temple under consideration was probably begun early in the twelfth century A.D. and finally left unfinished in A.D. 1311 due to the Muslim invasions. The Hoyśaleśvara is a double temple and contains two shrines placed side by side. It was undoubtedly intended to raise two indented pyramidal towers over these two sanctuaries, but this is a part of the work that was never completed, and the structure stands today as shown in Fig. 64. If it could have been carried out fully the architectural design would have been most impressive, and the sculptured decorations which adorn the entire building as it stands are of an almost incredible variety and beauty. A succession of friezes runs around the temple exterior, following all of its indentations. These friezes show beasts and birds, horsemen, scenes from the Ramayana, gods and heavenly beings. Among the animal friezes, that of the elephants may be specially mentioned. It is the first frieze above the temple terrace and extends in length for some seven hundred and ten feet. It contains not less than two thousand sculptured representations of elephants, many with riders and trappings, and all shown in an exceedingly lifelike and striking way. Among the gods every great figure of the Hindu pantheon appears, including Brahma, Śiva with Parvati, and Vishnu in the forms of his various avatars.[190]

For another example of exceedingly rich sculptural ornamentation in a central Indian temple of the Medieval Period, reference may be

[189] Fergusson, *History of Indian and Eastern Architecture*, I, pp.362-364; CHIIA p.122, Fig. 235; G. Jouveau-Dubreuil, *Dravidian Architecture*, ed. S. Krishnaswami Aiyangar. 1917.
[190] Fergusson, *History of Indian and Eastern Architecture*, I, pp.444-446; CHIIA p.118, Fig. 211.

made to the main temple at Palampet, a small village in the Warangal district in the Deccan.[191] This structure is built on a cruciform plan. Its exterior is adorned with long panels of carved figures, including gods, goddesses, warriors, acrobats, musicians and dancing girls. The interior likewise is filled with sculptures, which depict scenes from early myths, the Ramayana, the Puranas, and later Hindu texts. One of the four central columns of the main hall in this temple, with its very intricate ornamentation, is shown in Fig. 65.[192]

The northern type of Indian temple is represented by very numerous examples found in the Punjab, Rajputana, the Ganges Valley, the central provinces, and Orissa. The outstanding feature of this style is its lofty and aspiring vertical development. Here the entire temple is called the *śikhara*, and is distinguished by its curvilinear form. The *śikhara* is usually surmounted by an *amalaka*, a circular, corrugated coping stone carrying a flat dome in the center of which is a vaselike pinnacle.

Some of the finest northern Indian temples of the Medieval Period are at Khajuraho, which was the ancient capital of the Chandel kings, in Bundelkhand. There are some thirty important temples here, most of which are dated from their style and from inscriptions in the century between A.D. 950 and 1050. About one-third belong to the religion of Jainism, one-third to Vaishnavism and one-third to Śaivism, and all are very similar architecturally. In each group there is one large temple, sometimes more than one, with smaller ones in its vicinity. The chief temple in the Śaiva group, and the most imposing of all the Hindu structures, is the Kandarya Mahadeva which is pictured in Fig. 66. The pinnacle of the tower rises to an elevation of one hundred and sixteen feet above the ground, and the effect of height is greatly accentuated by the vertical lines in the structure and by the way the tower is built up of duplications of itself. Except for the tower all parts of the structure are covered with elaborate sculptures, featuring both floral themes and figures, and giving prominence to the erotic element. On and in the temple no less than eight hundred and seventy-two separate statues have been counted.[193]

Likewise of exceeding magnificence are the northern-style temples in Orissa. The greatest of these is the Lingaraja (Fig. 67) which was built at Bhuvaneśvara around A.D. 1000, and which has been

---

[191] Ghulam Yazdani, *The Temples at Palampet* (MASI, 6). 1922.
[192] *ibid.*, pl. XXXI,a.
[193] Fergusson, *History of Indian and Eastern Architecture*, II, pp.141-143; CHIIA p.109, Fig. 214.

called "perhaps the most majestic Indian temple now standing."[194] Here the *śikhara* is massive and solemn, yet lofty and impressive. Almost infinite labor has also been bestowed upon the carvings with which the entire structure is decorated. Other notable Orissan temples of the next century or so include the one at Puri, dedicated to Vishnu as Jagannatha or "Lord of the World," and popularly known as Juggernaut; and the one at Konarak, known as the Sun Temple or Black Pagoda, and evidently once devoted to the worship of Vishnu in the form of Surya or the sun.

As the foregoing descriptions have shown, much of Indian sculpture was an integral part of temple buildings. There were also detached works of art, however, and for illustration we show in Fig. 69 a stone statue of Brahma which came from Kuruvatti in the Bellary district, Madras, and is now in the University Museum of the University of Pennsylvania. The entire carving is about five and one-half feet in height. Brahma is portrayed with four faces, and the face at the back is bearded. The inscription at the bottom records the name of the maker of the statue. The date of the work is probably in the eleventh century.

The bronze image shown in Fig. 68 also comes from south India, and is perhaps to be dated in the twelfth century. It is a relatively early and completely intact example, over forty inches in height, of an important type of representation. The figure is known as Nataraja, the Lord of the Dance, and the subject portrayed is the cosmic dance of Śiva. Śiva is here considered not only as the destroyer but also as the sustainer, and indeed as the supreme lord of the universe. He stands within the flaming circle of the cosmos, and performs the five-fold dance of life. The details of the symbolism may be interpreted as follows. One hand holds a drum which marks the rhythm of creation; another hand is uplifted to reassure against fear and signify preservation; yet another hand carries a ball of fire which stands for destruction; the stationary leg gives the idea of repose; the uplifted one symbolizes the divine activity leading to the liberation of all beings. The seven streams of water extending from each side of the head recall the myth that Śiva once kept the heavenly Ganges imprisoned in his hair before finally releasing it in seven streams, one of which is the great river of India. Among the streams is a small figure of the river goddess Ganga.[195]

[194] CHIIA p.115, Fig. 215.
[195] F. St.G. Spendlove in *Gazette des beaux-arts*. 6th Series. 25 (1944), pp.59f.; cf. Ananda Coomaraswamy, *The Dance of Śiva*. 1924, pp.56-66; Heinrich Zimmer,

RAMANUJA

The greatest Hindu philosopher of the Medieval Period was Ramanuja, who is probably to be dated around A.D. 1100. He lived in his
youth at Kanchi or Conjeeveram, and later settled at Srirangam near
Trichinopoly. He taught and wrote extensively, and like Śankara composed a commentary on the Vedanta-Sutras.[196] Ramanuja agreed with
Śankara that Brahman is the total reality, but unlike Śankara he
taught that Brahman has positive qualities of love and grace, and
that individual souls and the external world exist within the body
of God. Through personal devotion (*bhakti*) the soul gains an in-
tuitive perception of God, and upon release from earthly bondage
passes into the enjoyment of personal bliss in the eternity of Brahman.

"We know from Scripture," says Ramanuja, "that there is a Supreme Person whose nature is absolute bliss and goodness; who is
fundamentally antagonistic to all evil; who is the cause of the origi-
nation, sustentation, and dissolution of the world; who differs in
nature from all other beings, who is all-knowing, who by his mere
thought and will accomplishes all his purposes; who is an ocean of
kindness as it were for all who depend on him; who is all-merciful;
who is immeasurably raised above all possibility of any one being
equal or superior to him; whose name is the highest Brahman. And
with equal certainty we know from Scripture that this Supreme
Lord, when pleased by the faithful worship of his devotees—which
worship consists in daily repeated meditation on him, assisted by the
performance of all the practices prescribed for each caste and *ashra-
ma*—frees them from the influence of nescience which consists of
karma accumulated in the infinite progress of time and hence hard
to overcome; allows them to attain to that supreme bliss which consists in the direct intuition of his own nature: and after that does
not turn them back into the miseries of *samsara*."[197]

In the early and advanced Medieval Periods, then, Hinduism
reached a definitive stage in its development. The implications of
its fundamental philosophy were fully expounded on the monistic
and theistic sides by Śankara and Ramanuja. The expression of its

---

Myths and Symbols in Indian Art and Civilization. ed. by Joseph Campbell. Bollingen
Series, 6. 1946, pp.151-175.

[196] George Thibaut, *The Vedânta-Sûtras with the Commentary of Râmânuga.* SBE
XLVIII; A. Berriedale Keith in HERE X, pp.572-574.

[197] SBE XLVIII, p.770.

character in art and architecture culminated in such magnificent works as the Kailasanatha at Elura and the Kandarya Mahadeva at Khajuraho. Such achievements of thought and craftsmanship crowned thirty-five hundred years of Indian civilization.

THE MUSLIM INVASIONS

Then came the Muslim invasions, which were begun by the Arabs and continued by the Turks. The greatest threat originated at Ghazni in Afghanistan. There a Turk named Sabuktigin (A.D. 976-997), established a powerful Muslim kingdom, and his son Mahmud (A.D. c.999-1030) raided India repeatedly and in 1022 annexed the Punjab. In his most famous expedition Mahmud went all the way to Somnath on the coast of Gujarat and sacked the temple which was there dedicated to Śiva as the Lord of the Moon.

AL-BIRUNI

Two famous men of letters were active at Ghazni in Mahmud's time, Abul Kasim Mansur or Firdausi (A.D. c.940-c.1020), author of the epic history of Persia, the Shah Namah or Book of Kings; and Abu Rihan Muhammad, called al-Biruni, "the foreigner" (A.D. c.973-c.1048), who wrote an extensive work on India.[198] Al-Biruni had studied in India, and he gives much information about the country and people in this age in which the Muslim conquests were just beginning. Concerning Mahmud's aggression in India he writes with a freedom presumably only possible after the death of that king: "Mahmud utterly ruined the prosperity of the country, and performed there wonderful exploits, by which the Hindus became like atoms of dust scattered in all directions, and like a tale of old in the mouth of the people."[199]

Al-Biruni tells little or nothing of Buddhism or Jainism, but a great deal of Hinduism, with which he seems to have been most familiar in the form of Vaishnavism. His description bears the marks of a reasonably critical and impartial mind, and is reinforced by numerous quotations from Hindu writings. Concerning the faith of the educated people he writes, "The Hindus believe with regard to God that he is one, eternal, without beginning and end, acting by free-will, almighty, all-wise, living, giving life, ruling, preserving; one who in

[198] Edward C. Sachau, *Alberuni's India, An Account of the Religion, Philosophy, Literature, Geography, Chronology, Astronomy, Customs, Laws and Astrology of India about* A.D. *1030.* 2 vols. 1888.
[199] I, 11. Sachau, I, p.22.

his sovereignty is unique, beyond all likeness and unlikeness, and that he does not resemble anything nor does anything resemble him."[200]

A great deal of stress is laid upon transmigration or metempsychosis, which al-Biruni regards as the characteristic and distinctive doctrine of Hinduism. "As *the word of confession,* 'There is no god but God, Muhammad is his prophet,' is the shibboleth of Islam, the Trinity that of Christianity, and the institute of the Sabbath that of Judaism, so metempsychosis is the shibboleth of the Hindu religion." Continuing with a description of this belief, al-Biruni says, "The migration begins from low stages, and rises to higher and better ones. . . . The difference of these lower and higher stages depends upon the difference of the actions. . . . This migration lasts until the object aimed at has been completely attained both for the soul and matter; the *lower* aim being the disappearance of the shape of matter, except any such new formation as may appear desirable; the *higher* aim being the ceasing of the desire of the soul to learn what it did not know before, the insight of the soul into the nobility of its own being and its independent existence, its knowing that it can dispense with matter after it has become acquainted with the mean nature of matter and the instability of its shapes, with all that which matter offers to the senses, and with the truth of the tales about its delights. Then the soul turns away from matter; the connecting links are broken, the union is dissolved. Separation and dissolution take place, and the soul returns to its home. . . . The intelligent being, intelligence and its object, are united and become one."[201]

The Muslim author further reports on the caste system which he found to be very prominent. The castes, he says, are called *varna* or "colors," and are four in number: the Brahmans, Kshatriyas, Vaisyas, and Sudras, who were created respectively from the head, from the shoulders and hands, from the thighs, and from the feet of the supreme Brahman. Below the four castes are eight guilds of fullers, shoemakers, jugglers, basket and shield makers, sailors, fishermen, hunters of wild animals and birds, and weavers. Below these are classes of people like the Candalas who belong neither to a caste nor to a guild, and who are occupied with unclean work like the cleansing of the villages. From his own emancipated point of view, al-Biruni says concerning the institution of caste, "We Muslims, of course, stand entirely on the other side of the question, considering

[200] II, 13. Sachau, I, p.27.   [201] V, 24f. Sachau, I, pp.50f.

all men as equal, except in piety; and this is the greatest obstacle which prevents any approach or understanding between Hindus and Muslims."[202]

Al-Biruni also gives descriptions of various Hindu idols, of which one was of bronze and nearly the size of a man, and another of wood, covered with red leather, and with two red rubies for eyes.[203] Pilgrimages were frequent to various sites and particularly to rivers for bathing festivals. According to the author, such pilgrimages were not obligatory but were meritorious. "A man sets off to wander to some holy region, to some much venerated idol or to some of the holy rivers. He worships in them, worships the idol, makes presents to it, recites many hymns and prayers, fasts, and gives alms to the Brahmans, the priests, and others. He shaves the hair of his head and beard, and returns home."[204] Among the places of pilgrimage Benares had become one of the most sacred, as it still is today.[205]

In the time of Mahmud, the Muslim impact upon India was largely in the form of plundering raids, but a later ruler of Ghazni, Muhammad Ghori, seriously undertook the conquest of the land. He extended Muslim sway almost to Delhi, and established his slave Qutb-ud-din Aibak as governor of his Indian dominions. Aibak continued the Muslim conquests, and after the death of Muhammad Ghori in A.D. 1206 became the first Muslim sultan of Delhi and the founder of the dynasty of Slave Kings at that place.

From this time on, for centuries, Islam was the dominant religious force in India. Buddhism had already declined and now was virtually obliterated; Hinduism was greatly weakened and its material possessions much devastated. Hinduism did not perish, however, and eventually its remarkable vitality reasserted itself. A renascence took place, and in modern India the age-old belief in Śiva and Vishnu, in *samsara* and *karma*, lives on.

[202] IX, 48f. Sachau, I, pp.100f.
[203] XI, 56. Sachau, I, pp.116f.
[204] LXVI, 273. Sachau, II, p.142.
[205] E. B. Havell, *Benares, The Sacred City.* 1905.

CHAPTER IV

Jainism

JAINISM was founded by certain great ascetics, of whom the last, Mahavira, was the perhaps slightly elder contemporary of Gautama Buddha. Mahavira himself is believed to have been but the final one of a long line of twenty-four teachers which reaches back into the most remote past. These founders of the faith are known as Jinas or Conquerors, and their adherents are Jains or Jainas. The number of believers in this religion in India today is over one million.

1. THE JAINA SCRIPTURES

ACCORDING to Jaina belief, the great truths of their faith were set forth by all the Jinas of the past and were embodied in definite scriptural works in each successive age.[1] The teachings of the last founder of the religion, Mahavira, were transmitted to posterity by his followers, the Ganadharas, in the form of works known as Puvvas and Angas. These and other compositions constituted the canon, which was faithfully preserved at first but later fell into confusion. In order to restore it, a council was held at Pataliputra shortly before 300 B.C. under Sthulabhadra, a disciple of Bhadrabahu, the head of the church who was then away in another region. Despite the council's best efforts and the sending of Sthulabhadra to consult with Bhadrabahu, it was found impossible at this time to reconstitute the canon completely. Bhadrabahu could indeed recite all of the texts but he forbade the communication of the last four Puvvas to the congregation. In later years the remaining ten of the original fourteen Puvvas were also lost to knowledge, but the other sacred works were preserved and were again revised and edited in the fifth century A.D. at a council held at Valabhi under the presidency of Devarddhi. It is also indicated in Jaina traditions that the sacred texts were for the first time committed to written form at the Council of Valabhi. Since, however, perishable materials such as birch bark and palm leaves were commonly used for Indian manuscripts our oldest extant copies

[1] GJ pp.81-104.

[182]

date only from around the fourteenth century and later. The language of the oldest works is Prakrit, a later form of Sanskrit.

It must also be explained that from the time of the Council of Pataliputra on, a schism deepened within Jainism between two sects known as the Śvetambaras and the Digambaras, and that while the former cherish the canon whose origin we have just described, the latter hold that not only the Puvvas but also the Angas and all the original texts have been lost and that the scriptures of the Śvetambaras are therefore not genuine. They, the Digambaras, consequently adhere to a secondary and relatively modern (A.D. c.600-c.900) canon of works on history, cosmography, philosophy and ethics.

CANONICAL WORKS

Returning to the scriptures of the Śvetambaras we find that they are collectively known as the Siddhanta and that they comprise the following divisions:[2] The first group contains the fourteen Puvvas (Purvas) which, as we have already explained, are no longer extant. They are frequently mentioned in other works, however, and thus we are able to give the following list of their titles and brief indication of some of their subject matter: (1) Uppaya. Origin of substances. (2) Agganiya. Basic truths. (3) Viriyappavaya. Powers of substances. (4) Atthinatthippavaya. Nature of substances from seven logical standpoints. (5) Nanappavaya. True and false perception. (6) Saccappavaya. True and false speech. (7) Ayappavaya. Characteristics of souls. (8) Kammappavaya. Nature of Karma. (9) Paccakkhanappavaya. Renunciation as the means to the eradication of Karma. (10) Vijjanuppavaya. Various sciences. (11) Avamjha. High points in the lives of 63 great men. (12) Panavaya. Medicine. (13) Kiriyavisala. Music, poetry and other arts. (14) Logavindusara. Ceremonies and salvation.

The twelve Angas make up the second division of the canon. Their titles and subject matter are as follows: (1) Ayara (Acaranga).[3] Manner of life of the ascetic. (2) Suyagada (Sutrakritanga).[4] Instructions for monks and refutation of heretical teachings. (3) Thana. Jaina concepts arranged by categories. (4) Samavaya. Continua-

[2] Walther Schubring, *Die Lehre der Jainas nach den alten Quellen dargestellt* (Grundriss der indo-arischen Philologie und Altertumskunde. Encyclopedia of Indo-Aryan Research. III, 7). 1935, pp.52-84; A. Guérinot, *Essai de bibliographie Jaina, Répertoire analytique et méthodique des travaux relatifs au Jainisme avec planches hors texte* (Annales du Musée Guimet, Bibliothèque d'Études, 22). 1906, pp.129-145.
[3] tr. Hermann Jacobi in SBE XXII.
[4] tr. Hermann Jacobi in SBE XLV.

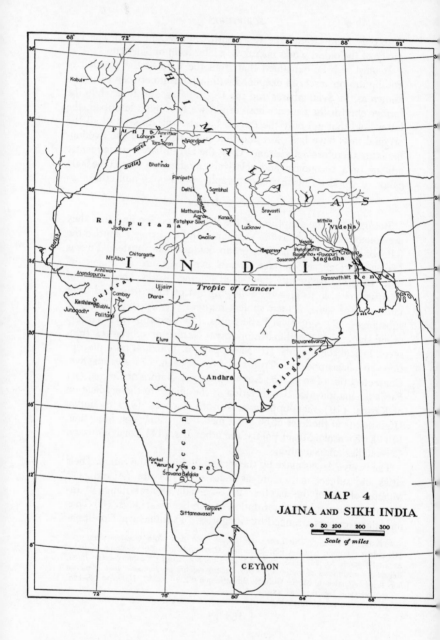

MAP 4

JAINA AND SIKH INDIA

0 50 100 200 300

Scale of miles

tion of the preceding work. (5) Viyahapannatti (Bhagavati). Jaina teachings in dialogues and legends. (6) Nayadhammakahao (Jnatadharmakatha). Narratives and parables. (7) Uvasagadasao. Legends concerning pious laymen who became adherents of Jainism. (8) Antagadadasao.[5] Narratives of ten ascetics who overcame their Karma. (9) Anuttarovavaiyadasao.[6] Legends of saints who attained to the highest heavens. (10) Panhavagaranaim. Commandments and prohibitions. (11) Vivagasuya. Legends concerning the recompense for good and evil deeds. (12) Ditthivaya. This Anga is no longer extant, but once contained five groups of texts among which were the fourteen Puvvas described in the preceding paragraph.

The third division of the canon is that of the twelve Uvangas (Upangas). (1) Uvavaiya. The preaching of Mahavira to King Kunika (Ajataśatru) at Champa. (2) Rayapasenaijja. The conversion of King Paesi by Keshi, a disciple of Pasa (Parśva). (3) Jivabhigama. The world and the beings that are in it. (4) Pannavana. Characteristics of living beings. (5) Surapannatti. Concerning the sun and moon. (6) Jambuddivapannatti. Jambuddiva, the central continent of the universe, on which India and this world are. (7) Candapannatti. Similar to Surapannatti. (8) Nirayavaliyao. War of Kunika and ten stepbrothers against King Cetaka of Vesali. (9) Kappavadimsiyao. Conversion and salvation of sons of the princes mentioned in the preceding work. (10) Pupphiyao. Pre-existences of certain deities who did reverence to Mahavira. (11) Pupphaculao. Similar to the preceding work. (12) Vanhidasao. Conversion of certain princes by Aritthanemi (Arishtanemi).

Ten Painnas (Prakirnas) constitute the fourth section of the canon: (1) Causarana. Prayers. (2) Aurapaccakkhana. Rites in preparation for death. (3) Bhattaparinna. Similar to the foregoing text. (4) Samthara. Also about matters connected with death. (5) Tandulaveyaliya. Embryology and anatomy. (6) Candavejjhaya. Concerning teachers and pupils. (7) Devindatthaya. Enumeration of god-kings. (8) Ganivijja. Astrology. (9) Mahapaccakkhana. Formulas of confession. (10) Viratthaya. Praise of Mahavira and enumeration of his names.

In the fifth group of scriptural texts we find six Cheyasuttas (Chedasutras): (1) Nisiha. Duties of monks and penalties for transgressions. (2) Mahanisiha. Moral transgressions, confession and penance.

---

[5] tr. L. D. Barnett, *The Antagaḍa-Dasāo and Anuttarovavāiya-Dasāo, Translated from the Prakrit* (Oriental Translation Fund, New Series, xvii). 1907.
[6] *ibid.*

(3) Vavahara. Instructions for monks and nuns. (4) Ayaradasao. Various teachings concerning the monastic life. The eighth section of this work is the Kalpasutra,[7] which contains biographies of Mahavira and the earlier Jinas. (5) Brihatkappa. Instructions for monks and nuns. (6) Pancakappa. Similar to the preceding.

The sixth section of the canon is composed of only two works: (1) Nandi. Modes of perception. (2) Anuogadara. An encyclopedia of the most varied sciences.

The seventh section comprises four Mulasuttas (Mulasutras): (1) Uttarajjhaya (Uttaradhyayana).[8] Legends, parables, dialogues and sermons. (2) Avassaya. Daily duties. (3) Dasaveyaliya. Rules for the ascetic life. (4) Pindanijjutti. The food of monks.

NONCANONICAL WORKS

In addition to the canonical works of which the chief have now been listed, the Jains also have an extensive noncanonical literature which includes theological and scientific compositions, stories, poetry and drama.[9] Several authors and works in the theological category may be mentioned here.

Umasvati (Umasvami) was the first great dogmatic writer. He lived sometime between the second and fifth centuries A.D., and wrote a work entitled Tattvarthadhigama-Sutra.[10] In this for the first time the entire system of Jaina belief was reduced to a series of condensed statements. His book is accorded the highest authority by both the Śvetambaras and the Digambaras.

Among the Śvetambaras the outstanding theological writers included Divakara (seventh century A.D.), Haribhadra (eighth century A.D.), and Hemachandra (A.D. 1088-1172). The last named was the most important of all, and his works included grammars and commentaries, an exposition of asceticism called Yogaśastra, a long epic poem entitled Trishashtiśalakapurushacaritra[11] in which the

---

[7] tr. Hermann Jacobi in SBE XXII; J. Stevenson, The Kalpa Sútra and Nava Tatva: Two Works Illustrative of the Jain Religion and Philosophy, Translated from the Mágadhi with an Appendix Containing Remarks on the Language of the Original. 1848.

[8] tr. Hermann Jacobi in SBE XLV.

[9] GJ pp.105-134.

[10] tr. J. L. Jaini, Tattvarthadhigama Sutra (A Treatise on the Essential Principles of Jainism), by Sri Umasvami Acharya, Edited with Introduction, Translation, Notes and Commentary in English (The Sacred Books of the Jainas, II). 1920.

[11] tr. Banarsi Das Jain, Jaina Jātakas or Lord Rshabha's Púrvabhavas, Being an English Translation of Book I Canto I of Hemacandra's Trishashtiśalakāpurushacaritra Originally Translated by Prof. Amūlyacharan Vidyābhushana Revised and Edited

previous births of the Jinas and other great figures of the faith to the number of sixty-three are recounted, and a work named Pariśishtaparva in which a sort of history of the Jaina church is given.

Among the Digambaras, notable theological authors included Kundakunda, who lived sometime before A.D. 600 and possibly as early as the beginning of the Christian era, and wrote Panchastikayasara,[12] Samayasara,[13] Niyamsara[14] and other works; and Nemichandra, who flourished around A.D. 1000 and wrote Davva-Samgaha,[15] Gommatsara with two parts, Jivakanda[16] and Karmakanda,[17] and other compositions.

---

with Notes and Introduction (The Punjab Sanskrit Series, VIII). 1925; Helen M. Johnson, *Triṣaṣṭiśalākāpuruṣacaritra* (Gaekwad's Oriental Series, 51, 77). 2 vols. 1931-37.

[12] tr. A. Chakravartinayanar, *The Building of the Cosmos or Panchastikayasara (The Five Cosmic Constituents) by Svami Sri Kundakundacharya,* Edited with Philosophical and Historical Introduction, Translation, Notes and an Original Commentary in English (The Sacred Books of the Jainas, III). 1920.

[13] tr. J. L. Jaini, *Samayasara (The Soul-Essence) by Shri Kunda Kunda Acharya,* The Original Text in Prakrit, with Its Sanskrit Renderings, and a Translation, Exhaustive Commentaries, and an Introduction (The Sacred Books of the Jainas, VIII). 1930.

[14] tr. Uggar Sain, *Niyamsara (The Perfect Law) by Shri Kunda Kunda Āchārya,* The Original Text in Prakrit, with Its Sanskrit Renderings, Translation, Exhaustive Commentaries, and an Introduction, in English (The Sacred Books of the Jainas, IX). 1931.

[15] tr. Sarat Chandra Ghoshal, *Davva-Saṃgaha (Dravya-Saṃgraha) by Nemichandra Siddhānta-Chakravarti,* with a Commentary by Brahma-Deva, Edited with Introduction, Translation, Notes and an Original Commentary in English (The Sacred Books of the Jainas, I). 1917.

[16] tr. J. L. Jaini, *Gommatsara Jiva-Kanda (The Soul) by Shri Nemichandra Siddhanta Chakravarti,* Edited with Introduction, Translation and Commentary (The Sacred Books of the Jainas, V). 1927.

[17] tr. J. L. Jaini, *Gommatsara Karma-Kanda (Part I) by Shri Nemichandra Siddhanta Chakravarti,* Edited with Introduction, Translation and Commentary (The Sacred Books of the Jainas, VI). 1927.

2. THE FOUNDERS OF JAINISM

THE TIRTHANKARAS

Among the great figures of Jainism the most important are the twenty-four Tirthankaras, the title Tirthankara probably meaning one who is a guide over the ocean of Samsara.

In the introduction to the Trishashtiśalakapurushacaritra, Hemachandra addresses words of praise and prayer to the twenty-four as follows:[18]

We praise the Lord Rishabha, who was the first king, the first ascetic, the first head of a congregation.

I praise the Arhat Ajita, the sun to the lotus-bed in the form of the universe, in the clear mirror of whose omniscience the world is reflected.

May the words of the Lord of the World, Holy Sambhava, prevail at the time of his preaching—words that resemble rivers in the garden of all the souls who can attain emancipation.

May the Blessed Abhinandana, the moon for the exhilaration of the ocean of Anekanta-doctrine[19] give great joy.

May the Blessed Lord Sumati, whose toe-nails are sharpened on the whetstone of the gods' diadems,[20] grant your desires.

May the splendor of the Lord Padmaprabha's body, red as if from a burst of anger in crushing internal enemies, promote your emancipation.

Homage to the Lord of Jinas, Holy Suparśva, whose feet are honored by Mahendra (Śakra),[21] the sun to the sky in the form of the fourfold congregation.[22]

May Lord Chandraprabha's form, bright as a mass of moonbeams, as if made of embodied pure meditation, be for your prosperity.

May Suvidhi, who considers the universe as plain as a myrobalan lying in the hand by means of his wealth of omniscience, the depository of inconceivable power, be for your enlightenment.

May the Jina Śitala, a new cloud for making shoot up the bulb of the people's supreme joy, who pours forth the nectar of Syadvada, protect you.

May Śreyamsa, the sight of whom is a physician for creatures afflicted with the disease of existence, the lover of the Śri[23] of emancipation, be for your emancipation.

[18] tr. Johnson, *Triṣaṣṭiśalākāpuruṣacaritra*, I, pp.1-7; cf. Banarsi Das Jain, *Jaina Jatakas*, pp.1-5.

[19] The Anekanta doctrine is the "many-sided doctrine" or Syadvada, a distinctive feature of Jaina logic, which considers everything from seven points of view and implies that a true assertion is true only under certain conditions of time and space.

[20] The gods bow their heads so low before this great being that the jewels on their crowns come in contact with his feet.

[21] The Indra of the first heaven, the most important of the sixty-four Indras of the Jaina pantheon.

[22] The Jaina Sangha or congregation is made up of monks, nuns, laymen and laywomen.

[23] The Sanskrit *śri* means fortunate, holy or reverend, and is commonly employed when speaking of a person, king or deity with special respect. Hemachandra uses

May Vasupujya, whose acquisition of Tirthankara-nama-karma[24] has been beneficial to the whole universe, entitled to worship from gods, asuras and men, purify you.

May the words of the Lord Vimala which are like powdered clearing-nut,[25] be successful in clarifying the water of the mind of the three worlds.

May Ananta, rivaling the Svayambhuramana ocean[26] with water of the feeling of compassion, bestow on you the boundless wealth of happiness.

We worship Dharmanatha, the teacher of fourfold dharma,[27] like a kalpa-tree for attainment of creatures' desires.

May the Jina Santinatha, who has brightened the quarters of the sky by the moonlight of his nectar-like words, be a moon to you for dispelling (mental) darkness.

May the Blessed Sri Kunthunatha, lord of the wealth of the supernatural powers, supreme lord of the lords of gods, asuras and men, be for your emancipation.

May the Blessed Aranatha, the sun in the sky of the fourth division of time, grant us pleasure with the Sri of the fourth object of existence.

We praise Malli, a new cloud for the peacocks[28] in the form of lords of gods, asuras and men, Hastimalla [Indra's elephant] for the rooting up of the tree of karma.

We praise Munisuvrata's preaching, which resembles the dawn for the sleep of the world's great delusion.

May the rays of light from Nami's toe-nails which, falling on the heads of his worshipers, purify them like streams of water, protect you.

May the Blessed Arishtanemi, the moon to the ocean of the Yadu-family, a fire to the straw of karma, destroy your misfortunes.

May the Lord Parsvanatha, whose attitude of mind was the same toward Kamatha and Dharanendra[29] while each was performing actions characteristic of himself, be for your emancipation.

May there be good fortune from Holy Vira's eyes whose pupils are wide with compassion even for sinful people, moist with a trace of tears.

This and other Jaina sources provide much information about the various Tirthankaras and enable the construction of a table like the following in which are shown not only the color and emblem customarily associated with each but also his height and age and the

---

the word frequently in such a way that, as here, it might be translated "goddess," without reference, however, to Lakshmi who is known by this name in Hinduism.

[24] Tirthankara-nama-karma ensures that one will at last become a Tirthankara.

[25] This powder is said to remove all impurities from water in which it is dissolved.

[26] The last and largest circular ocean on this earth.

[27] Of dharma, usually translated "law" or "religion," Hemachandra later says: "Dharma bestows heaven and emancipation. Dharma shows the road for crossing the wilderness of samsara. Dharma nourishes like a mother, protects like a father, pleases like a friend, and is loving like a kinsman. . . . It is fourfold with the divisions of liberality, good conduct, penance, and state of mind." tr. Johnson, pp.18f.

[28] With reference to the proverbial love of peacocks for clouds.

[29] The demon Kamatha was the enemy of Parsvanatha, and the god Dharanendra his friend.

interval to the next Tirthankara.[30] While there is some variation among sects as to details this will provide the general picture of Jaina belief in this regard.

NAME	COLOR	EMBLEM	HEIGHT	AGE	INTERVAL TO NEXT TIRTHANKARA
1. Rishabha	Golden	Bull	500 dhanushas	84 lakhs of purvas	50 lakhs of krores of sagaras
2. Ajita	Golden	Elephant	450 "	72 lakhs of purvas	30 lakhs of krores of sagaras
3. Sambhava	Golden	Horse	400 "	60 lakhs of purvas	10 lakhs of krores of sagaras
4. Abhinandana	Golden	Ape	350 "	50 lakhs of purvas	9 lakhs of krores of sagaras
5. Sumati	Golden	Heron	300 "	40 lakhs of purvas	90,000 krores of sagaras
6. Padmaprabha	Red	Red Lotus	250 "	30 lakhs of purvas	9,000 krores of sagaras
7. Suparśva	Golden	Swastika	200 "	20 lakhs of purvas	900 krores of sagaras
8. Chandraprabha	White	Moon	150 "	10 lakhs of purvas	90 krores of sagaras
9. Suvidhi (or Pushpadanta)	White	Dolphin	100 "	2 lakhs of purvas	9 krores of sagaras
10. Śitala	Golden	Śrivatsa	90 "	1 lakh of purvas	9,999,900 sagaras
11. Śreyamsa	Golden	Rhinoceros	80 "	84 lakhs of years	54 sagaras
12. Vasupujya	Red	Buffalo	70 "	72 lakhs of years	30 sagaras
13. Vimala	Golden	Boar	60 "	60 lakhs of years	9 sagaras
14. Ananta	Golden	Falcon	50 "	30 lakhs of years	4 sagaras
15. Dharma	Golden	Thunderbolt	45 "	10 lakhs of years	3 sagaras less 3/4 palya
16. Śanti	Golden	Antelope	40 "	1 lakh of years	½ palya
17. Kunthu	Golden	Goat	35 "	95,000 years	¼ palya less 6,000 krores of years
18. Ara	Golden	Nandyavarta	30 "	84,000 years	1,000 krores less 6,584,000 years
19. Malli	Blue	Jar	25 "	55,000 years	54 lakhs of years
20. Munisuvrata (or Suvrata)	Black	Tortoise	20 "	30,000 years	9 lakhs of years
21. Nami	Golden	Blue Lotus	15 "	10,000 years	5 lakhs of years
22. Arishtanemi (or Nemi)	Black	Conch Shell	10 "	1,000 years	84,000 years
23. Parśva	Blue	Hooded Snake	9 hastas	100 years	250 years
24. Mahavira	Golden	Lion	7 "	72 years	

[30] Johnson, *Triṣaṣṭiśalākāpuruṣacaritra*, I, pp.347-349; Jagmanderlal Jaini, *Outlines of Jainism* (Jain Literature Society). 1916, table facing p.6; Hermann Jacobi in HERE VII, p.466.

The above table is self-explanatory except for the appearance of certain technical terms and statistical units. The Śrivatsa, the emblem of the tenth Tirthankara, is a curl of hair on the breast, well known as a mark of Vishnu too. The Nandyavarta, the symbol of the eighteenth Tirthankara, is a mark resembling a swastika.[31] As used by the Jains, the units of number and measure, including also a few appearing elsewhere in the present chapter, are as follows. In some cases different authorities give different values.

NUMBERS

1 lakh (Sanskrit, laksha) = 100,000[32]
1 krore (Sanskrit, koti) = 100 lakhs = 10,000,000[33]
1 kotikoti = 10,000,000 x 10,000,000 = 100,000,000,000,000[34]

MEASURES OF LENGTH AND DISTANCE

1 hasta = 18 inches[35]
1 dhanus = 4 hastas = 72 inches = 6 feet[36]
1 krośa = 8,000 hastas = 12,000 feet = 2¼ miles [37]
1 yojana = 4 krośas = 9 miles [38]
1 rajju = the distance a god can go in 6 months when he goes 100,000 yojanas in the winking of an eye[39]

MEASURES OF TIME

1 purva = 8,400,000² years[40]
1 palya (or, palyopama) = the length of time required to empty a receptacle one yojana (9 miles) wide and deep, which is filled with new lamb's hairs grown within seven days, when one hair is taken out every hundred years.[41]
1 sagara (or, sagaropama), "ocean of years" = 10 krores of palyas = 100,000,000 palyas[42]

Applying these units to the table of Tirthankaras, we find, for example, that Rishabha was three thousand feet in height, and that the interval between his Nirvana and that of Ajita was 50 x 100,000 x 10,000,000 "oceans of years" (sagaras), or 50 x 100,000 x 10,000,-000 x 100,000,000 palyas.

---

[31] CJ pp.383f.
[32] Monier Monier-Williams, *A Sanskrit-English Dictionary Etymologically and Philologically Arranged with Special Reference to Cognate Indo-European Languages.* New ed. 1899, p.891.
[33] *ibid.*, p.312.
[34] cf. Champat Rai Jain, *Riṣabha Deva, the Founder of Jainism.* 1929, p.50.
[35] Monier-Williams, *A Sanskrit-English Dictionary*, p.1294.
[36] *ibid.*, p.509.　　　[37] *ibid.*, p.322.　　　[38] *ibid.*, p.858.
[39] Johnson, *Triṣaṣṭiśalākāpuruṣacaritra*, I, p.103 n.140.
[40] *ibid.*, I, p.84 n.125.　　　[41] *ibid.*, I, p.29 n.50.　　　[42] *ibid.*, I, p.71 n.97.

The most striking fact in the entire table is that, whereas enormous magnitudes of size and time are involved throughout most of the chart, there is a progressive diminution in the measurements until at the bottom of the table the figures come almost or entirely within the realm of actual earthly possibilities. Specifically, the last two Tirthankaras appear as persons of exaggerated but not utterly fantastic size, of thoroughly reasonable age-lengths of 100 and 72 years respectively, and with a relatively brief interval between them of only 250 years. The conclusion is suggested, therefore, that while the earlier Tirthankaras are purely mythological beings, Parśva and Mahavira were actual historical persons and the real founders of the religion.[43]

PARŚVA

The life of Parśva (or Parśvanatha) is narrated in the Kalpasutra, a work which contains a date nine hundred and eighty years after the death of Mahavira and is said to have been read publicly before a certain King Dhruvasena of Anandapura[44] to comfort him upon the death of his son.[45] While it is characteristic of the Jaina literature to portray all of the Tirthankaras according to one stereotyped pattern, and while the account of Parśva's life no doubt contains much that is legendary, nevertheless the kind of experience that is ascribed to him fits naturally into the background of Indian life as known from the time of the Upanishads on, and the record may not be entirely devoid of historical value.[46]

According to the Kalpasutra[47] Parśva was born in Benares as the son of King Aśvasena and Queen Vama. A commentary says that the name Parśva was bestowed upon him because before his birth Queen Vama saw a black serpent crawling about; and in the text he is given the appellation Purisadaniya, which means "the people's favorite" or "who is to be chosen among men because of his preferable Karma."

After living for thirty years as a householder, Parśva left the world behind to practice asceticism and seek salvation. He attained the en-

---

[43] Within Jainism itself, of course, the belief is held that even the first Tirthankara, Rishabha, was an actual man who lived "very very far back in the remoteness of hoary antiquity," who attained immortality, and who through his teachings founded the true religion. Champat Rai Jain, *Riṣabha Deva, The Founder of Jainism*, p.i.

[44] Anandapura was about a hundred and twenty miles northwest of Valabhi according to Hiuen Tsang (xi, 8f. tr. Beal, *Buddhist Records of the Western World*, ii, p.268; cf. Cunningham, *The Ancient Geography of India*, i, pp.493f.).

[45] SBE XXII, p.270.   [46] GJ p.19.   [47] SBE XXII, pp.271-275.

lightenment he sought after eighty-three days, and then spent the remainder of his life preaching his doctrine to others. At last, having abstained from food and water for an entire month, he died at the age of a hundred upon the summit of Mount Sammeta, now known in his memory as Parasnath Mountain.

The work of Parśva was very successful according to the Kalpa-sutra, which records that he won 164,000 men and 327,000 women as lay adherents, and 16,000 men and 38,000 women as monks and nuns. His Ganadharas or chief disciples were eight in number, Śubha (or Śubhadatta), Aryaghosha, Vasishta, Brahmacari, Saumya, Śrid-hara, Virabhadra and Yaśas. Of these Śubha became the leader of the church after the death of the master, and was followed in turn by Haridatta, Aryasamudra, Prabha and Keśi.[48]

MAHAVIRA

Concerning the life of Mahavira we have an extended and legend-embellished account not only in the Kalpasutra[49] but also in the Acarangasutra.[50] In these sources we learn that Mahavira was a na-tive of Kundagrama, which was a suburb of Vesali and is probably represented by the modern village of Basukund.[51] He was going to be born of a Brahman mother, Devananda, a highly legendary por-tion of the narrative relates, but through the intervention of the god Śakra (Indra) an embryonic transfer was accomplished and he was born of a Kshatriya mother named Triśala. The latter was the wife of a certain Kshatriya named Siddhartha, and was herself the sister of the Licchavi king Chetaka of Vesali, whose daughter Chellana later married King Bimbisara and became the mother of King Ajataśatru. Prior to her son's birth Triśala learned, it is said, through fourteen dreams that she was to be the mother of a great saint. In these dreams she saw a white elephant, a white bull, a white lion, the goddess Śri, a garland of flowers, the white moon, the red sun, a banner, a vase, a lotus lake, a milk ocean, a celestial abode, a heap of jewels and a blazing ghee-fed fire.

At the birth of the son, it is declared, "there was a divine luster originated by many descending and ascending gods and goddesses, and in the universe, resplendent with one light, the conflux of gods occasioned great confusion and noise."[52] In Kundagrama, the parents and the townsfolk joined in extended celebrations of the auspicious event.

[48] GJ pp.22f.   [49] SBE XXII, pp.217-270.   [50] ibid., pp.189-202.
[51] Jarl Charpentier in CHI I, p.157.   [52] SBE XXII, p.251.

The personal name bestowed upon the son was Vardhamana, which is explained as follows: "In the night in which the Venerable Ascetic Mahavira was brought into the family of the Jnatris their silver increased, their gold increased, . . . the intensity of their popularity and liberality highly increased. At that time the following personal, reflectional, desirable idea occurred to parents of the Venerable Ascetic Mahavira: 'From the moment that this our boy has been begotten, our silver increased, our gold increased, . . . the intensity of our liberality and popularity highly increased. Therefore when this our boy will be born, we shall give him the fit name, attributive and conformable to his quality—Vardhamana (the Increasing One).' "[53]

It may also be noted in the foregoing passage that the family bore the name of Jnatri (Prakrit, Naya or Nata), and on this account the masculine members were designated as Jnatriputras or Nataputtas. Thus is explained the name Nataputta by which Mahavira is often called.

For thirty years Vardhamana lived the life of a householder, and then his parents died. We are told that the parents "were worshipers of Parśva and followers of the Śramanas (or Samanas; 'ascetics')," and that at the end of their lives they fasted to the death as Parśva himself had done.[54] Upon the death of his parents Vardhamana resolved to renounce the world, and first disposed of his treasures as gifts to the poor. Then "he, after fasting two and a half days without drinking water, put on a divine robe, and quite alone, nobody else being present, he tore out his hair and leaving the house entered the state of houselessness."[55]

There is reason to believe that at first Vardhamana remained in the vicinity of his home as a member of the ascetic order founded by Parśva and with which his parents seem to have been in contact.[56] Evidently finding their rules insufficiently strict, he departed from them for an utterly possessionless wandering. The Kalpasutra records: "The Venerable Ascetic Mahavira for a year and a month wore clothes; after that time he walked about naked, and accepted the alms in the hollow of his hand."[57]

For more than twelve years he sought thus for perfect salvation. A brief description of his manner of life says: "The Venerable One lived, except in the rainy season, all the eight months of summer

[53] SBE XXII, pp.248f.   [54] SBE XXII, p.194.   [55] *ibid.*, p.259.
[56] GJ p.24.   [57] SBE XXII, pp.259f.

and winter, in villages only a single night, in towns only five nights; he was indifferent alike to . . . straw and jewels, dirt and gold, pleasure and pain, attached neither to this world nor to that beyond, desiring neither life nor death, arrived at the other shore of the Samsara, and he exerted himself for the suppression of the defilement of Karma."[58] Extreme in his asceticism, he slept and ate but little, suffered attacks from animals and men without defending himself, bore pain in silence, and even if wounded never desired medical treatment.[59]

In the thirteenth year thus devoted to utterly self-forgetful meditation Vardhamana at last attained perfect understanding. "Outside of the town Jrimbhikagrama,[60] on the northern bank of the river Rijupalika, in the field of the householder Samaga, in a northeastern direction from an old temple, not far from a sal tree, in a squatting position with joined heels exposing himself to the heat of the sun, with the knees high and the head low, in deep meditation, he reached Nirvana, the complete and full, the unobstructed, unimpeded, infinite and supreme, best knowledge and intuition, called Kevala ('total'). When the Venerable One had become an Arhat and Jina, he was a Kevalin ('possessed of Kevala'), omniscient and comprehending all objects, he knew all conditions of the world, of gods, men, and demons; whence they come, where they go, whether they are born as men or animals . . . ; he saw and knew all conditions in the whole world of all living beings."[61]

Henceforth properly called Mahavira or Great Hero, the victorious ascetic lived for almost thirty years longer and preached his message widely. As before, he wandered from place to place during two-thirds of the year and only in the four months of the rainy season remained in some single city. A precise catalogue is given in the Kalpasutra of the cities in which his rainy seasons were spent throughout all forty-two years of his life as an ascetic: "Mahavira stayed the first rainy season in Asthikagrama, three rainy seasons in Champa and Prishtichampa, twelve in Vesali and Vanijagrama, fourteen in Rajagriha and the suburb of Nalanda, six in Mithila, two in Bhadrika, one in Alabhika, one in Panitabhumi, one in Sravasti, one in the town of Papa in King Hastipala's office of the writers: that was his very last rainy season."[62] Many of these places are well

[58] ibid., p.262.   [59] ibid., pp.79-87.
[60] Perhaps in the vicinity of Parasnath Mountain. Mrs. Sinclair Stevenson, *The Heart of Jainism* (The Religious Quest of India). 1915, p.38.
[61] SBE XXII, pp.201f.   [62] SBE XXII, p.264.

known, such as Champa the capital of Anga, Vesali Mahavira's own native metropolis, Rajagriha the capital of Magadha, Mithila in the kingdom of Videha, and Sravasti, celebrated in the annals of Buddhism.

Mahavira enjoyed family relationship to several of the leading rulers of his time as we have seen, and both Bimbisara (or Srenika) who ruled at Rajagriha around 540-490 B.C. and Ajatasatru (or Kunika) who succeeded his father on the same throne about 490-460 B.C. are said to have regarded his teachings with favor. The actual conversion of King Srenika by a young disciple of Mahavira is recounted in Lecture xx of the Uttaradhyayana,[63] but since that king is also claimed as a patron of Buddhism in the traditions of that religion we may suppose that he manifested a broad interest in the doctrines of various teachers rather than committing himself to any single sect.

As intimated in the quotation from the Kalpasutra given just above, death came to Mahavira in the town of Papa (or Pava). This was a place not far from Rajagriha, and is today a small village called Papapuri or Pavapuri in the region of the modern city of Bihar.[64] In the words of the Kalpasutra which follow immediately after the quotation just given: "In the fourth month of that rainy season, . . . in the town of Papa, in King Hastipala's office of the writers, the Venerable Ascetic Mahavira died, went off, quitted the world, cut asunder the ties of birth, old age, and death; became a Siddha, a Buddha, a Mukta, a maker of the end [to all misery], finally liberated, freed from all pains."

The success of Mahavira's work is indicated by the statement of the Kalpasutra that he gathered "an excellent community of 14,000 Sramanas with Indrabhuti at their head; 36,000 nuns with Chandana at their head; 159,000 lay votaries with Sankhasataka at their head; 318,000 female lay votaries with Sulasa and Revati at their head."[65] The four groups here designated, namely monks, nuns, laymen and laywomen, constitute the four orders or Tirtha of Jainism. Associated with Gautama Indrabhuti (as his full name was) in the leadership of the monks were ten other Ganadharas or chief disciples, Agnibhuti, Vayubhuti, Akampita, Arya Vyakta, Arya Sudharma, Manditaputra, Mauryaputra, Acalabhrata, Metarya and Prabhasa. All of the disciples who had wholly severed their connections with the

[63] SBE XLV, pp.100-107.
[64] Chimanlal J. Shah, *Jainism in North India 800 B.C.-A.D. 526.* 1932, p.27 n.5.
[65] SBE XXII, pp.267f.

world, that is both the monks and the nuns, were known as Nir-granthas (Niganthas) meaning "without any ties," a designation which had perhaps already been borne by Parśva's followers.[66]

THE DATES OF MAHAVIRA AND PARŚVA

The death of Mahavira, or in the language of religious faith his Nirvana, is the basic point in Jaina chronology. According to the tradition of the Śvetambaras this took place four hundred and seventy years before the beginning of the Vikrama Era (58/57 B.C.); and according to the Digambaras it was six hundred and five years before the beginning of the Śaka Era (A.D. 78).[67] By either mode of calcula-tion the date was therefore 527 B.C. Since at death the Tirthankara had attained the age of seventy-two, his birth must have been around 599 B.C. To date the life of Mahavira around 599-527 B.C. is to make him a slightly elder contemporary of Gautama Buddha who probably lived about 567-487 B.C. This is substantiated by Bud-dhist sources, in which there are many references to Nataputta and the Niganthas, meaning Mahavira and the Jains; although in the Jaina canonical books there seem to be no corresponding notices of Gautama and the Buddhists. Three passages in the Buddhist canon refer specifically to the death of Nataputta the Nigantha at Pava at a time when the Buddha was still engaged in his work of teach-ing.[68] "Once while the lord was staying among the Sakyans at Sama-gama," it is written, "Nataputta the Nigantha had died recently at Pava."

It is true that Hemachandra states that the death of Mahavira took place one hundred fifty-five years before the accession to the throne of Chandragupta, an event which transpired in about 322 B.C. This would lead to a date around 549-477 for Mahavira and would place his death slightly later than that of the Buddha. This is supported by some scholars who criticize the Buddhist notices referred to just above as unreliable.[69]

At all events, the two great teachers, Mahavira and Gautama Bud-

[66] CJ pp.22,32.

[67] Schubring, *Die Lehre der Jainas nach den alten Quellen dargestellt*, p.30.

[68] Samagama Sutta. Majjhima Nikaya III, i, 104 (II, 243). tr. Chalmers, *Further Dialogues of the Buddha*, II, p.139; Pasadika Suttanta and Sangiti Suttanta. Digha Nikāya XXIX (III, 117); XXXIII (III, 209f.). tr. Rhys Davids, *Dialogues of the Buddha*, III, pp.111,203. For bibliographical details on the Buddhist sources see the chapter on Buddhism.

[69] Hermann Jacobi in *Sitzungsberichte der preussischen Akademie der Wissen-schaften*. 1930, phil.-hist. Kl., XXVI, pp.557-561.

dha, were substantially contemporaries. In the Buddhist sources the followers of the two teachers are for the most part represented as in controversy with each other, and, as is not surprising in texts emanating from only the one group, the Buddhists are always pictured as victorious. For an example we may cite the Upali Sutta in the Majjhima Nikaya.[70] In this Sutta a prosperous householder named Upali, who is an adherent of Mahavira, enters into a conversation with Gautama Buddha, intending to refute him on a point of philosophical doctrine. Instead of succeeding, Upali finds himself not only overcome in argument but also, to his surprise, deeply impressed with both the wisdom and the magnanimity of Buddha. He forthwith announces himself to be a follower of Gautama, and closes his house to the Niganthas although at Buddha's behest he still distributes alms to them at a distance. Mahavira cannot believe the report which comes to him of the defection of his erstwhile disciple, and goes to visit Upali. The latter treats him with haughty condescension, and utters a lengthy eulogy of the Buddha. "Then and there," the Sutta concludes, "from the mouth of Nataputta the Nigantha, who could not bear to hear the lord extolled—there gushed hot blood."

While we are dealing with Buddhist notices of the Jains we may add a report on their teachings which is found in the Devadaha Sutta of the Majjhima Nikaya.[71] Gautama is supposed to be speaking: "Hereupon those Niganthas told me that Nataputta the Nigantha was all-knowing and all-seeing, with nothing beyond his ken and vision, and that he affirmed of himself that, whether walking or standing, sleeping or awake, he was always, without a break, at his spiritual best. These, they added, were his words: You have done misdeeds, Niganthas, in past existences; wear it out by severe austerities; every present restraint on body, speech and mind will undo the evil-doings of the past; hence, by expiation and purge of past misdeeds and by not doing fresh misdeeds, nothing accrues for the future; as nothing accrues for the future, misdeeds die away; as misdeeds die away, Ill dies away; as Ill dies away, feelings die away, and as painful feelings die away, all Ill will wear out and pass away. This doctrine, they added, commends itself to us and

[70] II, i, 56 (I, 371-387). tr. Chalmers, *Further Dialogues of the Buddha*, I, pp.267-278.

[71] III, i, 101 (II, 217f.). tr. Chalmers, *Further Dialogues of the Buddha*, II, p.125; cf. Culadukkhakkhandha Sutta, Majjhima Nikaya I, ii, 14 (I, 92f.). tr. Chalmers, *ibid.*, I, p.67.

has our approval, and we rejoice in it." Needless to say, in this Sutta the Buddha proceeds immediately to the refutation of the Jaina philosophy.

Having seen, then, that Mahavira and Gautama Buddha were indisputably contemporaries, and that the most probable dates for Mahavira are 599-527 B.C., we may turn to the question of the date of Parśva. There is no doubt that Parśva preceded Mahavira, since the parents of the latter were already worshipers of Parśva. Also the most reasonable explanation of the nature of Mahavira's work is that he was not the inventor of a new doctrine but the reformer of a movement already long in existence and derived from Parśva. Four vows had been enjoined on his followers by Parśva, namely: (1) not to destroy life (*ahimsa*); (2) not to speak untruth; (3) not to steal; and (4) not to own property. To these Mahavira added as a fifth the vow of chastity. This was indeed thought of as already implied in the fourth vow of Parśva, but on this point laxity had developed within the order and Mahavira deemed it necessary to make the rule explicit as a fifth regulation, additional to the four of his predecessor.[72] Furthermore, it seems that Parśva had allowed his followers to wear an under and an upper garment, but that Mahavira went to the extreme position of forbidding his monks to wear any clothing whatsoever.

There is a very interesting section (Lecture XXIII) in the Uttaradhyayana[73] in which these and other points of difference between the disciples of Parśva and those of Mahavira are set forth, and in which it is related that through an amicable discussion between Keśi, leader of the followers of Parśva, and Gautama, foremost disciple of Mahavira, the two groups were united in acceptance of the reformations of Mahavira. The following quotations will give the essence of the account:

There was a Jina, Parśva by name, an Arhat, worshiped by the people, who was thoroughly enlightened and omniscient, a prophet of the law and a Jina.

And there was a famous disciple of this light of the world, the young Śramana Keśi, who had completely mastered the sciences and right conduct.

He possessed the light of Śruta and Avadhi knowledge,[74] and was surrounded by a crowd of disciples; wandering from village to village he arrived in the town of Śravasti.

[72] A. F. R. Hoernle in HERE I, p.264.   [73] SBE XLV, pp.119-129.
[74] The second and third grades of knowledge according to the Jains.

In the district of that town there is a park, called Tinduka; there he took up his abode in a pure place to live and sleep in.

Now at that time there lived the prophet of the law, the Jina, who in the whole world is known as the venerable Vardhamana.

And there was a famous disciple of this light of the world, the venerable Gautama by name, who had completely mastered the sciences and right conduct.

He knew the twelve Angas, was enlightened, and was surrounded by a crowd of disciples; wandering from village to village he, too, arrived in Śravasti.

In the district of that town there is a park Koshtaka; there he took up his abode in a pure place to live and sleep in.

The young Śramana Keśi and the famous Gautama, both lived there. . . .

The pupils of both, who controlled themselves, who practiced austerities, who possessed virtues, and who protected their self, made the following reflection:

"Is our law the right one, or is the other law the right one? are our conduct and doctrines right, or the other?

"The law as taught by the great sage Parśva, which recognizes but four vows, or the law taught by Vardhamana, which enjoins five vows?

"The law which forbids clothes [for a monk], or that which [allows] an under and upper garment? Both pursuing the same end, what has caused their difference?"

Knowing the thoughts of their pupils, both Keśi and Gautama made up their minds to meet each other.

Gautama, knowing what is proper and what is due to the older section [of the church], went to the Tinduka park, accompanied by the crowd, his pupils.

When Keśi, the young monk, saw Gautama approach, he received him with all becoming attention. He at once offered Gautama the four pure kinds of straw and hay to sit upon.

Keśi, the young Śramana, and the famous Gautama, sitting together, shone forth with a luster like that of sun and moon.

There assembled many heretics out of curiosity, and many thousands of laymen; gods, . . . Gandharvas, Yakshas, . . . [assembled there], and there came together invisible ghosts too. . . .

[Here follows an extended conversation between Keśi and Gautama on the points at issue between the two groups, including not only the questions concerning vows and clothes but also various problems in the philosophy of religion. On each matter Gautama made such a convincing presentation that Keśi was fully persuaded, and the passage closes with these words describing the accord to which they came:]

Keśi, of enormous sanctity, bowed his head to the famous Gautama. And in the pleasant [Tinduka park] he sincerely adopted the law of the five vows, which was proclaimed by the first Tirthankara, according to the teaching of the last Tirthankara.

In that meeting of Keśi and Gautama, knowledge and virtuous conduct were for ever brought to eminence, and subjects of the greatest importance were settled.

The whole assembly was greatly pleased and fixed their thoughts on the right way. They praised Keśi and Gautama: "May the venerable ones show us favor!"

Parśva, then, was indubitably prior to Mahavira, and sufficient time had elapsed since his day that a decay in the morals of the monastic order had occurred which led to the reformation carried out by Mahavira. This situation is in satisfactory agreement with the more exact indication given in Jaina tradition that a period of two hundred and fifty years had separated the two Tirthankaras. This tradition is represented in the Kalpasutra[75] where it is stated that from the death of Parśva to the time of the writing of the Kalpasutra 1,230 years had elapsed, and from the death of Mahavira 980 years. Reckoning two hundred and fifty years before the death of Mahavira in 527 B.C. we reach 777 B.C. as the date of Parśva's death, and if the latter lived for one hundred years his inclusive dates were 877-777 B.C. Such an early date for the foundation of Jainism is consonant with the animistic character of its basic philosophy which will appear in the succeeding section.

[75] SBE XXII, pp.270,275.

3. THE TEACHINGS OF JAINISM

THE essential ideas of Jainism, which may be supposed to go back at least as far as to Parśva,[76] include a conception of the cosmos as divided into three parts, a higher world of the gods, a middle world of men, animals and plants, and a lower world of demons; and a belief that this entire universe is filled with an infinite number of eternal, indestructible individual souls. These souls, which are called Jivas from the Sanskrit root *jiv* meaning "to live," are in themselves purely spiritual and possess unlimited wisdom, power and goodness, but their true nature is at least partially obscured by the fact that at present most of them are enveloped in matter. In other words the souls are now incarnated in the bodies of gods, men, animals, plants and demons, and are even to be found in particles of earth, cold water, fire and wind.[77] The thoughts and deeds of each embodied soul, moreover, continue to draw into itself more invisible atoms of matter which become the Karma of that soul. The eradication of this Karma and the setting free of the soul from its involvement in base matter can only be accomplished by the most rigorous regulation of all thinking and doing. To this end Parśva instituted the four vows already mentioned, which in their positive connotations call for kindness, truth, honesty and poverty. By the practice of such a way of life and by constant meditation upon its own real character, the soul may at last rise to that realm of blessedness which is lifted up like an island above the surging waves of the ocean of Samsara.

Such was the philosophical animism of early Jainism which has ever since remained characteristic of that faith. When Mahavira entered into this heritage of thought he seems not so much to have made innovations as to have systematized, and when he accepted Parśva's four vows he simply made their import unmistakable by adding the explicit fifth vow of chastity.

In its fuller development Jaina thought retained these essential foundations and built upon them an extensive system of which certain main outlines may now be indicated.[78]

WORLD STRUCTURE

As to the structure of the universe, three worlds, lower, middle and higher, are conceived as rising one above the other, all enveloped

---

[76] GJ pp.20-22.　　　　　　　　　　[77] Jacobi in SBE XLV, p.xxxiii.
[78] Schubring, *Die Lehre der Jainas nach den alten Quellen dargestellt*, pp. 84-207.

in three atmospheres. Dimensions of this cosmos are given in rajjus, and it is said that the universe is fourteen rajjus high and at the base seven rajjus from north to south and seven rajjus from east to west. At the middle it tapers, however, to a width of only one rajju; above that it increases again and at half of its remaining height reaches a maximum breadth of five rajjus. The earth, which is in the middle world, is a very large circular body made up of a number of concentric rings called islands, separated from each other by ring-shaped oceans. At the center stands Mount Meru, at the foot of which is the island-continent, Jambuddiva, surrounded by the Lavanasamudra or Salt Sea. Jambuddiva itself is divided into several regions, and of these, that between the Indus and the Ganges is known as the land of Bharata. Beyond Jambuddiva and Lavanasamudra come the other continents and seas. Around Mount Meru revolve two suns, two moons and two sets of constellations.[79]

WORLD CHRONOLOGY

As to chronology, it is believed that in this world two ages follow one upon the other in constant succession. They are the "descending" age or Avasarpini, which begins with everything in the best possible condition and goes through successive periods of degeneration to the worst possible state of affairs. Then the "ascending" age or Utsarpini begins, in which conditions progressively improve again. The two ages, each with its six periods, are charted below. The quality of each period is shown by the word Sushama meaning good, or by the word Duhshama signifying bad, or by some combination of the words indicating something better or worse than the average represented by one of them alone. The duration of each period is given in units which have already been explained.

AVASARPINI

1. Sushama-sushama, "best" period, 4 kotikotis of sagaras
2. Sushama, "good" period, 3 kotikotis of sagaras
3. Sushama-duhshama, "good-bad" period, 2 kotikotis of sagaras
4. Duhshama-sushama, "bad-good" period, 1 kotikoti of sagaras less 42,000 years
5. Duhshama, "bad" period, 21,000 years
6. Duhshama-duhshama, "worst" period, 21,000 years

UTSARPINI

1. Duhshama-duhshama, "worst" period, 21,000 years

[79] Jaini, *Outlines of Jainism*, pp.119-125.

2. Duhshama, "bad" period, 21,000 years
3. Duhshama-sushama, "bad-good" period, 1 kotikoti of sagaras less 42,000 years
4. Sushama-duhshama, "good-bad" period, 2 kotikotis of sagaras
5. Sushama, "good" period, 3 kotikotis of sagaras
6. Sushama-sushama, "best" period, 4 kotikotis of sagaras[80]

The total duration of each age is ten kotikotis of sagaras. A descending and an ascending age taken together represent one complete revolution of the Kalacakra or Wheel of Time, the spokes of which are the periods of each age. The Wheel turns forever at constant speed, and thus Avasarpinis and Utsarpinis follow each other in ceaseless succession throughout eternity.

In the two periods Sushama-duhshama and Duhshama-sushama, sixty-three "great men" regularly appear, namely, 24 Tirthankaras, 12 Cakravartis (world-rulers) and 27 heroes (9 Baladevas, 9 Vasudevas and 9 Prativasudevas). It is these sixty-three who are the heroes of Hemachandra's Trishashtiśalakapurushacaritra already mentioned. One Tirthankara and one Cakravarti live in Sushama-duhshama, all the others have their existences in Duhshama-sushama, and this is so regardless of whether it is an "ascending" or "descending" age. It should also be added that various such series of "great men" appear in various portions of the world during the periods in question. Furthermore, in his life on earth each Tirthankara is accompanied by a special Yaksha and Yakshi (or Śasanadevata), and also is served by Sarasvati as a messenger goddess.

The present age of the world is Avasarpini, and it is during this age's periods of Sushama-duhshama and Duhshama-sushama that there appeared in the land of Bharata the twenty-four Tirthankaras whom we listed above and their accompanying world-rulers and heroes. Rishabha and the Cakravarti Bharata lived in Sushama-duhshama; the remaining Tirthankaras from Ajita to Mahavira, and their associates, lived in Duhshama-sushama. The Duhshama-sushama period came to an end three years and eight and one-half months after the Nirvana of Mahavira, and the world is now in the Duhshama or "bad" period of twenty-one thousand years, which will be followed by the Duhshama-duhshama or "worst" period of twenty-one thousand years. As things go thus from bad to worse, Jainism itself will disappear, but at last the time will come for the "ascending" age of Utsarpini to begin, and when the periods of

[80] Johnson, *Triṣaṣṭiśalākāpuruṣacaritra*, I, pp.93f.

Duhshama-sushama and Sushama-duhshama come, twenty-four new Tirthankaras will reestablish the true religion. The names of these future Tirthankaras will be: (1) Padmanabha; (2) Śuradeva; (3) Suparśva; (4) Svayamprabha; (5) Sarvanubhuti; (6) Devaśruti; (7) Udaya; (8) Pedhala; (9) Pottila; (10) Śatakirti; (11) Suvrata; (12) Amama; (13) Nishkashaya; (14) Nishpulaka; 15) Nirmama; (16) Citragupta; (17) Samadhi; (18) Samvara; (19) Yaśodhara; (20) Vijaya; (21) Malli; (22) Deva; (23) Anantavirya; (24) Bhadrakrit.[81]

WORLD RENUNCIATION

The teachings of the true religion lead to that mode of life through which the soul may disentangle itself from attachment to the material and ascend from the lowest reaches of the universe to the highest. This manner of life is regulated by the five vows already given and is followed in all its austerity by monks and nuns. Since, however, only a relatively small number of persons can be expected to practice extreme asceticism, lay members, both men and women, are also admitted to the Sangha or religious community. They are expected to keep the great commandments too, but only after such a fashion as is possible for those who still live in the world. Thus in the Purushartha Siddhyupaya, a treatise of high authority for all Jains, the fourth vow, not to own property, is reduced for the householder to this: "And if one is unable to wholly renounce cattle, corn, servants, buildings, wealth, etc., he also should at least limit them; because renunciation is the right principle."[82] Again the same work says: "Ratna-Traya, the Three Jewels (right belief, right knowledge, right conduct) should be followed, even partially, every moment of time without cessation by a householder desirous of everlasting liberation. . . . Even when Ratna-Traya is partially followed, whatever bondage of Karma there is, is due to its antithesis, because Ratna-Traya is assuredly the way to liberation, and can never be the cause of bondage."[83]

In yet another passage the Purushartha Siddhyupaya gives this admonition to the lay follower of the religion:

Having due regard to one's own status and capacity, a [householder] should practice the conduct of a saint, as described in the Scriptures.

[81] CJ pp.244-310.
[82] Ajit Prasada, *Purushartha-Siddhyupaya (Jaina-Pravachana-Rahasya-Kosha) by Shrimat Amrita Chandra Suri, Edited with an Introduction, Translation, and Original Commentaries in English* (The Sacred Books of the Jainas, IV). 1933, p.55, §128.
[83] *ibid.*, p.80, §209,211.

Equanimity, praising, bowing, repentance and renunciation, and giving up attachment for the body are the six [daily] duties, which should be observed.

One should carefully observe the three controls, proper control of body, proper control of speech, and proper control of mind. . . .

Forgiveness, humility, straightforwardness, truth, contentment, restraint, austerities, charity, non-attachment, and chastity are the [ten] observances to be followed. . . .

(1) Hunger, (2) thirst, (3) cold, (4) heat, (5) insect bite (6) nudity, (7) ennui, (8) women, (9) walking, (10) sitting, (11) resting, (12) abuse, (13) beating, (14) begging, (15) non-obtaining, (16) disease, (17) contact with thorny shrubs, etc., (18) dirt, (19) respect and disrespect, (20) conceit of knowledge, (21) lack of knowledge, (22) slack belief, are twenty-two sufferings. These should be ever endured without any feeling of vexation by one who desires to get rid of all cause for pain.[84]

WORLD CONQUEST

When, through the manner of life just indicated, the soul finally eradicates its karma and overcomes its worldly entanglements, it becomes a Siddha or Perfected One and is free to rise by its own nature to the highest realm of blessedness. This is a beautiful place called Ishatpragbhara, which is situated yet twelve yojanas above the highest heaven (Sarvarthasiddha)[85] of the gods. It is described as follows in Lecture XXXVI of the Uttaradhyayana:

Where do the perfected souls reside? Where do they leave their bodies, and where do they go, on reaching perfection?

Perfected souls . . . reside on the top of the world; they leave their bodies here [below], and go there, on reaching perfection.

Twelve yojanas above the Sarvartha is the place called Ishatpragbhara, which has the form of an umbrella; [there the perfected souls go].

It is forty-five hundred yojanas long, and as many broad, and it is somewhat more than three times as many in circumference.

Its thickness is eight yojanas, it is greatest in the middle, and decreases toward the margin, till it is thinner than the wing of a fly.

This place, by nature pure, consisting of white gold, resembles in form an open umbrella, as has been said by the best of Jinas.

[Above it] is a pure blessed place [called Sita], which is white like a conch-shell, the anka-stone, and Kunda-flowers; a yojana thence is the end of the world.

The perfected souls penetrate the sixth part of the uppermost krosa of the [above-mentioned] yojana.

There at the top of the world reside the blessed perfected souls, rid of all transmigration, and arrived at the excellent state of perfection. . . .

[84] *ibid.*, pp.78-80, §200-202,204,206-208.
[85] It was from the Sarvarthasiddha Vimana (or heaven) that Rishabha descended to earth (SBE XXII, p.281).

They have no [visible] form, they consist of life throughout, they are developed into knowledge and faith, and they possess paramount happiness which admits of no comparison.

They all dwell in one part of the world, and have developed into knowledge and faith, they have crossed the boundary of the Samsara, and reached the excellent state of perfection.[86]

THE NINE CATEGORIES

The extent to which the schematization and analysis of various items in the Jaina philosophy is carried is nothing less than amazing and may be indicated by a résumé of the nine categories in which the later Jaina writers organized the fundamental truths of the religion.[87]

The *first category* is Jiva or soul. All Jivas may be divided into two classes, (1) the perfected Siddhas that live in Ishatpragbhara, and (2) the unperfected jivas of samsara that live in the world. The Samsari, as the latter are called, may be divided into three groups, (1) male, (2) female and (3) neuter. According to the place where they were born, jivas may be classed in four divisions, namely those born (1) in hell, (2) in a subhuman state as in plants or animals, (3) as human beings, and (4) as spirits (*devata*), either gods or demons. A fivefold classification is possible depending upon the number of senses possessed by the jivas. (1) Ekendriya jivas possess only one sense, that of touch. Such jivas exist in stones, water, fire, wind and vegetables, which consequently are capable of pain and suffering. The length of time for which a jiva may be compelled by its karma to reside in things of this sort may extend anywhere from one moment to as much as twenty-two thousand years. According to the strictest interpretation of Jainism, the vow of Ahimsa or non-killing begins to be applicable with this very first class of jivas: therefore monks often refuse to touch a stone or fire; insist on boiling and straining water they use; make it a practice to breathe through a cloth; and avoid the eating of many vegetables—all in order to avoid injuring or destroying these jivas. (2) Beindriya jivas have two senses, touch and taste. Here are grouped animalcules, worms and creatures living in shells. The maximum term of such an existence is twelve years. For the Jaina layman the vow of non-killing is held to be in effect first with regard to this class. (3) Triindriya jivas have three senses, touch, taste and smell. Included in

[86] SBE XLV, pp.211-213.
[87] Stevenson, *The Heart of Jainism*, pp.94-172; Johnson, *Triṣaṣṭiśalākāpuruṣacaritra*, I, pp.437-450.

this group are ants, bugs and moths. The period of time for which a jiva may exist in such a form varies from one moment to forty-nine days. (4) Corendriya jivas possess four senses, touch, taste, smell and sight. Such creatures as wasps, scorpions, mosquitoes, gnats, flies, locusts and butterflies belong to this group. Six months is the maximum period for life in this division. (5) Pañcendriya jivas are those which enjoy five senses, namely the four hitherto enumerated plus hearing. Within this group there are four divisions: hell beings, lower animals, human beings and demigods. Remarkably enough, disease germs are classed as Pañcendriya and treated as human beings. A jiva may spend from ten thousand years to thirty-three sagaras as a hell being or demigod; from one instant to three palyas of time as a lower animal or human being (including as a disease germ).

Jivas, again, may be divided into six groups, including (1) earth, (2) water, (3) fire, (4) wind and (5) vegetable lives, with which we already have some acquaintance, and then also (6) Trasakaya. The class of Trasakaya includes all the jivas which have the power of mobility and which, when impelled by *trasa* or dread can endeavor to remove themselves from danger. A sevenfold classification of jivas divides them into (1) hell beings, which are neuter, (2) male lower animals, (3) female lower animals, (4) male human beings, (5) female human beings, (6) male demigods and (7) female demigods.

Eight classes of jivas are distinguished according to the emotions by which they are swayed or according to their complete freedom from emotion. (1) Those moved by any of the three good or three bad emotions are Saleśi and form the first class. (2) The second class comprises those dominated by Krishnaleśya, the worst of the three evil emotions, a temper so bad that it is as black as a thundercloud and rougher than a saw. (3) Jivas in the third class are ruled by Nilaleśya, an emotion blue as indigo, in which envy, gluttony and laziness are mingled. (4) Jivas of the fourth group are swayed by Kapotaleśya, a gray crookedness in thought and deed. (5) The fifth division of jivas is constituted of those who are ruled by Tejoleśya, the first of the three good emotions, red like the rising sun and sweeter than ripe mangoes. It removes evil thoughts and makes men humble and straightforward. (6) The sixth class includes the jivas whose emotion is Padmaleśya, yellow in color and named for the lotus flower. Like the lotus expanding to the sun, so their hearts are opened to all good things. (7) Śuklaleśya is the highest of the emotions and rules the jivas of the seventh class. It is white as pearls and sweeter than sugar. It brings a harmony with all nature. (8) The eighth group comprises the jivas which have risen above all emotions. Only the Siddhas are found here.

Beyond this point, further classes are made chiefly by introducing subdivisions into groupings already mentioned. Thus the classification of jivas is carried forward until a fourteenfold division is achieved; some authorities go on until they have enumerated no less than five hundred and sixty-three groupings.

The *second category* is Ajiva or non-soul. This is the realm of inanimate things, with which Jiva is entangled but toward separation from which it is struggling. Here, too, there are numerous divisions and subdivisions. The two main classes of Ajiva are Arupi, without form, and Rupi, with form. Motion, space and time are examples of divisions within Arupi. Various groupings of Pudgala, roughly translatable as "matter," are found in Rupi. Jiva and Ajiva together account for the universe; there is no need to speak of a creator.

The *third category* is Punya or merit. Here it is observed that there are nine ways of performing actions which lead to a good karma and bring peace of mind. These include (1) feeding the hungry, (2) giving drink to the thirsty, (3) offering clothes to the poor, (4) providing residence or (5) a seat or bed for a monk, (6) wishing others well or (7) exerting ourselves in their service, (8) speaking without hurting another's feelings, and (9) making reverent salutations to religious men. The reward of merit attained in these nine ways may be reaped in no less than forty-two ways, such as enjoying bodily strength or beauty.

The *fourth category* is Papa or sin. Eighteen classes of sin are recognized: (1) killing (*himsa*), (2) untruthfulness, (3) dishonesty, (4) unchastity, (5) excessive love of possessions, (6) anger, (7) conceit, (8) intrigue, (9) greed, (10) over-fondness for a person or thing, (11) envy, (12) quarrelsomeness, (13) slander, (14) telling of stories to discredit another, (15) fault-finding, (16) lack of self-control in the presence of joy or sorrow, (17) hypocrisy and (18) false faith. Among the foregoing, special emphasis is laid upon the sins of anger, conceit, intrigue and greed, these four together being called Kashaya. The results of sin are enumerated under no less than eighty-two headings. Sin affects the class of beings into which one is born in the next incarnation, it results in ugliness and deformity, it is the cause of every illness and ailment.

The *fifth category* is Aśrava which has to do with the channels for the acquisition of karma. There are forty-two channels through which karma enters a jiva. These include the senses, the emotions and various kinds of activities, all of which are carefully listed.

The *sixth category* is Samvara, meaning methods of impeding Karma. This obviously is the converse of the preceding. Here fifty-seven ways are stated in which the inflow of karma may be arrested. These include the manner of walking so as not to injure any living thing, the guarding of the words of one's mouth, the exercise of circumspection in eating, the restraint of emotion, the endurance of hardship and illness, the performance of meditation with eyes and limbs immovable, the practice of fasting and austerity, and the cultivation of reflection aimed at a recognition of the true nature of the soul and of the manner of its release from the world.

The *seventh category* is Bandha or bondage. The enslavement of the soul to karma, it is here taught, is due to the union of the jiva with pudgala, which as has already been pointed out is roughly the equivalent of matter. The classification of such bondage is fourfold: (1) As to its nature, karma is bitter or sweet, varying with the character of the individual person. (2) As to the time required for its expiation, some karma can be eradicated in a day, some will require a thousand years. (3) In intensity, some karma is heavier than some other. (4) In thickness and thinness, karma varies with the amount of pudgala which has been attracted.

The *eighth category* is Nirjara or destruction of karma. The eradication of accumulated karma is a slow and difficult process. Exterior and interior austerities are two of the chief means. Exterior or bodily austerities include: (1) fasting for a fixed period of time or for the remainder of one's life (as Parśva and many others did); (2) partial fasting, by gradually decreasing the quantity of food consumed; (3) limited eating, involving for example a reduction in the varieties of food taken or in the number of places where one will eat; (4) abstention from certain foods in which one takes particular delight; (5) ill-treatment of the body, such as the pulling out of the hair by the roots; (6) control of the senses and restriction of exercise. Interior or spiritual austerities are also six in number: (1) confession and penance; (2) reverence to superiors; (3) service to the poor; (4) study; (5) meditation; (6) the practice of indifference to the body, to the extent of standing motionless in some sacred place until death comes.

The *ninth category* is Moksha or deliverance. As we have already seen, one who attains the state of complete deliverance is called a Siddha. He is then, by Jaina definition, "without caste, unaffected by smell, without the sense of taste, without feeling, without form, without hunger, without pain, without sorrow, without joy, without birth, without old age, without death, without body, without karma, enjoying an endless and unbroken calm."[88] Only a human being can pass directly to the state of a Siddha. If he has previously been a Tirthankara he is called a Tirtha Siddha. Interestingly enough, while a Tirthankara is an object of worship, upon becoming a Siddha he no longer receives worship since he no longer has a body. In all there are fifteen kinds of Siddhas. Factors taken into account in classification include not only previous status in life but also previous sex, influences which led to Siddhahood, and whether moksha was attained alone or in a group with others.

THE ANALYSIS OF KARMA

Prominent as karma is in the above outline, we have even yet scarcely more than hinted at the complexity of the analysis to which this central concept is subjected by the Jaina theologians. In briefest summary this analysis includes the four following points:[89]

Karma has four sources: (1) Mithyatva, false belief; (2) Avirati, attachment; (3) Kashaya, greed; (4) Yoga, adherence to worldly things. It is of two main types: (1) Nikacita, firmly bound karma which must be endured; (2) Śithila, loose karma which can be destroyed. There are one hundred and forty-eight (and some say one hundred and fifty-eight) specific kinds of karma, grouped under eight main divisions. Listing only the main divisions, we find that (1) Jñanavaraniya karma hides knowledge from us; (2) Darśanavaraniya karma keeps us from beholding the true faith; (3) Vedaniya karma determines whether we experience the feeling of pleasure or of pain; (4) Mohaniya karma causes delusion; (5) Ayu karma fixes the period of time which a jiva must spend in a given form; (6) Nama karma determines the condition of the jiva's existence as to genus of being and nature of body; (7) Gotra karma decides a man's destiny in his next existence as to whether he will be born in a high-caste or low-caste family; (8) Antaraya karma obstructs the efforts of a person toward various accomplishments.

Of the foregoing eight main kinds of karma, the first, second,

[88] Stevenson, *The Heart of Jainism*, p.169.
[89] Stevenson, *The Heart of Jainism*, pp.173-192; Johnson, *Triṣaṣṭiśalākāpuruṣacaritra*, I, pp.402-436.

fourth and eighth are the most difficult to eliminate; the others can more easily be destroyed. Three tenses are also recognized in relation to karma. (1) Satta is the name for the karma accumulated in past existences. All one hundred and forty-eight different kinds of karma are involved in satta. (2) Bandha is the karma which is being taken on even now in the present life. One hundred and twenty of the one hundred and forty-eight kinds are concerned in bandha. (3) Udaya is the karma, the fruits of which, whether good or evil, are maturing and ripening and now being experienced. One hundred and twenty-two kinds of karma are involved here.

On the ladder by which the soul climbs to emancipation from karma there are fourteen steps or Gunasthanas. (1) When a jiva is on the first step (Mithyatvagunasthana) it is in a state of delusion and does not know the truth. There are two subdivisions of this step: in the first the soul cannot tell the difference between a god and a non-god; in the second the soul knows that there is a difference but mistakes a non-deva for a deva. (2) In the second step (Saśvasadanagunasthana) the soul possesses a faint remembrance of the often forgotten distinction between truth and falsity. (3) On the third rung of the ladder (Miśragunasthana) the jiva is in the condition of knowing the truth one moment and doubting it the next. (4) In the fourth phase (Aviratisamyagdrishtigunasthana) the soul attains to faith but is not yet strong enough to take any of the vows of the Jaina life. (5) On the fifth level of progress (Deśaviratigunasthana) the soul is able to take the various vows which delimit the highest kind of life possible for the Jaina layman. (6) Step six (Pramattagunasthana) can only be ascended by the professed ascetic. Here the soul has complete self-control but is still subject to five "negligences," namely pride, enjoyment of the senses, Kashaya (i.e. anger, conceit, intrigue and greed), sleep, and idle talk. (7) At the seventh stage (Apramattagunasthana) many of the "negligences" are overcome, particularly anger, but pride, deceit and greed remain. (8) It is in the eighth stage (Niyatibadaragunasthana) that pride is conquered. (9) In the ninth (Aniyatibadaragunasthana) deceit disappears. (10) On the tenth level (Sukshmasamparayagunasthana) all pleasure in beauty and all perception of pain and fear are gone. (11) On the eleventh (Upaśantamohagunasthana) the most critical of all sins has been overcome, even greed. (12) The twelfth step (Kshinamohagunasthana) finds the soul freed from the kinds of karma which are difficult to destroy although those which are easy to destroy still persist. (13) In the thirteenth phase (Sayogikevaligunasthana) a man may preach to others, form a Tirtha or community, and become a Tirthankara, in which state he is an object of worship. (14) The fourteenth and final step (Ayogikevaligunasthana) witnesses the destruction of all remaining karma, the separation from the body, and the attainment of moksha or release. The jiva has now become a Siddha and reached the blessed consummation of its long ascent. "Omniscience, boundless vision, illimitable righteousness, infinite strength, perfect bliss, indestructibility, existence without form, a body that is neither light nor heavy," it is declared, "such are the characteristics of the Siddha."[90]

[90] Stevenson, *The Heart of Jainism*, p.192.

4. THE LATER HISTORY OF THE RELIGION

JAINA theory conceives the present age of the world to be one of decline, and Jaina traditions describe a progressive diminution in spiritual authority on the part of the leaders of the church who came after the last Tirthankara. Mahavira's leading disciple was Indrabhuti, but he attained complete enlightenment in the very night in which his master died and, as a Kevalin, was no longer expected to be active in the administration of church affairs. Of the other Ganadharas nine had attained Nirvana even before this, and thus there was only one left to be the head of the church, namely Arya Sudharma. He served in this capacity for twelve years, at which time Indrabhuti died and he himself entered into complete enlightenment, and after that his disciple Jambusvami was the leader of the church. Jambusvami himself reached the great enlightenment one year after the death of Sudharma and then later, sixty-four years after the Nirvana of Mahavira, died. From this time on, according to Jaina belief, no man was able to achieve the great enlightenment. Since there were now no more Kevalins who possessed the authority of personally won insight into the true nature of things, understanding depended upon study of the traditions derived from the great men of the past. The next five leaders of the church were believed to possess complete knowledge of all the original texts, and hence were called Srutake-valins. The last of these was Bhadrabahu, who is said to have died a hundred and seventy years after the Nirvana of Mahavira. After this, as we have seen, knowledge of the canonical texts tended gradually to disappear, and while the Svetambaras think that some authentic scriptures remain the Digambaras believe that all the original texts are now lost.[91]

Despite the discouraging theory that the world has been in a "bad" period of decline since the time of Mahavira, Jainism has made many achievements of importance and has created monuments which bear witness to its significance as the faith of many believers. We will now sketch the course of the religion through several successive periods in Indian history and will mention a number of its archeological sites and remains.

[91] CJ pp.302-304.

5. THE ŚIŚUNAGA AND NANDA PERIODS, c.642-c.322 B.C.

MAHAVIRA himself lived in the Śiśunaga Period (c.642-c.413 B.C.), the first clearly defined epoch in Indian history. As we have seen, he enjoyed the favor of Kings Bimbisara and Ajataśatru. This royal patronage seems also to have been bestowed by King Udaya, son of Ajataśatru, upon the Jains of his day. Likewise the succeeding Nandas (c.413-c.322 B.C.) appear to have been friendly toward the religion. Tangible evidence for this fact is found in a badly damaged inscription of the later (second century B.C.) King Kharavela of Kalinga in which reference is made to "King Nanda" in connection with "an idol of the first Jina."[92]

[92] Charpentier in CHI I, p.164.

6. THE MAURYA PERIOD, c.322-c.185 B.C.

THE Maurya Period inaugurated by the powerful ruler Chandragupta (c.322-c.298 B.C.) is of much interest in the history of Jainism.

BHADRABAHU AND CHANDRAGUPTA

The head of the Jaina church in the time of Chandragupta's reign
was Bhadrabahu, the last of the Śrutakevalins. According to Jaina
tradition which is recorded with not a few variations in the Brihat-
kathakośa (written by Harishena in A.D. 931), the Bhadrabahucha-
rita (fifteenth century), the Munivamśabhyudaya (seventeenth century) and the Rajavalikathe (nineteenth century), Bhadrabahu
prophesied a twelve-year famine and advised or even led a migration
of a large body of Jaina monks to the south. They are supposed to
have settled in the vicinity of Śravana Belgola in Mysore, where
perhaps Bhadrabahu himself died. King Chandragupta, who was
already an adherent of the Jaina faith, left his throne at this time
and also went to Śravana Belgola where he lived for a number of
years in a cave as an ascetic, worshiping the footprints of Bhadrabahu, and finally himself died by the Jaina rite of starvation.[93]

Remarkable as this account is, it receives some substantiation from
ancient rock inscriptions at Śravana Belgola, which refer to the connection of both Bhadrabahu and Chandragupta with that place,
and speak of the king as the disciple of the great saint. The oldest
inscriptions are on a hill which is known as Chandragiri after the
king. Inscription No. 1, dating from around A.D. 600, includes this
statement: "Bhadrabahuswami, of a lineage rendered illustrious by
a succession of great men . . . , who was acquainted with the true
nature of the eightfold great omens and was a seer of the past, the
present and the future, having learned from an omen and foretold in
Ujjayani a calamity lasting for a period of twelve years, the entire
community (*sangha*) set out from the North to the South and
reached by degrees a country counting many hundreds of villages
and filled with happy people, wealth, gold, grain, and herds of cows,
buffaloes, goats and sheep."[94]

Another inscription (No. 67) also on the Chandragiri hill and
dated in A.D. 1129, contains the sentence: "Say, how can the greatness

[93] R. Narasimhachar, *Epigraphia Caranatica*, II *Inscriptions at Sravana Belgola*
(Mysore Archaeological Series). rev. ed., 1923, pp.36-42; Hiralal Jain in *The Cultural
Heritage of India* (Sri Ramakrishna Centenary Memorial). I, p.221.

[94] Narasimhachar, *Epigraphia Caranatica*, II, Translations, p.1.

be described of Bhadrabahu whose arms have grown stout by subduing the pride of the great wrestler delusion, and through the merit
of being whose disciple the renowned Chandragupta was served for
a very long time by the forest deities."[95]

Yet another text (No. 258), this one found on the Vindhyagiri hill
and dated in A.D. 1432, mentions "the lord of ascetics, Bhadrabahu,"
who "arose on the earth . . . as the full moon in the milk ocean," and
continues: "Pre-eminent for the wealth of perfect intelligence, of
brilliant perfection of conduct, breaker of the bond of karma, of a
fame increased by the growth of penance, Bhadrabahu of supernatural powers lifted up here the pure doctrine of the Siddhas beautifully
composed with faultless words. Though the last of the lords of sages,
the Śrutakevalins, on earth, Bhadrabahu became the foremost leader
of the learned by his exposition of the meaning of all the scriptures.
His disciple was Chandragupta, who was bowed to by the chief
gods on account of his perfect conduct and the fame caused by the
greatness of whose severe penance spread into other worlds."[96]

THE GREAT SCHISM

This is also the time when the Council of Pataliputra was held and
when the cleavage between the Śvetambaras and the Digambaras
began to appear. It will be recalled that even in the time of Keśi and
Gautama there was discussion on questions of monastic vows and
clothing, but that such agreement was reached that all the Jains
could be together in one community. With the great famine the
question relative to clothing became more acute. It is supposed that
the monks who went to south India were the younger and more
vigorous members of the order, who were able to maintain their
discipline in full severity and go unclad. Those who remained in
Magadha were allowed, perhaps because of age and infirmity, to
wear clothes. When the famine was over many of the emigrant monks
returned and were displeased with the laxity which had developed
among those who had remained in the north. Also they disapproved
of the Council of Pataliputra which had been held in their absence,
and questioned the validity of its revision of the canon. This estrangement developed across the succeeding years and led finally (perhaps
around A.D. 80) to actual separation between the two communities.
The spiritual descendants of the stricter southern monks became the
Digambaras (literally, sky-clad), who taught that a monk who has

[95] *ibid.*, p.25; cf. No. 64 (A.D. 1163), p.16.   [96] *ibid.*, p.116.

any property, even clothes, cannot reach Nirvana, and who disowned the canonical books as revised at Pataliputra. The others became the Svetambaras (literally, white-clad), who maintained that the practice of dispensing with clothing had no longer been requisite since the time of the last Kevalin, Jambusvami, and who accepted the canon of Pataliputra.[97]

BINDUSARA AND AŚOKA

If Chandragupta was a complete convert to radical Jainism the same cannot be said of his two successors. His son Bindusara (c.298-c.273 B.C.) is described in the Mahavamsa[98] as supporting sixty thousand Brahmans; and his grandson Aśoka (c.273-c.232 B.C.) was deeply interested in the furtherance of Buddhism. Aśoka was tolerant, however, of all denominations and required the same attitude on the part of his officials who were in charge of religious affairs. In his seventh Pillar Edict, after telling of his own concern for the material and spiritual welfare of his subjects, he continues: "My Censors of the Law of Piety, too, are occupied with many objects of the [royal] favor, affecting both ascetics and householders, and are likewise occupied with all denominations. I have arranged, also, that they should be occupied with the affairs of the Buddhist clergy, as well as among the Brahmans and the Ajivikas, the Jains, and, in fact, various denominations. The several ordinary officials shall severally superintend their respective charges, whereas the Censors of the Law of Piety shall superintend all other denominations in addition to such special charges."[99]

As far as we know, the foregoing is the oldest actual inscriptional mention of the Jains. The passage is also of interest for its reference to the Ajivikas, another ascetic group whose founder, Gosala, was at one time closely associated with Mahavira.[100] The Ajivikas are mentioned as if they were a sect of considerable prominence at the time, and this is further borne out by the fact that both Aśoka and his grandson Daśaratha dedicated caves for the use of members of this order in the Barabar Hills near Gaya.[101]

97 Margaret Stevenson in HERE XII, pp.123f.

98 v, 34. tr. Geiger, pp.28f.

99 Vincent A. Smith, *The Edicts of Asoka*, p.34.

100 A. F. R. Hoernle in HERE I, pp.259-268.

101 Vincent A. Smith, *Asoka, The Buddhist Emperor of India*. 3d ed. 1920, pp.134f.; Fergusson and Burgess, *The Cave Temples of India*, pp.37-43.

SAMPRATI

Daśaratha, whom we have just mentioned, seems to have ruled the eastern part of his grandfather's territories, while another grandson, Samprati, resided in Ujjain and held sway over the western regions. Samprati was converted by a famous Śvetambara monk named Suhastin, and became very zealous in the promotion of Jainism and in the building of Jaina temples. This is known on the authority of Hemachandra, who writes as follows concerning Samprati: "He showed his zeal by causing Jaina temples to be erected over the whole of Jambuddiva. During Suhastin's stay at Ujjain, and under his guidance, splendid religious festivals and processions in honor of the Arhat were celebrated, and great was the devotion manifested by the king and his subjects on this occasion. The example and advice of Samprati induced his vassals to embrace and patronize his creed, so that not only in his kingdom but also in adjacent countries the monks could practice their religion." Hemachandra also tells how Samprati had missionaries sent out, doubtless of the Śvetambara persuasion, as far as to south India: "In order to extend the sphere of their activities to uncivilized countries, Samprati sent there messengers disguised as Jaina monks. They described to the people the kind of food and other requisites which monks may accept as alms, enjoining them to give such things instead of the usual tax to the revenue collector who would visit them from time to time. Of course these revenue collectors were to be Jaina monks. Having thus prepared the way for them, he induced the superior to send monks to those countries, for they would find it in no way impossible to live there. Accordingly missionaries were sent to the Andhras and Dramilas, who found everything as the king had told. Thus the uncivilized nations were brought under the influence of Jainism."[102]

[102] Quoted by Shah, *Jainism in North India 800 B.C.-A.D. 526*, p.145.

7. BETWEEN THE MAURYA AND KUSHAN PERIODS

THE years preceding and shortly following the inception of the Christian era are relatively dark in the history of Jainism. We do know, however, that the city of Ujjain, just mentioned in connection with Samprati, continued to be an important center of the religion. A narrative known as the Kalakacaryakatha or Story of the Teacher Kalaka[103] has to do with events which took place there in the first century B.C. when a certain Gardabhilla was king.

THE STORY OF KALAKA

Although the account is legendary, and was probably not put into the form of a single written text until between the tenth and thirteenth centuries A.D., the Story of Kalaka may contain a kernel of historical truth. It relates that King Gardabhilla of Ujjain carried off the Jaina nun Sarasvati, who was the sister of the famous monk Kalaka. When Kalaka found his protests unavailing, he journeyed west of the Indus and persuaded the Sakas (Scythians) to come and attack Ujjain and overthrow Gardabhilla. The Sakas did this and established themselves in the city, where it is said that "the time passed happily for them as they devoted themselves to honoring the teaching of the Jinas, and sported like bees about the lotus-feet of the *suri* [Kalaka]."[104] Soon afterward, however, Vikramaditya, son of Gardabhilla, expelled the invaders and reestablished the native dynasty. Vikramaditya is supposed also to have adhered to the Jaina faith, and the Vikrama Era which he inaugurated in 58/57 B.C. is still in use among the Jains of north India. After one hundred and thirty-five years the Sakas regained the ascendancy and instituted their own era (A.D. 78), by which Jaina dates also are still reckoned.

THE CAVES OF ORISSA

We also know that Jainism was of importance in eastern India at this time as well as in the western regions of Ujjain. This is indicated by the existence of Jaina caves not far from Bhuvanesvara in Orissa, the oldest of which probably date from the second century B.C. The caves are excavated in some sandstone hills known as Khandagiri, Udayagiri and Nilagiri, and served as viharas or monasteries for

---

103 W. Norman Brown, *The Story of Kālaka, Texts, History, Legends, and Miniature Paintings of the Śvetāmbara Jain Hagiographical Work, The Kālakācāryakathā* (Smithsonian Institution, Freer Gallery of Art, Oriental Studies, 1). 1933.

104 *ibid.*, p.60.

Jaina monks. Two of these caves in particular may be mentioned here. The Hathigumpha or Elephant Cave, as it is now known, was an extensive natural cave which was improved by the Jaina king, Kharavela of Kalinga. There is a badly damaged inscription of this king in the cave, dating around the middle of the second century B.C.,[105] which tells among other things of how he constructed rock-dwellings and gave abundant gifts to Jaina devotees. The cave now called Rani ka Naur or Queen's Palace is arranged with two stories of cells, both originally fronted by pillared verandas, and with a large courtyard cut out of the hillside. There are sculptured adorn-ments, probably the finest of any in this entire group of caves, which include fighting scenes, the hunting of a winged deer, the carrying off of a woman, and other subjects. Although they have not been further identified, it is supposed that the portrayals are taken from Jaina legends more or less similar to the Jatakas which provided such abundant themes for Buddhist sculptures.[106]

[105] E. J. Rapson in CHI I, pp.534f.
[106] Fergusson, *History of Indian and Eastern Architecture*, II, pp.9-18; CHIIA pp.37f.

8. THE KUSHAN PERIOD, A.D. c.50-c.320

THE most famous king of the Kushan Period was Kanishka (second century A.D.), and he is well known for his patronage of Buddhism. Nevertheless Jainism also flourished in his reign and throughout this period.

MATHURA

The city of Mathura on the Jumna River was now a prominent center of Jainism as indeed it had already been for a considerable time. The ruins of a Jaina stupa as well as of two temples have been excavated in the mound called Kankali Tila at Mathura, and a second century A.D. inscription has been found which says that the stupa was "built by the gods." Evidently at that time the stupa was regarded as of immemorial antiquity. Later, in a legendary work of the fourteenth century, it is said that the stupa was built originally of gold by the goddess Kubera in honor of the seventh Jina, Suparśva, and was encased in bricks in the time of Parśva.[107]

The most important Jaina inscriptions and sculptures at Mathura, however, date probably from the first and second centuries A.D. and thus fall within the Kushan Period of which we are now speaking. The numerous inscriptions from these two centuries are of particular interest in supplying corroboration for many of the points found in the later Jaina traditions. Already, for example, the series of twenty-four successive Tirthankaras, each with his distinctive emblem, was firmly believed in, women had an influential place in the church and an order of nuns was in existence, the division between the Śvetambaras and Digambaras had come into being, and the sacred texts were being recited with verbal exactitude.[108]

The sculptures as well as the inscriptions found at and near Mathura are of much interest for the history of Jainism. A characteristic production was an Ayagapata or "tablet of homage" which was sculptured in relief and erected in a temple for purposes of adoration. Such a small sculptured tablet, dating probably from the first century A.D. and now in the Mathura Museum, is shown in Fig. 70. The inscription on the tablet begins with the words "Adoration to the

---

[107] Vincent A. Smith, *The Jain Stûpa and Other Antiquities of Mathurâ* (Archaeological Survey of India, New Imperial Series, xx). 1901, pp.10-13.

[108] G. Bühler in *Wiener Zeitschrift für die Kunde des Morgenlandes*. 1 (1887), pp.165-180; 2 (1888), pp.141-146; 3 (1889), pp.233-240; 4 (1890), pp.169-173,313-331; 5 (1891), pp.59-63,175-180; cj pp.42f.

Arhat Vardhamana," and indicates that it was the gift of a courtesan named Vasu, daughter of Lonaśobhika. The main representation is of a Jaina stupa, or hemispherical memorial mound, which has the same general appearance as the stupas of the Buddhists. In this case the stupa stands on a high platform surrounded by a railing, and is approached by nine steps which lead up to an ornamental gateway. On either side are Yakshis and tall columns.[109]

Another such Jaina tablet from Mathura is pictured in Fig. 71. It probably also comes from the first century A.D., and is now in the Lucknow Museum. The figure in the center is that of a seated Jina surrounded by various symbols. On the left is a pillar with a dhamma-cakka capital, and on the right a pillar with an elephant capital. The accompanying inscription reads: "Adoration to the Arhats! A tablet of homage (*ayagapata*) was set up by Sihanadika, son of the Vanika Sihaka and son of a Kośiki, for the worship of the Arhats."[110]

Larger cult images of the Jinas were also made at this time and have a general appearance similar to that of contemporary statues of the Buddha. An example is given in Fig. 72, which shows a mottled red sandstone statue found at Mathura and now in the Lucknow Museum.[111] The date is probably in the first or early second century A.D. The figure is that of the Tirthankara Parśvanatha protected by the Naga Dharanendra. The portrait type is comparable to that of the Buddha from Mathura which will be shown in Fig. 107; the sheltering of the figure beneath the hood of the snake king is a theme also familiar in Buddhist art as will be seen later (Fig. 123).[112]

[109] J. Ph. Vogel, *La sculpture de Mathura* (Ars Asiatica, xv). 1930, p.27; Smith, *The Jain Stûpa and Other Antiquities of Mathurâ*, p.61.

[110] Smith, *The Jain Stûpa and Other Antiquities of Mathurâ*, p.14.

[111] CHIIA p.57, Fig. 86.

[112] J. Ph. Vogel, *Indian Serpent-Lore or the Nāgas in Hindu Legend and Art*. 1926, p.104.

9. THE GUPTA PERIOD, A.D. C.320-C.600

MATHURA continues to provide illustration of Jaina art in the Gupta Period. From that site we show in Fig. 73 a seated image of a Tirthankara which is similar to the Buddha representation typical of the Gupta epoch (cf. Fig. 109). Thus is emphasized again the fact which is often evident, that all the Indian religions drew upon the common art of their time and place. Nevertheless, the statue is clearly Jaina rather than Buddhist. Among the points distinguishing this work from an image of the Buddha are the lack of clothing, the absence of the ushnisha and urna (p.284), and the presence of the Srivatsa symbol on the chest. Since the Srivatsa appears on various figures of Tirthankaras it may be supposed to be a general Jaina emblem at this time rather than the designation of a single Jina. The lions on the pedestal of the statue may then give us the clue to the identification of this Tirthankara as Mahavira. Between the lions are two kneeling figures and a sacred wheel.[113]

SITTANNAVASAL

In painting as well as in sculpture the Jaina art of the period may be compared with the Buddhist. Important Jaina paintings have been discovered at Sittannavasal not far from Tanjore, which are executed in the Gupta style like the Buddhist paintings at Ajanta and like some of them belong to a time around A.D. 600 or a little later. The paintings are preserved on the ceilings, capitals and upper parts of the pillars of a rock-cut Jaina temple, which was once fully decorated. The chief subject still to be seen is a large fresco adorning the entire ceiling of the veranda of the shrine. It shows a tank covered with lotus flowers, and also depicts fish, geese, buffaloes, elephants and three men. The men hold lotuses in their hands and are portrayed in a very attractive way. This is presumably some unidentified scene from Jaina history. On the capitals of the pillars are elegant painted lotuses, and on the pillars themselves are figures of *devadasis* or dancing girls of the temple.[114]

[113] Vogel, *La sculpture de Mathura*, pp.112f.; Smith, *The Jain Stûpa and Other Antiquities of Mathurâ*, p.51.
[114] G. Jouveau Dubreuil in *The Indian Antiquary, A Journal of Oriental Research.* 52 (1923), pp.45-47.

10. THE MEDIEVAL PERIOD, A.D. c.600-c.1200

DURING the Medieval Period, Jainism for the most part enjoyed the tolerance of rulers who looked upon the various religious sects with broad sympathy, and in not a few instances it was the recipient of special favor and patronage. Of this general situation several specific illustrations may be given. The great monarch Harsha (A.D. c.606-c.647) who ruled from Kanauj over most of north India, and the Pawar king Bhoja (A.D. c.1010-c.1065) who reigned at Dhara and was celebrated as an ideal Indian ruler, were both exponents of genuine tolerance. The Solanki king Siddharaja (A.D. 1094-1143) of Anhilwar, although himself a worshiper of Śiva, was pleased to have the distinguished Jaina writer, Hemachandra (A.D. 1088-1172), work at his court; and his successor, Kumarapala (A.D. 1143-1173), was actually converted by Hemachandra to Jainism. In the south the Gangas, Rashtrakutas and early Hoyśalas were Jains and supporters of the faith. The great minister Chamunda Raja or Chamunda Raya (end of the tenth century), who served under the Ganga kings Marasinha II and Rachamalla (Rajamalla) IV and whose spiritual adviser was the Jaina scholar Nemichandra, provided a notable example of active patronage of the religion. Under these favorable circumstances the religion of the Tirthankaras expanded and flowered.[115]

Tangible evidence of the splendor which Jainism attained is still to be seen in architectural monuments throughout India, several of which will now be mentioned. As in sculpture and in painting, so, too, in architecture the style of Jaina work is often not peculiar to that sect but is simply the Indian style of the time and place in which it is done. Thus we shall encounter both cave temples and structural temples which are very similar to examples of Hindu work with which we are already familiar.

ELURA

The best-known Jaina cave temple of the Medieval Period is doubtless the so-called Indra Sabha ("Court of Indra"),[116] one of

[115] GJ pp.45-60.
[116] Fergusson, *History of Indian and Eastern Architecture*, II, pp.19f.; Fergusson and Burgess, *The Cave Temples of India*, pp.496-500; James Burgess, *Report on the Elura Cave Temples and the Brahmanical and Jaina Caves in Western India, Completing the Results of the Fifth, Sixth, and Seventh Seasons' Operations of the Archaeological Survey, 1877-78, 1878-79, 1879-80; Supplementary to the Volume on "The Cave Temples of India"* (Archaeological Survey of Western India, V). 1883, pp.44-48.

several Jaina caves at Elura in Central India. There are also Buddhist and Hindu caves at Elura, and the Hindu Kailasanatha, a complete monolithic temple, has been described earlier. Like the Kailasanatha, the Indra Sabha (Fig. 74) is cut out of the solid rock.[117] The courtyard is protected by a rock screen wall which faces south. Outside of this on the east is a chapel with two pillars in front and two at the back. Entering the courtyard, there is on the right an elephant on a pedestal and on the left a monolithic column (now fallen) surmounted by a quadruple image of a Tirthankara. In the center of the court is an elaborate square porch (*mandapam*) over another quadruple image. Beyond, a sort of double veranda gives access to the lower hall of the temple which is cut on back into the rock. At the left end of the veranda are two large images of Śanti, the sixteenth Tirthankara, with an accompanying inscription: "The image of Śantibhattaraka, [made by] Sohila, a Brahmacharin [i.e. pandit of the Digambara Jains]." At the other end is a stone stairway which leads to the upper hall of the temple. Both halls are adorned with pillars, although in the lower hall these have not been completely executed and the aisles have not been finished. In the upper hall the walls of the side and back aisles are divided into compartments and filled with sculptured figures of Jinas.

Among the many sculptured figures of Jinas in the cave and its chapels, the most prominent are Parśva, Mahavira, and Gommata. The last named, Gommata or Bahubali, was a son of the first Tirthankara, Rishabha, and is specially venerated by the Digambaras. In a typical relief panel in the Indra Sabha this saint is shown, accompanied by attendants and Gandharvas, but himself standing in such complete reverie that a creeping plant has grown up and wrapped its tendrils about him. Two other large figures which have an important place in the temple are commonly identified as Indra and Indrani his wife, but are possibly intended instead to represent the Yaksha and Yakshi who are the customary companions of a Tirthankara.[118]

ŚRAVANA BELGOLA

In south India the chief center of Jainism was Śravana Belgola, the legendary connections of which place with Bhadrabahu and

[117] Burgess, *Report on the Elura Cave Temples and the Brahmanical and Jaina Caves in Western India*, Pl. vi.

[118] W. Kirfel, *Die Religion der Jaina's* (in Hans Haas, ed., *Bilderatlas zur Religionsgeschichte*, 12). 1928, p.xxi.

Chandragupta have already been discussed. Here in medieval and later times almost innumerable shrines were constructed. These included an ordinary type of temple known as a Basti, which contained an image of a Tirthankara; and a specially arranged kind of sanctuary called a Betta, which consisted of cloisters around an open courtyard in which stood a colossal statue of a great man of the Jaina faith.

A remarkable example of the latter type of sanctuary may be seen on the summit of the Vindhyagiri hill at Sravana Belgola. In the center of an open court surrounded by corridors adorned with Jinas and other figures stands the enormous statue pictured in Fig. 75. This huge image measuring fifty-seven feet in height and standing erect and unclothed facing north, represents Gommata (Gommatesvara). Although the figure is treated in rather conventional form there is a calm and serene expression upon the face. Anthills rise on either side and, as in the relief in the Indra Sabha, creeping plants spring from the ground and twine around the thighs and arms of the saint. Thus is symbolized the profound abstraction of the great ascetic who stands in his place of seclusion neither moving nor noticing while ants build and plants climb around him. Inscriptions (Nos. 175, 176, 179) at the side of the statue state, "Chamunda Raja caused [this image] to be made," and thus we learn that it was none other than the famous minister of Rajamalla who was responsible for the making of the monument. The date must have been about A.D. 983.[119]

Another inscription (No. 234) found at Sravana Belgola, composed by the Jaina poet Sujanottamsa (or Boppana) and dating about A.D. 1180, tells something of the character ascribed to Gommata, relates how Chamunda Raya came to have the image made, and describes its wonderful character:

I shall praise the immeasurable Gommata Jina, worshiped by the lords of men, Nagas, gods, demons and Khacharas, destroyer of Cupid by the fire of meditation and worthy to be meditated upon by ascetics. Who else is so honorable as the high-souled Bahubali, son of Puru, who, having generously handed over the kingdom of the earth to his elder brother,— who on defeat in a regular hand-to-hand fight unjustly left off speaking and when even the discus thrown by him proved a failure was seized with shame,—went forth and destroyed by his penance the enemy Karma? The

[119] Narasimhachar, *Epigraphia Caranatica*, II, pp.10-23; Translations, p.89; Pl. I. Two other similar colossal statues of Gommata are known, one at Karkal, 41½ feet high, erected in A.D. 1432; and one at Venur, thirty-five feet high, set up in 1604.

emperor Bharata, conqueror of all kings, son of Purudeva, caused to be made near Paudanapura, with joy of mind, an image, 525 bows high, resembling the form of the victorious-armed Bahubali-kevali. After the lapse of a long time, a world-terrifying mass of innumerable *kukkuta-sarpas*[120] having sprung up in the region near that Jina, that enemy of sin obtained, indeed, the name Kukkutesvara. Afterward that region became invisible to the common people, though seen even now by many skilled in spells and charms. There might be heard the sound of the celestial drum; why say more, there might even be seen the details of divine worship; those who have seen the brilliant charming mirror of the nails of that Jina's feet, can see the forms of their former births;—the supernatural power of that god is renowned in the world. On hearing from people of the celebrated supernatural power of that Jina, a desire arose in his mind to see him, and when he prepared himself to go, he was told by his preceptors that the region of that city was distant and inaccessible; whereupon, saying, "In that case I will cause to be made an image of that god," Gomata had this god made. Combining in himself learning, purity of faith, power, virtuous conduct, liberality and courage, the moon of the Ganga family, Rachamalla was celebrated in the world. Was it not that king's matchless power, Chamunda Raya (*alias*) Gommata, an equal of Manu, that thus caused this god to be made with great effort?

When an image is very lofty, it may not have beauty; when possessed of loftiness and real beauty, it may not have supernatural power: loftiness, real beauty and mighty supernatural power being all united in it, how worthy of worship in the world is the glorious form, comparable to itself, of Gommatesvara Jina? When it is said that Maya, the king of heaven (Indra),[121] and the lord of serpents (Adisesha)[122] are unable respectively to draw a likeness, to take a full view and to undertake the praise of it, who else are then able to draw a likeness, to take a full view and to undertake the praise of the matchless form of wondrous beauty of the southern Kukkutesvara? Birds do not fly over it even in forgetfulness; . . . who can adequately praise the glorious form of Gommatesvara Jina? . . . Why in vain do you make yourself wander in the forest of births by foolishly mistaking the various dying deities of the land for gods? Think on Gommatadeva who is of the form of the supreme soul, and you will be rid of birth, old age and other sorrows. No man shall take pleasure in killing, lying, stealing, adultery and covetousness; if he does, he will lose for ever this world and the next: lo! Gommatadeva looks as if proclaiming this standing on high.[123]

KHAJURAHO

In north India one of the important centers of Jainism was Khajuraho. As we have already seen, this was also a seat of Hinduism,

---

[120] The *kukkuta-sarpa* is a fowl with the head and neck of a serpent.
[121] Even though possessed of one thousand eyes.
[122] Even though possessed of two thousand tongues.
[123] Narasimhachar, *Epigraphia Caranatica*, ii, Translations, pp.97-101.

and of the approximately thirty temples which stand there about one third are Vaishnavite, one third Śaivite and one third Jaina.[124] The proximity of the various temple groups to each other emphasizes their similarity, and we find that the Jaina temples are scarcely distinguishable from the Hindu except for the details of their sculptured representations.

Of all the Jaina sanctuaries the largest and finest is the Parśvanatha, which as its name indicates is dedicated to the twenty-third Tirthankara. Like most of the shrines at Khajuraho it probably belongs to the century between A.D. 950 and 1050. It is about sixty-two feet in length and half that in breadth. The outside walls are adorned with numerous bands of moldings and with three horizontal rows of sculptured statues. The appearance of the temple may be seen in Fig. 76, and may be compared with the Śaivite Kandarya Mahadeva at Khajuraho in Fig. 66.[125]

More distinctive of Jainism than the style of its individual buildings was its tendency to group its sanctuaries together into temple cities. While Buddhist stupas and viharas would of course cluster around a sacred spot as at Buddh Gaya and Hindu temples be multiplied at an important center of population such as Bhuvaneśvara, the erection of a Jaina temple was considered as a prayer in and of itself and many such structures were often built at some picturesque but relatively remote and uninhabited site. Such a temple city as would thereby arise would naturally become a place of pilgrimage (*tirtha*), but it might contain no human habitations and it might not even be permitted for men to cook or sleep within its environs.[126] Of such temple cities the greatest, where there are monuments probably dating from within the Medieval Period, are in Gujarat at Śatrunjaya, Girnar and Mount Abu.

ŚATRUNJAYA

Śatrunjaya or the Holy Mountain is one and one-half miles from Palitana, and rises to an elevation of almost two thousand feet above sea level. It is considered specially sacred to Rishabha, the first Tirthankara. The top of the hill consists of two main ridges with a valley between, and is protected by massive battlemented walls. The temples, of which there are said to be over five hundred, are

---

124 A general view of the Jaina group is given by Lepel Griffin, *Famous Monuments of Central India.* 1886, Pl. LI.

125 Fergusson, *History of Indian and Eastern Architecture,* II, p.50, Pl. XVIII.

126 *ibid.,* II, pp.24-26.

grouped in separate enclosures generally containing one principal temple with other smaller ones. There are elaborate sculptured ornamentations, and at one time approximately sixty-five hundred separate images of Tirthankaras were counted. As for date, some of the temples are believed to be as old as the eleventh century, while the majority range from around A.D. 1500 to the present time. A general view of a portion of this sacred city of temples is given in Fig. 77.[127]

GIRNAR

The hill of Girnar (Fig. 78) is not far from Junagadh, and rises to an elevation of some 3,664 feet. The foot of the hill was chosen as a place for the recording of his Rock Edicts by Aśoka, and in Jaina faith the mountain was deemed sacred to Nemi (or Arishtanemi), the twenty-second Tirthankara. The chief group of Jaina temples, some sixteen in number, forms a sort of fort on a spectacular ledge at the top of a great cliff only six hundred feet below the summit of the peak. Of these the largest and perhaps also the oldest is the Neminatha temple (Fig. 79) erected in honor of the Tirthankara just named. Since an inscription upon it records that it was repaired in A.D. 1278, its original erection must have been considerably earlier than that and well within the Medieval Period. The temple stands in a quadrangular courtyard 195 by 130 feet, surrounded by some seventy cells each containing a seated image of a Tirthankara, and itself consists of two halls with two porches (*mandapams*), and a shrine with a large image of Nemi.[128]

MOUNT ABU

Most famous of all are the temples of the Jaina Tirtha on Mount Abu,[129] an isolated and impressive mountain which rises out of the desert of southern Rajputana and attains an elevation of some four thousand feet above sea level. In an area known as Dilvara (from *deul*, "temple," and *vara*, "place" or "precinct") stand four large temples, of which the two most important are in certain respects unrivaled anywhere in India. The older of the two was built in A.D. 1031

[127] *ibid.*, II, pp.27-30; Fischer, *Die Kunst Indiens, Chinas und Japans*, p.247.

[128] *ibid.*, II, pp.32f.; *A Handbook for Travellers in India, Burma and Ceylon* (John Murray), pp.234-238.

[129] Fergusson, *History of Indian and Eastern Architecture*, II, pp. 36-44; Diez, *Die Kunst Indiens*, p.78; Otto Fischer, *Die Kunst Indiens, Chinas und Japans* (Propyläen-Kunstgeschichte, IV). 1928, p.55; A. A. Macdonell, *India's Past, A Survey of Her Literatures, Religions, Languages and Antiquities*. 1927, pp.76f.

by a wealthy Jaina banker, Vimala Shah, and named for its founder; the other was likewise erected by bankers, two brothers named Tejahpala and Vastupala, and was completed in A.D. 1230 and dedicated to the twenty-second Tirthankara, Neminatha. Both temples are constructed entirely of white marble which must have been quarried at a distance of at least twenty or thirty miles and transported up the mountain with enormous labor.

The two temples are similar in plan, and are relatively plain on the exterior but amazingly rich in interior decoration. Each stands in a rectangular walled area, surrounded by recesses with statues of Tirthankaras and other deities. The central structure is a cell with a pyramidal roof (*śikhara*), lighted only from its door, and containing a statue of a Tirthankara. Connected with this is a closed hall, and in front of it in turn is an extensive open portico or assembly hall adorned with free-standing columns and with a beautiful dome upheld by eight pillars.

Some indication of the intricate decoration lavished upon these white marble sanctuaries may be given by the two following photographs. Fig. 80 shows the dome in the temple erected by Vimala Shah; Fig. 81, the interior of the temple built by Tejahpala and Vastupala.

Other interesting Jaina temples, towers and sculptures are to be found at Parasnath, Ranpur in the Jodhpur territory, Chitorgarh and Gwalior, but for the most part they are of dates later than the first great age of Jaina architecture to which our survey has been limited.[130]

ILLUSTRATED MANUSCRIPTS

Yet another characteristic and interesting development in the artistic expression of Jainism was inaugurated toward the close of the Medieval Period. This was the ornamentation of sacred manuscripts with miniature paintings. A school which produced such paintings was flourishing in Gujarat, Kathiawar and Rajputana in the early part of the twelfth century, and such work continued to be done for many centuries thereafter. Up to about A.D. 1400 the texts and illustrations were placed on palm leaf manuscripts; after that paper came into use. The work was done chiefly among the Śvetambara Jains and the texts most frequently chosen for adornment were the

[130] Fergusson, *History of Indian and Eastern Architecture*, ii, pp.44-59.

Kalpasutra,[131] the Kalakacaryakatha,[132] and the Uttaradhyayanasu-
tra.[133] The earliest known examples of such miniatures are two paintings found in a palm leaf manuscript preserved in the Santinatha
Temple (Nagin Das) of the Svetambara Jains at the ancient port
city of Cambay in Gujarat. Here the text is that of the Jnatasutra
and next three Angas, together with the commentary of Abhayadeva,
a Svetambara scholar of the eleventh century A.D. The manuscript
itself bears a date equivalent to A.D. 1127.[134]

These two miniatures are shown in Figs. 82 and 83. In Fig. 82 the
personage in the center is a Jina, probably Mahavira, or possibly
Rishabha. He is seated upon a pedestal like that used for images in
temples; behind his head is a halo, and above an ornament of leaves.
On either side is a fly-whisk (*chauri*) bearer, presumably a god. In
Fig. 83 the chief figure is probably the goddess Sarasvati, often associated with Mahavira, although another interpretation would make
her Cakresvari, the Yakshi of Rishabha, the first Tirthankara. The
goddess is portrayed with four arms, and carries in her upper hands
lotuses and in her lower hands a rosary and a manuscript. In front
of her is a peacock, and on either side a worshiper, these perhaps
being the two laymen who were the donors of the entire manuscript.

The finest miniatures of the Jaina school were produced in the
fourteenth and fifteenth centuries.[135] While thus exceeding the chronological limits otherwise adhered to in this chapter, these paintings
are of such importance and interest that several examples may be
given. Two varieties of style are distinguished, the first of which
may be observed in Figs. 84 and 85. Here the composition and background remain relatively simple, as in the earlier miniatures already
shown. Both of the present paintings are from a palm leaf manuscript
of the Kalpasutra and Kalakacaryakatha which bears a date equivalent to A.D. 1370. The one illustration (Fig. 84) depicts the birth of
Mahavira; the other (Fig. 85), his bath at birth. The second style is
marked by richness of background and profusion of detail, executed

[131] W. Norman Brown, *A Descriptive and Illustrated Catalogue of the Miniature Paintings of the Jaina Kalpasūtra as Executed in the Early Western Indian Style* (Smithsonian Institution, Freer Gallery of Art, Oriental Studies, 2). 1934.

[132] W. Norman Brown, *The Story of Kālaka, Texts, History, Legends, and Minia-ture Paintings of the Svetāmbara Jain Hagiographical Work, The Kālakācāryakathā* (Smithsonian Institution, Freer Gallery of Art, Oriental Studies, 1). 1933.

[133] W. Norman Brown, *Manuscript Illustrations of the Uttarādhyayana Sūtra Re-produced and Described* (American Oriental Series, 21). 1941.

[134] Brown, *The Story of Kālaka*, pp.18,116; Figs.1,2.

[135] W. Norman Brown in *Journal of the Indian Society of Oriental Art*. June-Dec. 1937, pp.2-12; Figs.2,3,7,9.

usually with very fine lines. It may be studied in Figs. 86 and 87. Fig. 86 is a painting from a palm leaf manuscript of the Kalpasutra, not dated but belonging probably to the last half of the fourteenth century. Mahavira is shown giving away his possessions as he abandoned his worldly life. Fig. 87 is from a paper manuscript of the Kalpasutra, probably of the first half of the fifteenth century. The subject depicted is the recital by Queen Triśala to King Siddhartha of her fourteen wonderful dreams.

Index

Abagha, 530
Aban Yasht, 98
'Abbas, al-, 517
'Abbasid, 'Abbasids, 517-521, 526, 530, 532
'Abd Allah, 483, 492, *see also* 'Abdullah
'Abd Allah ibn-Najiyah, 518
'Abd Allah ibn-Yazid, 497
'Abd al-Malik, 498, 511, 512, 513
'Abd al-Muttalib, 495
'Abd al-Rahman I, 526
'Abd al-Rahman III, 526
'Abdullah, 495, *see also* 'Abd Allah
'Abdullah al-Husayn al-Shi'i, 524
abhaya, 284
abhaya mudra, 286
Abhayadeva, 232
Abhayagiri vihara, 297
Abhidhamma, 276, 277
Abhidhammapitaka, 240f.
Abhidhammattha-Sanga-ha, 242
Abhidharmakośa, 247
Abhinandana, 188, 190
Abikarib Yathi', 476
Abraham, 487, 488
Abu, Mount, 173, 229, 230f.
Abul Kasim Mansur, *see* Firdausi
Abyssinia, 477
Abyssinian, 498, 533
Acalabhrata, 196
Acaranga, 183, *see also* Ayara
Acarangasutra, 193
Acchariyabbhutadhamma Sutta, 250
Accomplished King, *see* Wen
Achaemenes, 73
Achaemenian influence, 474
Achaemenian kings, 121
Achaemenid, Achaeme-nids, 80, 83, 113
Achaemenid architecture and sculpture, 100-104

Achaemenid inscriptions, 93-100
Achaemenid Period, 73f., 78, 93, 100, 101
Acheulian epoch, 25
Activating Energy, *see* Chi
Adam, 502, 534, 559
Aden, Aden Protectorate, 461, 462, 468, 478
adhan, 498, 499, 508, 514
Adharakhsh, 117
Adharbaijan, *see* Azerbai-jan
Adharjushnas, 86, 117
Adi Granth, 541-543, 545, 546, 552, 557, 561, 563
Adiśesha, 228
Aditi, 133
Aditi, sons of, *see* Adityas
Adityas, 132, 133
Aditya, sons of, *see Aditya*
Admiralty Islands, 21
Admonitions of the In-structress to Court La-dies, 375
Adoration of a Stupa, 269
Adzuchi, 455
Aeshma, 90
Aethiopia, 466, *see also* Ethiopia
Afghan, Afghans, 536f., 538
Afghanistan, 65, 121, 179, 562
Afrasian culture, 123
Africa, 13, 14, 21, 38, 39, 40, 462; North, 511, 522, 523, 528; South, 35, 40; West, 19, 21, 22
Agamas, 164, *see also* Ni-kayas, Tantras
Agganiya, 183
Aghlabids, 522-525
Aghora, 170
Aglibol, 481
Agni, 129, 132, 162
Agni Purana, 161, 162, 163
Agnibhuti, 196
Agra, 537, 539
Agraeans, 66
Ahab, 463
Ahimsa, 199, 207

Ahmad Shah, 562
Ahmed, *see* Muhammad
Ahriman, 90, *see also* An-gra Mainyu
Ahunavaiti, 90
Ahura, Ahuras, 69, 89, 90, 92f., 98
Ahura Mazda, 84, 87, 89, 91, 93, 94, 95, 96, 97, 98, 100, 101, 103
Aibak, *see* Qutbud-din Ai-bak
Aihole, 164
Ainus, 420, 421, 424, 437
Airan-vej, 85
Airavata, 148
Airyana, *see* Iran
'A'ishah, 497, 498, 499, 506
Ajanta, 224, 290-293, 308, 313, 314
Ajataśatru, 141, 185, 193, 196, 215, 234, 248, 258, 259, 268, 306, 307, 309, *see also* Kunika
Ajita, 188, 190, 191, 204
Ajitavati, 295, *see also* Hi-ranyavati River
Ajiva, 209
Ajivikas, 218, 256
Ajmir, 173
Aka Manah, 90
Akal Takht, 556, 558, 563
Akal Ustat, 543
Akampita, 196
Akkadian cylinder inscrip-tion, 94
Akkadian inscription, 96
Aksum, 477
Alabhika, 195
Alaska, 48
'Ala-ud-din, 537
Albright, William F., 475
Alchemy, Taoist, 393-395
Alexander the Great, 74, 82, 105-107, 109, 110, 141, 142, 147, 276, called "the Ruman," 80, 81
Algonquins, 13
'Ali, 496, 507, 511, 518, 524, 534

[565]

INDEX

ILLUSTRATIONS

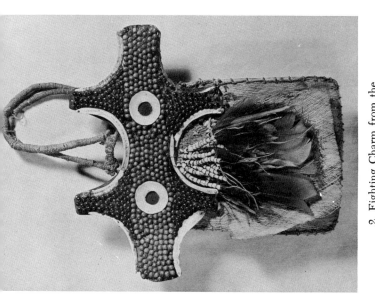

1. War Charm from the
Admiralty Islands

2. Fighting Charm from the
Gulf of Papua

3. Bird Mask from the
Gulf of Papua

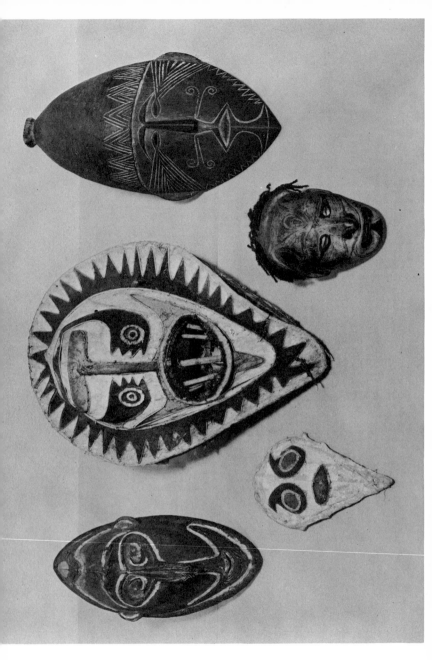

5. Wooden Mask from Borneo

6. Brass Mask from the Cameroons

7. Ancestral Figure from New Zealand

8. Ancestral Figure from New Zealand

9. Colossal Stone Images on Easter Island

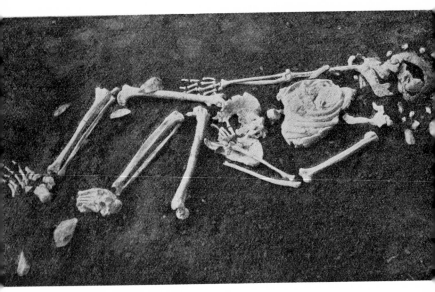

10. Aurignacian Burial at Combe-Capelle

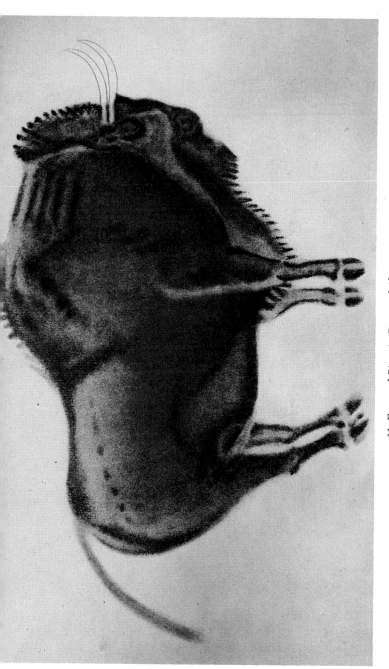

11. Fresco of Bison in Cavern of Altamira

12. Engraving of Rhinoceros in Cave of Les Combarelles

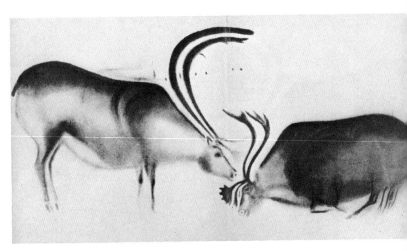

13. Polychrome Painting of Reindeer in Cave of Font-de-Gaume

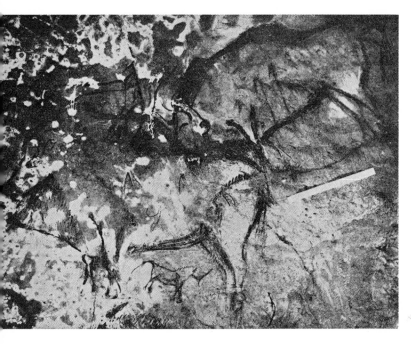

14. Painted Bison in Cavern of Niaux

15. Statue of Bison in Grotto of Tuc d'Audoubert

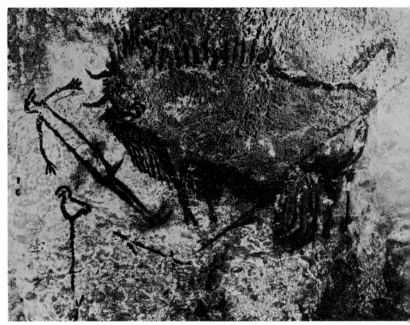

16. Bison Charging Hunter, Painting in Cave of Lascaux

17. Bushman Painting in South Africa

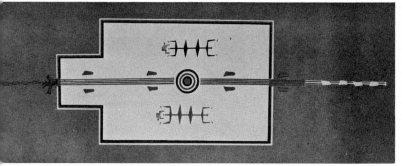

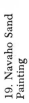

19. Navaho Sand Painting

18. Navaho Singers

20. Mescalero Apache Masked Dancers and Shaman

21. Governor and Women of Zuñi

22. Air View of Mount Demavend above the Plain of Ravy

23. Air View of Turang Tepe

24. Painted Pottery Bowl from the Early Mound near Persepolis

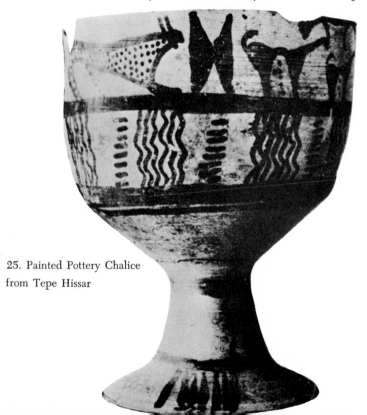

25. Painted Pottery Chalice
from Tepe Hissar

26. Air View of the Rock of Behistun

27. Air View of Persepolis

30. A Page of the Arda-Viraf Namak in Codex K20

29. A Page of the Bundahish in Codex K20b

31. Clay Tablet with Inscription of Darius I the Great

32. Symbol of Ahura Mazda on the Rock of Behistun

33. Carving above the Tomb of Artaxerxes III at Persepolis

34. Air View of the City Mound of Istakhr

36. The Ruins of the Palace of Ardashir I at Firuzabad

37. The Investiture of Ardashir I by Hormuzd, as Carved at Naqsh-i-Rustam

39. The Investiture of Bahram I by Hormuzd, a Rock Relief at Shapur

40. The Investiture of Narseh by Anahita, a Rock Relief at Naqsh-i-Rustam

41. Taq-i-Bustan

42. The Investiture of Ardashir II by Hormuzd and Mithra, at Taq-i-Bustan

43. Takht-i-Sulaiman, the Site of Ancient Shiz

44. Chosroes II on the Steed Shabdez, at Taq-i-Bustan

45. The Investiture of Chosroes II by Hormuzd and Anahita, at Taq-i-Bustan

47. Painted Pottery from Mohenjo-daro (*Copyright Government of India, by permission of Arthur Probsthain, London*)

46. Paleolithic Implements from Soan Valley

48. Portrait Statue from Mohenjo-daro (*Copyright*

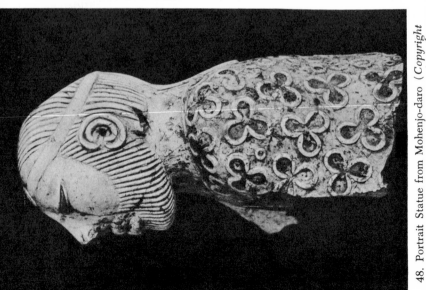

49. Seal from Mohenjo-daro with Three-faced God (*Copyright Gov-*

50. Hymn to Agni in a Manuscript
of the Rig-Veda

51. Statue of a Yaksha

Headless Statue of King Kanishka

54. Image of Vishnu as Trivikrama

55. Lad Khan Temple at Aihole

56. Lakshmana Temple
at Sirpur

57. Virupaksha Temple at Pattadakal

58. Kailasanatha Temple at Elura

59. Śiva and Parvati on Mount Kailasa

60. Central Aisle of the Cave Temple at Elephanta

61. The Three-headed Śiva

62. Kailasanatha Temple at Kanchi

63. Rajarajeśvara Temple at Tanjore

64. Hoyśaleśvara Temple at Halebid

65. Pillar in the Great Temple at Palampet

66. Kandarya Mahadeva Temple at Khajuraho

68. The Dancing Śiva

67. Lingaraja Temple at Bhuvaneśvara

69. Statue of Brahma

70. Jaina Tablet of Homage Showing a Jaina Stupa

Statue of the Tirthankara
Mahavira

74. The Indra Sabha Rock Temple at Elura

77. The Temple City of Śatrunjaya

78. The Hill of Girnar and the Stairway leading to the Jaina Temples

80. The Dome in the Temple of Vimala Shah

82. Miniature Painting of a Tirthankara

83. A Jaina Goddess

84. The Birth of Mahavira

85. The Bath of Mahavira

86. Mahavira Gives away his Earthly Possessions